Global Issues

Series Editor
Jim Whitman
Wakefield, West Yorkshire, UK

This series comprises three principal themes: the interaction of human and natural systems; cooperation and conflict; and the enactment of values. There is an underlying emphasis on the examination of complex systems and casual relations in political decision-making; problems of knowledge; authority, control and accountability in issues of scale; and the reconciliation of conflicting values and competing claims. The concentration throughout is on an integration of existing disciplines toward the clarification of political possibility as well as impending crises.

More information about this series at
http://www.palgrave.com/gp/series/15012

Roberto Belloni · Vincent Della Sala
Paul Viotti
Editors

Fear and Uncertainty in Europe

The Return to Realism?

Editors
Roberto Belloni
Department of Sociology and Social
 Research
University of Trento
Trento, Italy

Paul Viotti
Josef Korbel School of International
 Studies
University of Denver
Denver, CO, USA

Vincent Della Sala
Department of Sociology and Social
 Research
University of Trento
Trento, Italy

Global Issues
ISBN 978-3-319-91964-5   ISBN 978-3-319-91965-2   (eBook)
https://doi.org/10.1007/978-3-319-91965-2

Library of Congress Control Number: 2018941889

Cover credit: AtomicZen/Getty

Printed on acid-free paper

This Palgrave Macmillan imprint is published by the registered company Springer Nature Switzerland AG
The registered company address is: Gewerbestrasse 11, 6330 Cham, Switzerland

CONTENTS

NOTES ON CONTRIBUTORS

Roberto Belloni is professor at the Department of Sociology and Social Research; he is the holder of a Jean Monnet module on the European Union and Political Development in the Western Balkans (2015–2018). Previously, he held teaching and research positions at the University of Denver, Harvard, Johns Hopkins, and Queens Belfast. He published extensively on "International Intervention in Conflict Areas", "EU Foreign Policy", and "Peacebuilding", including the monograph *Statebuilding and International Intervention in Bosnia* (Routledge, 2008), as well as two co-edited volumes and one journal special issue (*The Politics of Hybrid Peace Governance*, published in Global Governance, 2012).

Fabrizio Coticchia is Assistant Professor of Political Science at the University of Genoa. His fields of research are foreign policy analysis, contemporary warfare, political parties, public opinion and military operations, Italian and European defense policy.

Vincent Della Sala is a Professor of Political Science at the University of Trento and is also adjunct professor at SAIS Europe of the Johns Hopkins University. He currently holds a Jean Monnet Chair on Narratives for a New Europe. His recent research interests focus on questions related to ontological security in the European Union and the role of domestic politics in shaping European policies.

Balkan Devlen is Associate Professor and Marie Sklodowska Curie Fellow in the University of Copenhagen. He focuses on the role of agency and individuals in foreign policy and international politics. His research is informed by Realism, the English School, and political psychology.

Jack Donnelly is the Andrew Mellon Professor in the Josef Korbel School of International Studies at the University of Denver. He has published extensively in the fields of international human rights and international relations theory, including *Realism and International Relations* (Cambridge, 2000).

Benedikt Erforth currently works as Teaching Fellow at Sciences Po's Euro-American program in Reims. His research interests include international relations theory, international security, and foreign policy analysis. He has published in Millennium, the *Cambridge Review of International Affairs*, and the *European Review of International Affairs*. He also is a contributor to Foreign Policy Blogs and former contributor to Think Africa Press.

Annette Freyberg-Inan is dean of the Graduate School of Social Sciences at the University of Amsterdam and Associate Professor of Political Science at the same university. Her research interests span the fields of International Relations, International Political Economy, and European Politics and Peripheries. Her relevant publications include A. Freyberg-Inan, E. Harrison, & P. James (eds.), *Evaluating Progress in International Relations: How Do You Know?* (London: Routledge, 2016) and A. Freyberg-Inan, E. Harrison, & P. James (eds.), *Rethinking Realism in International Relations: Between Tradition and Innovation* (Baltimore: Johns Hopkins University Press, 2009).

Catherine Gegout is Associate Professor in International Relations at the University of Nottingham. She has major research interests in international relations theories and European politics, with a focus on European foreign security and economic policies, and the role of the International Criminal Court. Her book *Why Europe Intervenes in Africa: Security, Prestige and the Legacy of Colonialism* was published in 2017 with Hurst and in 2018 with Oxford University Press.

Natalia Morozova is Associate Professor in the Department of Social Sciences at the Higher School of Economics, Nizhny Novgorod, Russia.

Her research interests include: Russian post-Soviet foreign policy and identity, international legitimacy, humanitarianism, international political theory, discourse analysis theory.

Özgür Özdamar teaches at Bilkent University's Department of International Relations. His research focuses on foreign policy analysis, international relations theories, and forecasting. He currently serves as editor of "All Azimuth: Journal of Foreign Policy and Peace" and director of research at Center for Foreign Policy and Peace Studies.

Alexander Reichwein is Assistant Professor of International Relations and PostDoc at the Justus-Liebig University in Giessen and Guest Lecturer at the University of Copenhagen. He is doing research on the history of the discipline IR and of Realism and on the Responsibility to Protect. He is co-editor of the book series *Trends in European IR Theory* (Palgrave Macmillan). His recent publications include *Reappraising European IR Theoretical Traditions* (Palgrave Macmillan, 2017), *Classical Realism*, in P. James, *Oxford Bibliographies Online: International Relations* (Oxford University Press, 2018), "Realism and European Foreign Policy: Promises and Shortcomings", in K. E. Jørgensen et al., *The SAGE Handbook of European Foreign Policy* (SAGE, 2015) and "The Tradition of Neoclassical Realism", in A. Toje and B. Kunz, *Neoclassical Realism in European Politics: Bringing Power Back In* (Manchester University Press, 2012).

Sten Rynning is Professor of international relations at the Department of Political Science, University of Southern Denmark, where he also heads the Center for War Studies. He is the author of numerous books and articles on "NATO and International Security Issues".

Pauline Schnapper is Professor of Contemporary British Politics at the University of Paris Sorbonne Nouvelle. Her research focuses on British European and foreign policy. She has published in the *Journal of Common Market Studies* and the *Cambridge Review of International Studies*. She is the author of *Le Royaume-Uni doit-il quitter l'Union européenne?*, Paris, La Documentation Française, 2014 and (with David Baker) of Britain and the Crisis of the European Union, Palgrave, 2015.

Paul Van Hooft is a 2016–2018 Max Weber Fellow at the European University Institute (EUI). He works on: trans-Atlantic relations; alliances; nuclear deterrence; national security decision making; and lessons of the past. He is particularly interested in the future of American power and leadership in Europe and its impact on European strategic autonomy. Van Hooft obtained his doctorate in Political Science at the University of Amsterdam (UVA). His dissertation on the impact of victory and defeat in war on grand strategy, and the propensity of states to use military force and diplomacy, was awarded the 2016 dissertation prize of the Dutch and Flemish political science associations.

Paul Viotti is a Professor at the University of Denver's Josef Korbel School of International Studies and Executive Director there of the Institute on Globalization and Security (IGLOS). He is the author of *American Foreign Policy* (Polity Press), *The Dollar and National Security* (Stanford University Press), *US National Security* (Cambria Press), five editions of two co-authored volumes: *International Relations Theory* and *International Relations and World Politics* (Pearson), and three co-edited editions of *The Defense Policies of Nations* (Johns Hopkins University Press).

CHAPTER 1

Introduction

Roberto Belloni and Vincent Della Sala

The election of Donald Trump to the American presidency, a growing sense of American disengagement in Europe, Russian's seeming readiness to challenge basic liberal institutions both internally and in Europe, the on-going Ukraine conflict, Brexit, the rise of extremism in European states, the migrant crisis, terrorist attacks in and outside Europe, and collapsing states in the Middle East and North Africa are just a few recent developments that have raised challenges to the post-war order in Europe. Europe, on the frontlines of both the Cold War and the multilateral system that governed the first decades of the post-war period, now faces the possibility that its transatlantic partner is no longer committed to the same international order at precisely the moment that the European Union and Europe faces serious internal and external challenges.

Order in post-war Europe was marked by two very different elements. On the one hand, being on the frontlines of the Cold War meant it was

R. Belloni (✉) · V. Della Sala
Department of Sociology and Social Research,
University of Trento, Trento, Italy
e-mail: roberto.belloni@unitn.it

V. Della Sala
e-mail: vincent.dellasala@soc.unitn.it

1

R. Belloni et al. (eds.), *Fear and Uncertainty in Europe*, Global Issues,
https://doi.org/10.1007/978-3-319-91965-2_1

at the very heart of power politics, with their attendant fear and uncertainty over material capacity and intentions in relations between states. On the other hand, the American security commitment contributed decisively to create the political space for the development of a political and economic order based on different principles, those that stressed a thick institutional and normative international order and a social market economy. In this context, European integration created an institutional architecture and normative foundation that would reduce, if not eliminate, fear and uncertainty and make calculations of material capability marginal in relations among a wide range of actors (Belloni 2016).

The end of the Cold War was thought to diminish the role of power politics in Europe and clear the way for the further development of peaceful relations. Theoretically, two influential components of structural realism—which was predominant in the United States in the 1980s and involved confidence in bipolar stability and power transition theory with its prediction of a clash among the superpowers—were challenged by the collapse of the Soviet Union and the peaceful end of the Cold War. While, as Paul Van Hooft and Annette Freyberg-Inan (Chapter 4, this volume) argue, realism can persuasively account for the end of the Cold War, the transformation of the global order, and the lack of major power conflict, the international system seemed to be moving in a direction that appeared to undercut realism's core tenets. This was no more the case than in Europe, as steps towards creating an 'ever closer union' with the European Union gave space to many new interpretative schemes that sought to understand an international order that seemed to be no longer driven by the dynamics of power politics and rational geopolitical calculations. Realists warned about the possibility that the end of bipolarity could result in increasing levels of instability (Mearsheimer 1990), but enthusiasm for European integration prevailed and reflected the hope that the second pillar of the post-war order—a thick normative and institutional architecture—would dominate and even extend beyond the expanding EU borders. It suggested that using "realism" as a cognitive map to understand the emerging European order, the behaviour of actors and the drivers of foreign policy was less useful than one that draws from liberal, or even interpretive and reflective, constructions of international relations.

As the euphoria over the end to Europe's division faded, the current political challenges stemming from the instability of the international system have raised questions about whether it may have been premature to herald the end of realism in Europe. As Paul Viotti explains in Chapter 3, "a shift away from multilateralism to bilateralism or unilateralism driven by the political right in various countries undermined the embedded liberalism in the elaborate architecture of multilateral institutions" that have been the bedrock of the international system since the end of World War II. With increasing levels of perceived insecurity and the lack of trust in the "civilizing" (Koskenniemi 2010) potential of international law and multilateralism, realism appeared once again as a promising tool to explain the return of forms of instability and uncertainty at the international level.

Not unlike previous historical moments when alternative paradigms—most notably institutional liberalism—seemed to take the upper hand, amended versions of realism claim to provide important insights to Europe's present-day predicament (Orsi et al. 2018). Realists' own self-reflexivity, as well as engagement with critics, have frequently contributed to the regeneration of this tradition of thought, rather than its marginalization (Guzzini 1998). Journalistic and popular accounts contribute to a persisting interest in realism, however defined. Realism maintains a certain attractiveness because of its apparently simple lexicon, including references to 'security', the 'heartland', and the dichotomy and dualism between 'self' and 'other'—understood in the current European context as Russia, the immigrant, financial capital, and everything else supposedly menacing the 'self'. In sum, even when both the theory and practice of realism appeared to be on the defensive, it may have gone underground rather than have disappeared.

REALISM'S MANY FACES

Any discussion of which conceptual map we might use to understand contemporary international relations, including Europe, requires sifting through the many ways in which the term "realism" can be and is used. There is no widely shared core of assumptions and claims that cover the entire spectrum of what is called realism: many claims made in the name of realism are not unique to it. Moreover, there is no immediate or clear answer to the question, "What is realism?".

As a rough approximation, two main traditions can be identified (Donnelly 2000; Wohlforth 2008). Classical or biological realists emphasize the importance of human nature, understood in essentially pessimistic and negative terms, in causing social conflict among groups.

By contrast, structural realists, often defined as neo-realists, stress the role played by international anarchy in creating the conditions for a perpetual struggle for power. Neo-realism is further divided into defensive and offensive realism on the basis of how much power states presumably require. Offensive realists, most notably John Mearsheimer (2001), argue that power predominance is the best safeguard for states' survival and thus states should maximize their relative power and become hegemonic. By contrast, defensive realists, such as Waltz (2008), contend that the maximization of power is ultimately counter-productive since it will eventually trigger the formation of an opposing coalition that will challenge their predominance. Whatever the merit of each position, power, along with its material manifestation to counter fear and uncertainty, is central to any type of realist analysis.

Both classical and structural realists have neglected the impact of domestic political factors in either constraining or enabling the ability of the executive to respond to systemic pressures and strategic challenges. In response to this limitation, a third major realist approach has been taking shape. Neoclassical realism affirms the primary importance of the international structure, but also includes in its analysis 'unit-level' variables such as domestic strategic leadership and power relationships (Rose 1998; Lobell et al. 2009; Toje and Kunz 2012). In this way, neoclassical realism 'brings the state back in' to the debates concerning systemic pressures on states and in the formulation of states' preferences and strategy. Several of the contributors to this volume draw from neoclassical realism to examine the foreign policy behaviour of states. In Chapter 4, Paul Van Hooft and Annette Freyberg-Inan explain recent security policy stances of states, such as France, as shaped primarily by domestic preoccupations and concerns, while being significantly moulded by their understanding of power relations in the international system, in particular in light of American relative decline over the last two decades or so. In Chapter 5, Alexander Reichwein adopts neoclassical realist lenses in order to elucidate dynamics of continuity and change in Germany's post-Cold War foreign policy. Along similar lines, Benedikt Erforth in Chapter 6 and Fabrizio Coticchia in Chapter 7 argue that neoclassical realism is well-suited to explain foreign policy decisions, in particular France's Operation Serval in Mali and Italy's Operation Prima Parthica in Iraq. Analogous dynamics are at play in non EU-members as well. In Chapter 9 Ozgur Ozdamar and Balkan Devlen elucidate Turkey's assertive policy towards the Middle East in the aftermath of the 2011 Arab revolutions as a result of both the perception of domestic elites with regard to Turkey's role in the region, and the lack of domestic constraints. This case is revealing of how domestic considerations shape foreign policy decisions but do not guarantee the adoption of the most rational or effective policy. In the case of Turkey, the assertive foreign policy caused a worsening of relationships with neighbours and eventually had to be reconsidered.

The different understandings of the realist tradition in international relations raise the question of whether it is possible to identify a set of essential realist principles. While disagreements on what to include are bound to persist, we understand these principles to consist of the following main concepts and ideas (drawing from Brooks 1997; Donnelly 2000; Guzzini 1998; Legro and Moravcsik 1999; Lobell et al. 2009). First, the international arena is anarchic. While in most IR scholarship "anarchy" is taken for granted, there are at least 20 different conceptions of the term (Donnelly 2015). This multiplicity is biased towards realist meanings involving primarily disorder, lawlessness, and the possibility that violence may break out at any time. Crucially, this anarchic structure does not compel a single particular type of behaviour, although it may favour the development of competition for scarce resources among states. As Donnelly argues in this volume, rather than a causal factor, anarchy is best understood as a permissive condition.

Second, the state is the primary unit of analysis. States with the greatest resources—great powers—are the most important because of their ability to shape international affairs. Primary among the states' priorities is security, which could be achieved through a variety of goals ranging form self-preservation to universal domination but always with keen attention to material conditions. Following the publication in 1979 of Waltz's seminal neo-realist work, *Theory of International Politics*, most IR literature, and above all structural realism, has focused on the systemic constraints on states' behaviour (for an assessment see Viotti, Forthcoming). Neoclassical realism does not neglect these constraints, but focuses on the internal characteristics of states to explain how |constraints (and opportunities) are understood, interpreted and acted upon. Structural realists may find this approach reductionist, but it does have the merit of problematizing the role of the state—thus far considered in realist analysis as a "black box." Neoclassical realism draws attention to the 'two-level game' (Putnam 1988) leaders play in devising and implementing their policies: while on the one hand they must assess and respond to the external environment, on the other hand they strive to gain or maintain the support of key domestic stakeholders, and to mobilize resources from domestic society. Thus, neoclassical realism combines structural realism's top-down approach with classical realism's bottom-up approach (Rose 1998: 154). As a number of the chapters in this volume demonstrate, understanding this dynamic may provide a useful interpretative key when examining recent foreign policy continuity and change in Europe.

Third, the view of human nature is profoundly pessimistic. Human nature is considered to be immutable, making moral progress impossible. Fear—understood as a reaction to a perceived threat or danger—is intrinsic to the human condition and urges us to defend ourselves from that threat or danger. Self-protection can be practiced through restraint or through aggressive behaviour. Whatever the preferred option, realists remain sceptical of the possibility of ameliorating international anarchy and thus reducing fear (Pashakhanlou 2017). The feasibility of establishing a pacific international order through international law and regimes is remote at best. Rather than relying on international institutions, states count on power to pursue their goals. Power is understood primarily, but not exclusively, in terms of material capabilities while politics is largely reduced to a struggle among states to acquire power in a world of uncertainty.

Reflecting on these different meanings attributed to the word 'realism', Jack Donnelly shows in Chapter 2 that the term has been used to capture a variety of uses. We can place them roughly on a spectrum that has theory on one end and tradition at the other, with models closer to the former, schools and approaches closer to the latter. Put succinctly, according to Donnelly, realism understands the international realm as one where self-interested states are driven by fear and uncertainty in a system based on states seeking power, at a minimum, to guarantee their survival. Each of these elements, either individually or collectively, does not necessarily constitute realism. What does is whether and how these elements shape the behaviour of actors and their understanding of international relations. Realists, whether as analysts or as foreign policy actors, "emplot" these elements in a particular way to shape their understanding of the social world and how to behave in it. For example, realists understand uncertainty as fear induced by anarchy and the possibility of predation (Rathbun 2007). This understanding gives meaning to the use of power and the thin normative and institutional order that serves strategic interests. The contributions in this volume want to explore whether this provides a useful conceptual map to understand how states and other actors face the growing uncertainty about the future of international order constructed over the last 75 years in Europe.

This Book

The aim of the chapters in this book is three-fold. First, they seek to assess whether foreign policy actors in Europe understand the international system and behave as realists and/or how realists would expect them to behave. They ask what drives their behaviour, how they construct material capabilities and to what extent they see material power as the means to ensure survival in a post-Cold War context apparently marked by growing instability. The contributors use or contest realism in its different forms as laid out in the chapter by Jack Donnelly. These authors also identify continuity or change in the foreign policy of key European actors. They ask whether the use of realism helps us to understand what might be critical junctures and why.

A number of important themes cut across most, if not all, of the chapters that deal with Europe in this volume. They address the question of how actors understand and use power. The conventional argument that European states are less driven by fear—the use of material power to achieve survival and security—is examined in a series of different cases. Countries such as Germany and France no longer engage in what Zaki Laïdi (2008: 12–17) described as 'power avoidance', that is, the preference for a limited engagement in international relations. In Chapter 5, Alexander Reichwein accounts for the rise of Germany as a 'responsible' and 'shaping power' in the international system and Benedikt Erforth in Chapter 6 discusses France's self-understanding as an 'influential power' with growing responsibilities and obligations. In Chapter 10, Pauline Schnapper discusses the consequences of 'Brexit' in the United Kingdom, including the return of what appears to be a traditionalist, power-based foreign policy detached from entanglements with European countries and based on British exceptionalism. The chapter has been placed in the section dedicated to non-EU European states to underscore that perhaps Britain's different understanding of fear and uncertainty had always distinguished it from its soon to be former EU partners.

Second, the chapters examine whether a thick normative order has developed and whether this has changed the ways in which actors understand fear and uncertainty along with how to manage this condition. This normative imperative is central to the discussion of European intervention in Africa, examined by Catherine Gegout in Chapter 13, and in the foreign policy of states such as France and Italy. In addition, it informs the analysis of recent Russian foreign policy. As Natalia Morozova argues in Chapter 8, Russia's subordinate position within the Western dominated normative order generates uncertainty not, as in the realist framework, about other states' intentions but rather about its own sense of identity and sources of agency. With an approach based on discourse analysis, Morozova examines Russia's attempt to ease its ontological insecurity through the adoption of a discursive framework based on 'Eurasianism' and 'geopolitics.' Even a security organization such as NATO experienced important normative developments. As Sten Rynning explains in Chapter 11, NATO's recent Protection of Civilians doctrine constitutes an important normative adaptation to the challenges presented by the organization's post-Cold War engagement in crisis management tasks.

Third, contributors examine what it means to act strategically in a world apparently dominated by fear and uncertainty. The foreign policy of states examined in this volume, as well as that of multilateral organizations such as the NATO and the EU, testified to the difficulty of formulating and implementing a coherent approach to the challenges that Europe has been facing since the end of the Cold War. In particular, in Chapter 12 Roberto Belloni and Vincent Della Sala discuss the EU's actions in the Balkans and its relations with Russia. Both areas present the EU not only with foreign policy challenges but also existential issues that point to its lack of ontological security. Both engagement with the Balkans and with Russia highlight the tension in the growing need to make strategic choices while remaining consistent with its narrative of a benign, normative power that looks to a thick institutional architecture to provide order.

Most of the chapters included in this volume originated from a conference held at the University of Trento on 11–12 November 2016, titled 'Realism and the Return of Geopolitics in Europe'. We are grateful to both the University's Jean Monnet Centre of Excellence and the Department of Sociology and Social Research for their generous financial and logistical support. We are also indebted to the conference participations as well as those colleagues who accepted to contribute a chapter at a later stage.

References

Belloni, Roberto. 2016. "Peace in Europe." In *The Palgrave Handbook of Disciplinary and Regional Approaches to Peace*, edited by Sandra Pogodda, Oliver Richmond, and Jasmin Ramovic. Houndmills: Palgrave.

Brooks, Stephen G. 1997. "Dueling Realisms." *International Organization* 51 (3): 455–477.

Donnelly, Jack. 2000. *Realism and International Relations*. Cambridge: Cambridge University Press.

Donnelly, Jack. 2015. "The Discourse of Anarchy in IR." *International Theory* 7 (3): 393–425.

Guzzini, Stefano. 1998. *Realism in International Relations and International Political Economy*. London and New York: Routledge.

Koskenniemi, Martti. 2010. *The Gentle Civilizer of Nations: The Rise and Fall of International Law, 1870–1960*. Cambridge: Cambridge University Press.

Laïdi, Zaki. 2008. *Norms Over Force: The Enigma of European Power*. New York: Palgrave Macmillan.

Legro, Jeffrey, and Andrew Moravcsik. 1999. "Is Anybody Still a Realist?" *International Security* 24 (2): 5–55.

Lobell, Steven E., Norrin M. Ripsman, and Jeffrey W. Tagliaferro, eds. 2009. *Neoclassical Realism in State and Foreign Policy*, Cambridge University Press.

Mearsheimer, John. 1990. "Back to the Future: Instability in Europe After the Cold War." *International Security* 15 (1): 5–56.

Mearsheimer, John. 2001. *The Tragedy of Great Power Politics*. New York: W.W. Norton and Company.

Orsi, Davide, J. R. Avgustin, and Max Nurnus, eds. 2018. *Realism in Practice: An Appraisal*. Bristol: E-International Relations. Available http://www.e-ir.info/wp-content/uploads/2018/01/Realism-in-Practice-E-IR.pdf.

Pashakhanlou, Arash Heydarian. 2017. *Realism and Fear in International Relations*. Houndmills: Palgrave Macmillan.

Putnam, Robert D. 1988. "Diplomacy and Domestic Politics: The Logic of Two Level Games." *International Organization* 42 (3): 427–461.

Rathbun, Brian C. 2007. "Uncertain about Uncertainty: Understanding the Multiple Meanings of a Crucial Concept in International Relations Theory." *International Studies Quarterly* 51: 533–557.

Rose, Gideon. 1998. "Neoclassical Realism and Theories of Foreign Policy." *World Politics* 51 (1): 144–172.

Toje, Asle, and Barbara Kunz, eds. 2012. *Neoclassical Realism in European Politics. Bringing Power Back In*. Manchester: Manchester University Press.

Viotti, Paul R. Forthcoming. *The Realism of Kenneth Waltz: Luminary to His Followers and Lighting Rod to His Critics*, New York: Columbia University Press.

Waltz, Kenneth. 1979. *Theory of International Politics*. New York: McGraw-Hill.
Waltz, Kenneth. 2008. *Realism and International Politics*. New York: Routledge.
Wohlforth, William. 2008. "Realism", in *The Oxford Handbook of International Relations*, edited by Christian Reus-Smit and Duncan Snidal. Oxford: Oxford University Press.

PART I

Context

CHAPTER 2

What Do We Mean by Realism? And How—And What—Does Realism Explain?

Jack Donnelly

Certainly, one would think, we know what we mean when we call an action, outcome, argument, or explanation "realist." In IR we do it "all the time," so we *must* know. Right?

Often, I want to suggest, only sort of. This essay tries to sort out and clarify some of the principal senses of "realism" and how (and what) realism explains.

"Defining" "Realism"

Consider the following "definitions" (presented in more or less heavily elided quotations or close paraphrases).

1. The fundamental unit of social and political affairs is the "conflict group."
2. States are motivated primarily by their national interest.
3. Power relations are a fundamental feature of international affairs (Gilpin 1996: 7–8).

J. Donnelly (✉)
University of Denver, Denver, CO, USA
e-mail: Jack.Donnelly@du.edu

© The Author(s) 2019
R. Belloni et al. (eds.), *Fear and Uncertainty in Europe*, Global Issues,
https://doi.org/10.1007/978-3-319-91965-2_2

1. The state-centric assumption: states are the most important actors in world politics.
2. The rationality assumption: world politics can be analyzed as if states were unitary rational actors seeking to maximize their expected utility.
3. The power assumption: states seek power and they calculate their interests in terms of power (Keohane 1986: 164–165).

1. Groupism. Politics takes place within and between groups.
2. Egoism. When individuals and groups act politically, they are driven principally by narrow self-interest.
3. Anarchy. The absence of government dramatically shapes the nature of international politics.
4. Power politics. The intersection of groupism and egoism in an environment of anarchy makes international relations, regrettably, largely a politics of power and security (Wohlforth 2008: 133; Donnelly 2008: 150).

1. Humans face one another primarily as members of groups.
2. International affairs takes place in a state of anarchy.
3. Power is the fundamental feature of international politics.
4. The nature of international interactions is essentially conflictual.
5. Humankind cannot transcend conflict through the progressive power of reason.
6. Politics is not a function of ethics.
7. Necessity and reason of state trump morality and ethics (Schweller 1997: 927).

1. The international system is anarchic.
2. States inherently possess some offensive military capability, which gives them the wherewithal to hurt and possibly destroy each other.
3. No state can ever be certain another state will not use its offensive military capability.
4. The most basic motive driving states is survival.
5. States are instrumentally rational (Mearsheimer 1994/1995: 9–10).

These are all "good definitions" that "point in the same direction." They range, though, from very broad (e.g., Gilpin and Keohane) to rather narrow (Schweller). And they only partially overlap.

Even more importantly, the widely shared elements, such as anarchy, power, selfishness, and rationality, are also central to many (most?) other leading perspectives. (Most strikingly, most IR scholars would readily agree with Gilpin's "defining" claims that social and political life is organized in groups that regularly engage in conflict, that states are motivated principally by their national interests, and that power is fundamental to international relations.)[1] In fact, although these definitions identify many *characteristically* "realist" features, few, even in combination, are *distinctively* "realist," in the sense that they demarcate "realist" from "non-realist."

Furthermore, the use of terms like "primarily," "fundamental," "most basic," and "essentially" make it unclear just what is being claimed. And how one gets from these "realist premises" to "realist conclusions" is, at best, obscure.

This variety and imprecision, I will argue, is inescapable. (If it is a "problem," it is irresolvable.) Realism has no defining core; no set of criteria by which we can sort arguments, explanations, actions, or outcomes as realist or non-realist. That does not, however, make "realism" an empty or confused term. Rather, I will argue, realism is a complex and diverse family of "things" that recurrently appear in our analytical practice in varied but patterned ways.

Realism as "Theory"

What kind of a "thing" is realism? One obvious answer is "a theory," in the broad sense of abstracted generalizations that purport to be of analytical or explanatory value. Here I identify five types of "realist theory," which I call theories, traditions, models, schools, and approaches.

Kenneth Waltz (1990b, 1991) drew a useful distinction between (realist) thought and (neorealist) theory. "Theory," Waltz argues (1979: 8–10, 12, 69), explains law-like regularities by showing them to be effects of underlying relations of cause or interdependency. I will adopt this fairly standard sense. *Theories* provide particular substantive explanations of patterned events. Waltz presents structural realism as a theory in this sense.

---

[1] Most would also agree with Mearsheimer's claims, at least if we interpret his claim that survival is the most basic motive driving states to to mean that states, if forced to choose, usually would rank survival above all other objectives.

"Thought" is a less clear category. I will use it here to refer to *traditions* of analysis, understood as persistent discursive communities and their associated bodies of work. Traditions of thought have no defining criteria. They do, however, have characteristic analytical perspectives and practices that typically are expressed in more or less widely shared parameters of conversation, common themes, characteristic elements and arguments, and exemplary authors and texts. The realist tradition is generally recognized as central to IR (although it long predates academic IR).

Models, as I will use the term, are combinations of interconnected analytical elements that say something significant about cause, process, mechanism, or outcome. Models, although more like theories than traditions, are too incomplete or underspecified to explain without (more or less substantial) supplementation.[2] Structural realism, I will argue below, is always used as a model.

"Schools" and "approaches", like traditions, are communities of practice that encompass multiple theories or models. They are, however, narrower and more coherent than traditions (of which they typically are parts). *Schools,* as I use the term, are fundamentally substantive. Their identity is tied to canonical texts or authorities or characteristic arguments or insights. Marxism is a school of social theory. Structural realism can also be read as a school. *Approaches* are much more centrally "methodological", defined more by shared analytical orientations and practices than by shared substance. Neo-classical realism, I will argue below, is an approach.

Finally, I suggest that it is useful to think of traditions, schools, and approaches as "perspectives", which inspire and guide, rather than provide, explanations. Theories and models, in this typology, explain (as do ad hoc and eclectic arguments).

These categories should not be taken too seriously. The dividing lines are not clear. Other fruitful categorizations are possible. (For example, I have not included research programs.) Nonetheless, this typology seems to me both insightful and useful for clarifying the diversity of "things" that fall within the realm of realist "theory" in IR.

---

[2] This distinction between theory and model is common in natural science disciplines that have been intensively formalized through mathematics. It also seems to me broadly consistent with standard usage in self-consciously social-scientific IR. See, for example, King et al. (1994: 49–53, 106–107).

What Is a Realist Explanation?

The rest of this chapter focuses on how and what "realism" explains. (For maximum clarity, I repeat that my focus is on realist *explanations*. The policies, actions, and outcomes that are being explained—which are the central concern of most of the other chapters in this volume—appear here only incidentally.) This section examines the character of realist (in any of the above senses) explanations. What makes an explanation "realist"?

Realist Explanations Versus Explanations that Employ Realist Elements

An explanation that employs "characteristically realist" premises in ways guided by and reflective of a realist tradition is, I will argue, "realist" in a strong and unambiguous sense. It is not enough that it gives a central place to one or more "characteristically realist" factors or forces—especially when those factors or forces are not *distinctively* realist.

For example, both neoliberal institutionalism[3] and structural realism[4] begin with anarchy and the problems for cooperation that it poses. Structural realism, however, focuses on self-help responses that pose power against power. Neoliberal institutionalism, by contrast, focuses on responses that develop and deploy international institutions. Structural realist theories and models (and the school or approach of structural realism) and neoliberal institutionalist theories and models (and the school or approach of neoliberal institutionalism) explore different kinds of responses to different things, producing divergent explanations.

Or consider neoclassical realism,[5] which, like neoliberal institutionalism, focuses on situations where structural explanations fall short or fail. Most of the work in neoclassical realist explanations is done by factors such as domestic political structure, perceptions, intentions, and processes of strategic interaction that not only have no special connection

---

[3] Keohane and Martin (2003), Stein (2008), and Keohane (2012) provide good brief overviews. I treat neoliberal institutionalism both as a school that is part of a broad tradition of liberal international thought and a part of a broad institutionalist approach that has generated a variety of theories and models.

[4] See section below on structural realism.

[5] See section below on neoclassical realism.

to realism but are widely employed by a great variety of other theories (broadly understood)—including neoliberal institutionalism. Nonetheless, we regularly (and I think rightly) describe neoclassical realism as a school or approach within realism and neoliberal institutionalism as a school or approach outside of (or even opposed to) realism.

If we look simply at the elements employed in the analysis and see neoliberal institutionalism as not realist, then we would seem to be compelled to say that neoclassical realism is not actually a form of realism. Conversely, though, looking only at the elements employed and seeing neoclassical realism as realist, we would seem compelled to say that neoliberal institutionalism is a form of realism. And there is no neutral position to adjudicate between these readings.

I have not mentioned "realist conclusions" because I am arguing that there are no such things *separate from the (realist) path(s) that produce them*. A realist conclusion is a conclusion reached by a realist path, guided by a realist perspective, largely irrespective of its content.

Because realism is not one thing with a precise and highly elaborated form, no particular conclusions follow necessarily from "realism." Therefore, there are no essential or defining realist conclusions. Conversely, any particular policy, action, outcome, or explanation usually can be reached by a variety of paths. Therefore, how one gets there (or explains getting there) is essential to whether it "is realist" (or not). In particular, simply reaching a characteristically realist conclusion (or behaving in a characteristically realist fashion) does not make an explanation (or action) realist.[6]

An explanation's perspective—features such as heuristics, emphases, discursive settings, analytic dispositions, and characteristic frames, elements, and arguments—is fundamental (and, I am suggesting, usually decisive) in determining its character. It matters, centrally, that neoclassical realists operate (and see themselves as operating) within the realist tradition, from which they draw their analytical frames, positive and negative heuristics, "unthinking" analytical and substantive predisposition, etc. And it matters, centrally, that others whose work might seem "very similar" employ different frames, for different purposes, to reach

---

[6]To argue otherwise is likely to lead us dangerously close to confusing "realist explanations" with "explanations often (or even typically) offered by realists." Were this error not so obvious, once noted, it might merit further discussion.

different conclusions (or the same conclusion by a different route)—and that they have different understandings of the meaning and significance of their accounts.

Realist Explanations Versus Explanations (Not In)Compatible with Realism

The central presence of "characteristically realist" actions, outcomes, variables, or conclusions probably does make an explanation (not in)*compatible* with realism. Although perhaps of interest for the "dueling theories" contests that are still popular in some parts of the discipline, this tells us little if anything about the character of an explanation—which is my concern here.

Few if any important features of international relations can be completely encompassed by realist (or any other type of) explanations. Therefore, few if any parts of international relations are the unquestionable provenance of realist explanations. Nonetheless, realism, as indicated by its persistent prevalence, has something to say about much of international relations.

This helps to explain why starting points, elements, and conclusions are not decisive—and why perspective is almost always both central and essential. How one weaves together the various threads of an argument or explanation is crucial to its character.

The point is especially clear if we turn, briefly, from explanation to action. *How* a state responds to external power in anarchy[7] is at least as important as *that* it does. One reasonable, and quite common, response is to seek to create rules or institutions that make such power less threatening. These, however, are institutionalist, not realist, responses.

Most if not all international actors take into account material capabilities and their distribution. (It would be a strange theory, model, or approach that suggested they did not.) "Realist" actors and actors employing other perspectives often will approach and respond to external power rather differently.

Explanations, it needs to be emphasized, do not sort neatly into realist and not realist. Realists have a "story"—or, rather, a genre of

---

[7] It may bear repeating that external power in anarchy is a universal feature of international systems and that has no special connection to realism (even if realism does have a special attachment to some of the problems it poses).

stories—about international relations. These stories tend to draw on a stock of situations, characters, themes, tropes, plot devices, and characteristic endings. If stories in other genres have certain similarities, though, that does not make them "realist." (That a pear is like an apple does not make it an apple.) Even self-conscious borrowing from the realist repertoire does not make a story realist (unless those borrowings, because of their quantity or overall impact, create a hybrid or genre-bending story).

There is a continuum of relations between explanations and realism. At one end, explanations converge with, have certain similarities to, and are congruent or compatible with realist explanations. At the other end, explanations are not incongruent with, not incompatible with, and, finally, (merely) not *entirely* incompatible with realist explanations.

Towards the tail end of this list, arguments are likely to be fundamentally non-realist or even anti-realist. But even at the head of the list, a central and substantial realist contribution does not make an explanation "realist" *in the sense that it is also* not "*not-realist.*"

Therefore, to *say* that an explanation that merely borrows from or has important similarities to an unquestionably realist explanation "is realist" *without also* saying *that it is* not *realist* is likely to be misleading. And unless there is some clear and particular reason to focus on just one side of the story, it is suspiciously partisan. It shifts attention to the uninteresting (because utterly uncontroversial) question of *whether* realism makes an analytical contribution to IR—every serious scholar agrees that it does—and away from the crucial question of *what* realism contributes, both absolutely and relatively; of how and how much of what realism explains.

To understand the contributions that realism has made and might make—and what it hasn't contributed and can't contribute—requires clarity, and a certain degree of precision, about the variety of "realist" explanations. In particular, I have argued, we need to distinguish clearly the sorts of strongly realist explanations that I have identified here from explanations that merely employ characteristically realist elements or are (not in)compatible with realism. And even with explanations that are firmly rooted in a realist perspective and that centrally employ characteristically realist elements, it is important not to ignore the presence and contribution of non-realist elements.

STRUCTURAL REALISM:
INDETERMINATE PREDICTIONS AND PERMISSIVE CAUSES

In academic IR today, self-consciously realist arguments usually are more or less "structural" or more or less "neoclassical." This and the following sections look in a bit more detail at the character of structural and neoclassical realist explanations.

Structural realism can be most precisely (and most determinately) identified as the "theory" developed by Waltz in *Theory of International Politics*. As every graduate student in IR knows, Waltz argued that international political structures are sparsely but exhaustively defined by anarchy and the distribution of capabilities. (Waltz 1979: 93–97. Cf. 82, 100–101). In practice, Waltz went even further, effectively reducing international structure to its ordering principle, anarchy.[8]

Waltz's account of anarchy/structure has been subjected to devastating criticism since at least the early 1990s.[9] We have long known that purportedly structural arguments almost always rely heavily and illicitly on additional non-structural assumptions about the actors or the environment in which they interact. We will return to this point in the next section. Here I set aside the substance of structural realist arguments and focus instead on Waltz's account of the character of structural realist "explanations"—which, on examination, turn out not to explain anything at all.

Waltz (1979: 124, 134. Cf. 54, 68–69) emphasizes that structural predictions are "indeterminate." An "indeterminate prediction," as Waltz presents it, claims that in some significant but unknown (and probably unknowable) number of instances the "predicted" outcome can be expected to occur, at some unspecified (and probably unspecifiable)

---

[8]"The essential structural quality of the system is anarchy" (Waltz 1988: 618). "The logic of anarchy does not vary with its content" (Waltz 1990b: 37). "The basic structure of international politics continues to be anarchic" (Waltz 1993: 59. Cf. Waltz 2000: 5, 10, 40). As the Index of *Theory of International Politics* put it "Structure, anarchy and hierarchy as the only two types of."

[9]In particular, the so-called effects of anarchy are not effects *of anarchy*. See, for example, Wendt (1992), Snidal (1991a, b), Milner (1991), and Powell (1994: esp. 314). Wagner (2007: 16–18, 21–29) offers a particularly spirited rationalist refrain. Donnelly (2015) comprehensively critiques IR's fundamentally Waltzian construction of anarchy.

times in some unspecified (and probably unspecifiable) places. Some
times, some where, some things turn out "as predicted."

Sometimes, though, for unexplained (and, from within the theory,
inexplicable) reasons, things turn out otherwise. Such non-occurrences,
however, even if they should prove to be the norm, are held not to count
against the theory, its explanatory power, or even its predictive power—
which remains "indeterminate." Heads I win. Tails we flip again—until I
win (and the explanatory power of structural realism is confirmed).

Furthermore, such "indeterminate predictions" provide no *explanation* at all. As Waltz puts it (1979: 69), to explain is "to say why the
range of expected outcomes falls within certain limits; to say why patterns of behavior recur; to say why events repeat themselves." Structure
(anarchy and the distribution of capabilities), however, provides not even
the outlines of an account of *why* (or even how[10]) "predicted" outcomes
occur.

"Indeterminate predictions" are mere correlations. No effort is made
to determine the expected correlation coefficient. And the correlation
with anarchy is "spurious."

Anarchy is a feature of all international systems. Therefore, it is correlated with *any* (all) patterned behavior or outcome—and thus explains
none. Anarchy tells us nothing about why this happened *instead of
that*—which is also (indeterminately) correlated with anarchy.

Consider the central substantive conclusion of structural realism,
namely, balancing. Waltz does not argue that units, states, or even
great powers *do* balance (rather than bandwagon). Quite the contrary,
he claims (only) that balances tend to form. "According to the theory,
balances of power recurrently form" (Waltz 1979: 124). "Only a loosely
defined and inconstant condition of balance is predicted" (Waltz 1979:
124. Cf. 118, 119, 126). In fact, Waltz (1996) argues that structural
theory *cannot* predict or explain the behavior of states. It only identifies a
constraining context within which states act.

This, though, is little more than a roundabout way of saying that a
states system is a states system, in which, by definition, there is some

[10]Waltz (1979: 74–77) does reference selection and socialization. Both, however, are, in
Waltz's terms, matters of interaction, not structure. (Socialization is especially distant from
structure.) And he offers not even a hint of an account of when we should expect these
mechanisms to work (or not work).

sort of loosely defined and inconstant condition of balance. As long as a "world hegemony," (Waltz 1979: 124) global empire, or world state does not arise—that is, as long as international relations remains international relations—anything that happens is (not in)consistent with the balancing prediction. (One does not need to be a fan of Popper or Lakatos to find such an "explanation" at best empty.)

Structural "explanations" cannot be rescued by arguing that anarchy is a "permissive cause", a feature of the world without which something could not occur; a necessary condition of that thing's possibility. Waltz's (1959: 232–234) classic argument that anarchy is a permissive cause of war, like his argument about balancing, has no explanatory content.

Even if it is true that war would not occur in the absence of anarchy, it is at least equally true that war would not occur in the absence of human life. And because anarchy is characteristic of all international systems at all times, calling anarchy a permissive cause (of anything) is not much more informative than calling human life a permissive cause.

Even more troubling, peace is far more frequent than war *in anarchic systems*. But anarchy *cannot* account for how, when, or why *either* war or peace is likely to occur. (A constant (anarchy) cannot explain variable outcomes (war and peace).) And as long as some wars occur at some times, almost any outcome is (not in)consistent with this "permissive cause."

Furthermore, if by "war" we mean organized collective violence, and if wars occur regularly in hierarchical systems (as they do if war is thus defined), then *anarchy is not a permissive cause of war.* If by "war," though, we mean violent inter-state conflict, then *the "permissive cause" of war is not anarchy* (absence of an international government) but rather the presence of a states system—which brings us back to the empty claim that if this were not a states system states would not war with one another.

Anarchy is not a cause. (It is more like a background condition.) And structural realism, understood as a theory that explains outcomes by reference to structure (anarchy and distribution of capabilities), explains nothing.

Augmented Structural Realism

This conclusion—that structure (anarchy and distribution of capabilities) explains nothing—is confirmed by the fact self-identified structural realists in practice rarely if ever even try to explain anything by structure alone.

Consider John Mearsheimer, arguably the leading realist of the generation following Waltz. Despite the fact that structure concerns only the *distribution* of capabilities (not the substance of power), he devotes a crucial chapter in his major book, *The Tragedy of Great Power Politics,* to "the primacy of land power" and emphasizes "the stopping power of water." Nonetheless, Mearsheimer insists (2001: 21) that "[his] theory of offensive realism is also [like Waltzian defensive realism] a structural theory of international politics."

Even Waltz regularly left structural accounts behind—out of a (sensible) desire to say something more than that balances tend to form. For example, in developing his theory he makes central use of the (nonstructural) proposition that "the first concern of states is not to maximize power but to maintain their positions in the system" (Waltz 1979: 126). And his explanation of the Cold War peace relies centrally, even primarily, on nuclear weapons (Waltz 1990a).

Or consider Stephen Walt, one of the first and most successful of Waltz's students following the publication of *Theory of International Politics.* Unwilling to settle for the claim that balances will form, Walt derived the determinate structural prediction that states in anarchy balance against external power. Even a superficial examination of the evidence, however, shows clearly that states balance against *threat*—leading Walt (1987, 1988) to advance a balance of threat theory. Threat, however, is a perceptual, "unit-level" variable, making the theory—as Waltz pointed out (1996: 916)—not a structural theory.

Although Walt insists that his theory is a *"refinement"* (1988: 281 [emphasis in original]) of structural balance of power theory, he does not say whether he considers balance of threat theory to be structural. This is in many ways an admirable orientation. If a structural theory can't explain what we want or need to explain, then so much the worse for structural theory. Aesthetics ought to give way to explanation. Purity does not justify willful analytical self-mutilation.

Problems, though, arise when (structural?) realists fail to confront the implications of combining structural and non-structural elements in a model, theory, or explanation. And such problems become especially severe when realists who make central reference to structure do not even acknowledge the non-structural nature of their explanations. The result is a tendency to wildly overstate the explanatory contribution of structure.

For example, Mearsheimer (2001: 10) argues that "structural factors such as anarchy and the distribution of power … matter most for explaining international politics." But he identifies only anarchy and the distribution of capabilities as structural. And in his account of the need to acquire power, which he sees as the central dynamic of international relations, structure does little of the explanatory work.

> The structure of the international system forces states which seek only to be secure nonetheless to act aggressively toward each other. Three features of the international system combine to cause states to fear one another: 1) the absence of a central authority that sits above states and can protect them from each other, 2) the fact that states always have some offensive military capability, and 3) the fact that states can never be certain about other states' intentions. Given this fear—which can never be wholly eliminated—states recognize that the more powerful they are relative to their rivals, the better their chances of survival. (Mearsheimer 2001: 2)

Note the shift from "the structure of the international system" to "features of the international system." Even more importantly, two of those three features are *not* structural; from uncertainty Mearsheimer jumps to fear—and what proves to be an almost overwhelming fear. And in the end fear does most of the analytical work. Structure (anarchy and the distribution of capabilities) may be part of, or even necessary, to the explanation. But it explains very little.

Or consider survival, which plays a central role in many ostensibly structural explanations. For example, Waltz (1979: 121) claims that "Balance-of-power politics prevail wherever two, and only two, requirements are met: that the order be anarchic and that it be populated by units wishing to survive." This might seem to be a very modest and uncontroversial non-structural addition. But a mere desire to survive explains nothing, not only because it is (close to) universal (and thus correlated with pretty much any form of behavior) but because the crucial question is the relative weights of survival and other interests—which vary dramatically both "in the world" and in different models and theories. Only when the desire to survive is close to paramount and pre-emptive is anything like a determinate prediction likely to be possible. And when it is not—which certainly is the situation in most of contemporary international relations—a desire to survive explains almost nothing (and probably can be left out of nearly all explanations).[11]

To repeat, not only is there nothing wrong with supplementing structural explanations, supplementation is necessary if we are to be able to offer real explanations of international events (rather than obscure gestures in the direction of anarchy and external material power). The only caveat—which I am afraid that most structural realists regularly ignore— is that these supplements be clearly acknowledged (and, at a minimum, not misrepresented).

If we acknowledge these supplementations, though, the typology that I have elaborated can give us a pretty good handle on the character of such "structural realist" explanations. In practice, they employ a very minimal structural model that is more or less extensively supplemented by non-structural elements. And these nonstructural elements are added in a way that may be guided by a realist perspective but it is not governed by the model.

The resulting "theories," it seems to me, are best described as *augmented structural realism*. Patrick James (1993) has described this kind of research strategy as "elaborated structural realism." But it involves not the further elaboration of the elements or character of structure but non-structural additions—and additions that are not governed by the logic of the structural starting point. Augmented thus seems to me a better description.

To be sure, structural realists *might* go about extending (elaborating) their conception of structure by developing an expanded account of the features that characteristically arrange (structure) the parts of international systems. I know of no realist, though, who has done that. The closest thing that I am aware of is Glenn Snyder's work on what he called "structural modifiers," such as technology and institutions, which he defines as "system-wide influences that are structural in their inherent nature but not potent enough internationally to warrant that description" (Snyder 1996: 169). And—quite unfortunately in my view—even this modest elaboration has not caught on.

---

[11] In Donnelly (2012: 610–616), I look at simple hunter-gatherer societies, which are anarchic and composed of people that wish to survive (who are also equal and equally armed) but who pursue security not through self-help balancing but by what I call binding through sharing. Waltz's only-two-requirements claim is simply empirically false. Where we see balancing, other factors are present and essential to the explanation.

"Structural realism" today thus is largely a set of variously augmented "structural realist" models and theories. Those models and theories, and the explanations derived from or associated with them, can fruitfully been seen as encompassed within a "school" that is insightfully described as both structural and realist. The realist tradition helps to guide the choice of additional elements and the ways in which they are deployed. And the focus of the school is on broad "structural" (in the ordinary-language sense of the term) constraints and opportunities.

But—and for my purposes here, these are the essential points—structure plays only a small part in most such explanations (because anarchy, which is indeed a generic feature of international relations, has no determinate effects and because very few international events can be explained primarily, let alone only, by the distribution of capabilities). Structural realism, thus understood, *cannot* be a general theory of international relations—because the additional factors required to produce explanations are specific to particular situations or types of international systems. And the realist contribution, as I emphasized above, lies not in the elements employed (either individually or in combination) but in shaping and applying a theory, model, or explanation.

Neoclassical Realism

The other principal strand of contemporary realism is usually labelled neo-classical.[12] Structure is moved to the background and attention is focused instead on, in Waltzian terms, "the unit level."

Waltz understands structure—fruitfully, I would argue—as the arrangement of the parts of a system; the *relations* between them. This makes not only what occurs within states (and what states do) but also how they inter-act "not structural." As Waltz puts it (1979: 80. Cf. 62, 69, 71, 110, 118), "structure is sharply distinguished from actions and interactions." There are thus two broad types of neo-classical realism, focusing on, respectively, the interactions of states and decision-making processes within states (and their results).

---

[12]The term was coined by Gideon Rose (1998). Schweller (2003) and Rathbun (2008) are lively expositions and defenses.

In both types, neoclassical realism is differentiated by *where* it looks for explanations; that is, the level of analysis on which it operates.[13] It is a (methodological) approach, not a (substantive) school.

A classic (and early) interactional example is Thomas Christensen and Jack Snyder's "Chain Gangs and Passed Bucks" (1990), which uses models of strategic interaction to explain certain alliance patterns (and their contribution to the outbreak of war). But even here, factors internal to states play a central role. And most neoclassical realist work focuses on foreign policy decision making.

We can usefully distinguish narrow and broad forms of such inward-looking neoclassical work.

In the narrow (or thin) form, illustrated by the literature on "under-balancing" (e.g., Schweller 2004, 2006), modestly augmented structural realism is treated as a rationalist model that sets a baseline of expectations. The focus then becomes explaining deviations from these expectations. Structural realism becomes a heuristic device, throwing up "puzzles" or "anomalies" to be explored non-structurally (although still from a realist perspective and with a realist style or sensibility).

The broad (or deep) form of neoclassical realism in effect treats anarchy and external material power as parameters within which decision-makers operate. The immediate sources of explanation are non-structural, lying in the full range of variables that foreign policy analysis regularly employs. A good recent example is Norrin Ripsman, Jeffrey Taliaferro, and Stephen Lobell's *Neoclassical Realist Theory of International Politics* (2016), which develops a fairly complex theory (I would say model) that focuses on how structural stimuli are processed through perception, decision making, and policy implementation (which in turn are influenced by leader images, strategic culture, state-society relations, and domestic institutions).

What makes neoclassical realist explanations *realist* is the special emphasis placed on external material power in anarchy. Even if decision-makers are in fact responding immediately to other factors and forces, those (ultimately preemptive) constraints are treated as nonetheless central to the explanation (for example, as internalized dispositions, unacknowledged assumptions about the context of action, or external forces that then act on the decisions that have been explained neoclassically).

---

[13] It is important that we not confuse levels of analysis in general, understood as the location of causal forces, with Waltz's particular three level (individual, state, system) model. For example, Waltz himself (1979: 62, 68, 99) speaks of "the level of (the) interacting units."

The principal explanatory variables employed by neoclassical realism, however, have no substantive focus or coherence. (Neoclassical realism is an approach.) We know very little about an explanation, and nothing about its substance, simply knowing that it is neoclassical realist. The wide range of nonstructural additions, many of which have no special connection to realism, bear most of the explanatory burden. The resulting explanations usually can best be described as eclectic or multi-perspectival.

That a model or explanation is appropriately described as neoclassical realist does *not* mean that "realism" does most, or even much, of the explaining. Realism helps to shape neoclassical realist explanations. Usually, though, "realism" does little of the explaining.

FEAR, UNCERTAINTY, AND THE RETURN TO (AND OF) REALISM

So far I have stressed the variety of realist "theories"—and thus the variety of ways and things that "realism" "explains." I have also stressed the role of realist perspectives in inspiring and guiding analysis (and thus defining a "theory" or explanation). I have had little to say, though, about the substance of realist perspectives.

Is there something like a core to those perspectives that we can use to help to identify (although not define) "realism"? I suggest that there is.

A realist sense or sensibility seems to me to lurk behind the definitions with which we began. And I think that I can see running through both structural realism and neoclassical realism, and "classical" realism as well, a fairly clear vision of the *nature* of international relations—and where that character comes from. My account, though, is very different from the accounts of most contemporary realists.

"Realism," as I see it, begins with self-interested states operating in a states system (i.e., an international system structured around states, which are its predominant actors). This states system has a narrow, thin, and weak normative-institutional structure that does not go much beyond what Hedley Bull (1977, ch. 1) calls rules of coexistence (in this case, establishing sovereign statehood and a system of contractual international law) and relies almost exclusively on self-help to enforce rules.

It is this normative-institutional structure—not the absence of an international government (anarchy)—that impels states to focus on the distribution of material capabilities. A thin and weak system of rules and a weak system of international governance pressures states towards self-help power politics by inducing fear and uncertainty (which are distinct problems that become especially acute when they interact and reinforce one another). What is frightening is not an "anarchic" world without an international government but a world with only minimal international rule and very few international rules.[14]

Neoliberal institutionalists, by contrast, see the international system as composed of a complex combination of states and (both public and private) nonstate actors, whose capabilities and authorities differ from issue area to issue area. *Their* international system has a fairly robust normative-institutional structure that provides not only an extensive system of rules but considerable international rule (both bilaterally and through international organizations and regimes). Fear and uncertainty—and the resulting pressures towards self-help balancing and power politics—thus often are mitigated, sometimes overcome, and occasionally even effectively eliminated.

International systems, I am suggesting, diverge most fundamentally in their *normative-institutional* structures. (This should not be surprising. International systems are *social* systems. And social systems are differentiated primarily by their norms and institutions.)

"Effects of anarchy" such as self-help balancing and the pursuit of relative gains actually arise from a particular institutional-normative structure (that is facilitated or enabled, but not caused, by the absence of an international government). And those effects work through fear and uncertainty, the nature and intensity of which varies considerably with time, place, and case. Whether realism has anything interesting or important to say about any particular international system, action, or outcome becomes, appropriately, an empirical question.

Now, finally, I come to the core questions of this volume. If, as I have suggested, a "realist world" is a states system with an anemic normative-institutional structure populated principally by states gripped by fear and uncertainty, then to the extent that such a world is actually realized "in the world," characteristically realist actions are likely to increase in number and salience and realist explanations are likely to gain weight. This, it seems to me, explains the "return" to (and of) realism in Europe—and, in reverse, its earlier "retreat."

---

[14] In Donnelly (2015: 210–211), I stress the importance of not jumping from absence of a "ruler" (government) to absence of "rule" or absence of "rules."

Anarchy, as I noted above, is a constant and thus cannot explain any sort of change. There has been no significant change in the distribution of material capabilities either. What *has* changed, as the title of this volume suggests, is fear and uncertainty—which are at the heart of the realist perspective; realism's comparative advantage, as it were. Thus realism's current return—and its earlier retreat as fear and uncertainty subsided in the immediate post-Cold War period.

My account also points, much more vaguely, towards where to look for explanations of this return. Structural realism offers only a perspective from which to develop a challenge to the retreat and return story. Neoclassical realism, I suspect, will have a variety of explanatory contributions. But what those contributions might be is radically unclear (because neoclassical realism is a methodological approach not a substantive school). If I am correct about the centrality of norms and institutions, though, we should expect to find—and, as a non-specialist at least, I think we can see—an erosion of peace-preserving norms (perhaps most strikingly in the Soviet annexation of Crimea and continuing intervention in Ukraine) and growing uncertainty about the continued conflict-ameliorating effects of regional institutions (perhaps most notably the EU—even before Brexit).

Realism is a set of theories, models, schools, and approaches that are "tuned" to operate in—and provide particular perspectives on—a dangerous international world. Realism is returning today in Europe, I would suggest, because many Europeans increasingly see similarities between the kinds of dangerous worlds that realists model and the world that they seem to be coming to live in. Some of the details of that world, and of what realism can (and cannot) tell us about it, are the subjects of the following chapters.

References

Bull, Hedley. 1977. *The Anarchical Society: A Study of Order in World Politics.* New York: Columbia University Press.

Christensen, Thomas J., and Jack Snyder. 1990. "Chain Gangs and Passed Bucks: Predicting Alliance Patterns in Multipolarity." *International Organization* 44 (2): 137–168.

Donnelly, Jack. 2008. "The Ethics of Realism." In *The Oxford Handbook of International Relations*, edited by Christian Reus-Smit and Duncan Snidal. Oxford: Oxford University Press.

———. 2012. "The Elements of the Structures of International Systems." *International Organization* 66 (4): 609–643.

———. 2015. "The Discourse of Anarchy in IR." *International Theory* 7 (3): 393–425.

Gilpin, Robert. 1996. "No One Loves a Political Realist." *Security Studies* 5 (3): 3–26.

James, Patrick. 1993. "Neorealism as a Research Enterprise: Toward Elaborated Structural Realism." *International Political Science Review / Revue internationale de science politique* 14 (2): 123–148.

Keohane, Robert O. 1986. "Theory of World Politics: Structural Realism and Beyond." In *Neo-Realism and Its Critics*, edited by Robert O. Keohane. New York: Columbia University Press.

———. 2012. "Twenty Years of Institutional Liberalism." *International Relations* 26 (2): 125–138.

Keohane, Robert O., and Lisa L. Martin. 2003. "Institutional Theory as a Research Program." In *Progress in International Relations Theory: Appraising the Field*, edited by Colin Elman and Miriam Fendis Elman. Cambridge: MIT Press.

King, Gary, Robert O. Keohane, and Sidney Verba. 1994. *Designing Social Inquiry*. Princeton: Princeton University Press.

Mearsheimer, John J. 1994/1995. "The False Promise of International Institutions." *International Security* 19 (3): 5–49.

———. 2001. *The Tragedy of Great Power Politics*. New York: W. W. Norton & Company.

Milner, Helen. 1991. "The Assumption of Anarchy in International Relations Theory: A Critique." *Review of International Studies* 17 (1): 67–85.

Powell, Robert. 1994. "Anarchy in International Relations Theory: The Neorealist-Neoliberal Debate." *International Organization* 48 (2): 313–344.

Rathbun, Brian. 2008. "A Rose by Any Other Name: Neoclassical Realism as the Logical and Necessary Extension of Structural Realism." *Security Studies* 17 (2): 294–321.

Ripsman, Norrin M., Jeffrey W. Taliaferro, and Stephen E. Lobell. 2016. *Neoclassical Realist Theory of International Politics*. Oxford: Oxford University Press.

Rose, Gideon. 1998. "Neoclassical Realism and Theories of Foreign Policy." *World Politics* 51 (1): 144–172.

Schweller, Randall L. 1997. "New Realist Research on Alliances: Refining, Not Refuting, Waltz's Balancing Proposition." *American Political Science Review* 91 (4): 927–930.

———. 2003. "The Progressivism of Neoclassical Realism." In *Progress in International Relations Theory: Appraising the Field*, edited by Colin Elman and Miriam Fendius Elman. Cambridge: MIT Press.

————. 2004. "Unanswered Threats: A Neo-Classical Realist Theory of Underbalancing." *International Security* 29 (2): 159–201.

————. 2006. *Unanswered Threats: Political Constraints on the Balance of Power.* Princeton: Princeton University Press.

Snidal, Duncan. 1991a. "International Cooperation Among Relative Gains Maximizers." *International Studies Quarterly* 35 (4): 387–402.

————. 1991b. "Relative Gains and the Pattern of International Cooperation." *American Political Science Review* 85 (3): 701–726.

Snyder, Glenn H. 1996. "Process Variables in Neorealist Theory." *Security Studies* 5 (3): 167–192.

Stein, Arthur A. 2008. "Neoliberal Institutionalism." In *Oxford Handbook of International Relations,* edited by Christian Reus-Smit and Duncan Snidal. Oxford: Oxford University Press.

Wagner, R. Harrison. 2007. *War and the State: The Theory of International Politics.* Ann Arbor: University of Michigan Press.

Walt, Stephen M. 1987. *The Origins of Alliances.* Ithaca: Cornell University Press.

————. 1988. "Testing Theories of Alliance Formation: The Case of Southwest Asia." *International Organization* 42 (2): 275–316.

Waltz, Kenneth N. 1959. *Man, the State and War: A Theoretical Analysis.* New York: Columbia University Press.

————. 1979. *Theory of International Politics.* New York: Random House.

————. 1988. "The Origins of War in Neorealist Theory." *Journal of Interdisciplinary History* 18 (4): 615–628.

————. 1990a. "Nuclear Myths and Political Realities." *American Political Science Review* 84 (3): 731–745.

————. 1990b. "Realist Thought and Neo-Realist Theory." *Journal of International Affairs* 44 (1): 21–37.

————. 1991. "Realist Thought and Neo-Realist Theory." In *The Evolution of Theory in International Relations: Essays in Honor of William T. R. Fox,* edited by Robert L. Rothstein. Columbia: University of South Carolina Press.

————. 1993. "The Emerging Structure of International Politics." *International Security* 18 (2): 44–79.

————. 1996. "International Politics is Not Foreign Policy." *Security Studies* 6 (1): 54–57.

————. 2000. "Structural Realism After the Cold War." *International Security* 25 (1): 5–41.

Wendt, Alexander. 1992. "Anarchy is What States Make of It: The Social Construction of Power Politics." *International Organization* 46 (2): 391–425.

Wohlforth, William C. 2008. "Realism." In *Oxford Handbook of International Relations,* edited by Christian Reus-Smit and Duncan Snidal. Oxford: Oxford University Press.

CHAPTER 3

Nationalism vs. Internationalism: Fears, Uncertainties and Geopolitics in Europe

Paul Viotti

The post-Cold War peace among great powers has given way to fears and uncertainties about security in Europe and in the world as a whole. A rightward, nationalist political turn in the domestic politics of a number of countries challenges the entire post-World War II liberal project marked by (a) increasingly open borders, (b) reliance on international organizations for managing relations among states, (c) maintenance of international monetary liquidity accompanied by fewer and fewer constraints on global trade and investment, (d) arms control and reduced allocation of resources to military spending, and (e) global promotion of democratic governments, economic development and human rights.

These concerns are a response to the rise of Vladimir Putin and the Russian-nationalist policies he has pursued vis-à-vis the former Soviet republics of Georgia, Ukraine, and elsewhere; Brexit—the U.K. withdrawal from the European Union (EU); the emergence of an America-first, nationalist rhetoric in the Trump administration in the United

P. Viotti (✉)
Graduate School of International Studies,
University of Denver, Denver, CO, USA
e-mail: pviotti@du.edu

© The Author(s) 2019
R. Belloni et al. (eds.), *Fear and Uncertainty in Europe*, Global Issues,
https://doi.org/10.1007/978-3-319-91965-2_3

States; and rising nationalist sentiments in other European countries, particularly in Central and Eastern Europe.

Do these events mark the beginning of the end of the multilateralist liberal order that has avoided general war and sustained the European peace? More specifically, are we returning to the kind of realist geopolitics among states that prevailed prior to the two world wars and, for that matter, in previous centuries? Given the rise of this nationalism, how durable are the liberal institutions and norms of the post-World War and post-Cold War orders? Can international and non-governmental organizations sustain the liberal project that created them?

These questions are the reason the authors in this volume came together as policy-oriented scholars to discuss and write about these fears and uncertainties that disturb the European peace. Balance-of-power, geopolitical realism in European thinking and liberal institutionalism—embedding liberal ideas in global and regional institutions—are the twin pillars upon which security rests. When one pillar is undermined or weakened, it affects the other adversely as well. The play between the two constructions relates directly to success or failure in maintaining international peace and security. If one becomes dominant or efforts are made to ignore or displace the other, security becomes ever more fragile. Engaging in realist discourse need not trash liberal or constructivist understandings of security. The two security constructs operate in tandem.

REALIST GEOPOLITICS AND LIBERALISM

Geopolitics—a realist focus on the balance of power—has dominated European thinking on security. In fact, as Ernest B. Haas argued as early as the 1950s, the balance of power in Europe has often produced as much war as it has peace (Haas 1953; see also Hass 1964). The critical question is the degree to which balance-of-power thinking in the realist tradition is accompanied by the more cosmopolitan, pluralist or liberal modes of thinking. From this perspective, peace cannot be assured by balance of power alone. Developing greater integration or connectedness of states and non-state actors, accompanied by liberal norms, has proven to be a more productive formula for maintaining international peace and security.

In this regard, the liberal aim of global institutions—the United Nations Organization (UNO) and its network of specialized agencies—and such regional ones as the European Union (EU), Organization of Security and Cooperation (OSCE), and the Council of Europe—is not only to manage conflicts and thus avoid war, but also to sustain and advance cooperative and collaborative measures among member states.

At the same time, however, alliances and other coalitions that form from time to time indicate the continuing presence of realist, geopolitical calculations. Both sets of considerations are fully consistent with the UN Charter, Chapters 7 and 8, that under Security Council auspices rely on both *collective security* and *collective defense* measures. The former is collective international law-enforcement to include both peaceful means and, under Article 42, the use of force against aggressor states. Individual states retain their sovereign right to self-defense but also, under Article 51, may take actions with others in alliances or coalitions.

In the paragraphs below we take up both liberal and realist or balance-of-power images of security both globally and within Europe. Even as the Cold War division between East and West was marked by competing alliances—the North Atlantic Treaty Organization (NATO) formed in 1949 and the Warsaw Pact in 1955—these were, at the same time, accompanied by global and regional institutions that focused on cooperative and collaborative measures.

The termination of the Warsaw Pact in 1991 and breakup of the Soviet Union in 1992 marked the end of the Cold War, but not the end of realist, balance-of-power thinking. Indeed, NATO extended its membership and security guarantee to former Warsaw Pact and, in 2004, to the post-Soviet, Baltic republics of Estonia, Latvia, and Lithuania. As NATO expanded, so did the EU either by extending membership or association agreements—the latter offered most recently to Georgia and Ukraine. In Moscow, this NATO and EU expansion was seen in realist terms merely as US and western European encroachment on what had been the Russian (previously Soviet) sphere of influence.

Policies pursued by Russian President Vladimir Putin then, are a reaction, at least in part, to what are understood as US-led, western encroachments. They are also a calculated effort by Putin's Russia to recover lost power and influence suffered by the end of Soviet dominance in Central and Eastern Europe. Some see Putin identifying most closely with Tsar Alexander III. It was he who "ended Alexander II's messy liberal experiment to restore conservative authoritarianism—as

Putin did after Yeltsin."[1] Violations of the Intermediate-range Nuclear Forces (INF) and the carefully crafted European conventional forces agreements[2] indicate a willingness to set aside inconvenient arms control commitments that constrain Russian military preparations.

For his part, President Donald Trump has pursued nationally oriented policies favored primarily by his southern-and-rural populist, working-class electoral base. The "America First," if not "America Alone," slogan is consistent with ending US participation in the Trans-Pacific Partnership (TPP), pulling out of the Paris climate accords, curtailing other environmental limitations that have negative implications both at home and abroad, putting limits on immigration, confronting allies and questioning alliance commitments and, as if that were not enough, allowing decimation of the US State Department. At the same time, he shares with Putin a liking for authoritarian regimes run by "strong" leaders with whom he can deal. As with his Russian counterpart, President Trump also has been the object of severe criticism, some of it very personal.[3]

It is somewhat ironic that German Chancellor Angela Merkel, now joined by French President Emmanuel Macron, are the principal liberal torchbearers left standing. The irony lies in the great success of American foreign policy in the post-World War II—its championing of the liberal project throughout its Western European sphere of influence and elsewhere in the world. With the US relinquishing its leadership role—at least for now—survival of this liberal order in Europe now depends primarily upon the efforts of American allies—particularly Germany, France, the United Kingdom, and Italy.

---

[1] Putin is quoted as saying: "The greatest criminals in our history were those weaklings who threw power on the floor—Nicholas II and Mikhail Gorbachev—who allowed power to be picked up by hysterics and madmen." Putin reveres both Tsar Nicholas II and Stalin. See the historian Simon Sebag Montefiore (2017: 656–657).

[2] These were made as part of the Conference on Security and Cooperation in Europe (CSCE) process that was institutionalized at the end of the Cold War as the Organization for Security and Cooperation in Europe (OSCE).

[3] In one anthology of essays by 27 psychiatrists and mental health experts, the consensus is that he suffers from malignant narcissism defined as including narcissistic personality disorder (NPD), antisocial behavior, paranoid traits, and sadism. Consistent with this assessment, one author identifies Trump with solipsism—seeing the world with oneself as the lens. See Lee (2017: 94–95, 114–115 *et passim*). Chronicling the turbulence of the president's first year in office is Wolff (2018).

Constructing Global Institutions

Following World War II, liberal norms became embedded in newly constructed global institutions. The foundation stones for constructing the great European post-war peace began to be put into place even while World War II was still raging on the continent. Optimistically looking forward, the British, American, and Soviet allies began meeting in London in 1943 to detail the occupation of Central Europe once victory over the Axis powers had been achieved. These arrangements were concretized later in summit meetings at Yalta and Potsdam in 1945.

Multilateral discussions including other countries were held in 1944 both at Dumbarton Oaks in Georgetown (Washington, DC) on establishing a United Nations (UN) organization and at Bretton Woods (New Hampshire) on constructing what became global financial institutions. The International Monetary Fund (IMF) has enabled and facilitated trade and commerce by providing a global mechanism for maintaining international monetary liquidity. The International Bank for Reconstruction and Development (IBRD) or World Bank has made capital available for investment, particularly for economic development. An early indicator of the Cold War division of Europe between East and West was the Soviet decision to opt out of the IMF and IBRD that were seen as dominated by US and other capitalist interests.

In 1945 the parties met in San Francisco figuratively to set the bricks and mortar in place for the UN that was to be headquartered in New York. The five "great powers" or victorious allies that had called themselves "united nations"—the US, Soviet Union, Britain, France and China—constituted the core of the Security Council. Although each member state had one vote in the General Assembly and other principal organs[4] in which they participated, as permanent members of the Security Council, each of the five retained veto power over any resolutions or actions that body might take. In addition to the IMF and World Bank, the parties constituted other specialized agencies linked loosely to one or another of the principal organs of the UN. These efforts established a global network of international organizations or specialized agencies in the UN system.

---

[4]The principal organs of the UN are the General Assembly, Security Council, Economic and Social Council, Trusteeship Council, International Court of Justice, and the Secretariat.

In Europe the peace also depended on a commitment to multilateralism embedded in the Brussels Pact that set up the West European Union (WEU) in 1948, the North Atlantic Treaty Organization (NATO) in 1949, the beginnings of the European Union (EU) with establishing a six-nation European Coal and Steel Community (1952) and two other six-nation communities under the Treaty of Rome (1958): one for economic cooperation (EEC) and the other for atomic energy (EURATOM). Germany, France, Italy, Belgium, the Netherlands, and Luxembourg were the charter members of these European Communities (EC)—the so-called "inner six." The European Free Trade Association (EFTA) or "Outer 7"[5] was a formation that allowed the UK to maintain its commonwealth ties while also engaging in multilateral trade agreements with non-EC countries in Europe. In the East, the Soviet Union led its own multilateral Council on Mutual Economic Assistance (CMEA or COMECON) from 1949 to the end of the Cold War in 1991.

THE BALANCE OF POWER AND NORMS OF CONDUCT IN MODERN EUROPEAN HISTORY

In this brief historical review, we underscore both balance-of-power geopolitics and the associated norms constructed to maintain the peace. Great powers mattered then, as they do now. Developing consensus among them on values underlying the order was essential. As such, peace had both ideational and material components—the latter in the distribution or balance of power or capabilities among them. In their own interests, lesser powers played an enabling role.

A key principal of the order was that no continental European power could become too strong. Maintaining a balance of power to keep contending parties at bay, accompanied by agreed norms to guide their conduct of both bilateral and multilateral diplomacy, was the formula for peace. By contrast, erosion of these norms or allowing one or another of the continental powers to become too strong were prescriptions for the outbreak of war.

Classic settlements of wars in Europe were accompanied by values agreed by the princes of the time on the ways and means by which they could work together, thus avoiding yet another outbreak of war.

---

[5] Austria, Denmark, Norway, Portugal, Sweden, Switzerland, and the United Kingdom.

The individualism of sovereign[6] states—the construct that emerged from the Peace of Augsburg (1555) and the Peace of Westphalia (1648)—was not in itself conducive to peace over the longer term.[7]

The French revolutionary period (1789–1815) had lasting impact on the European continent. Napoleon's popular army upset the balance in a French effort to transform Europe. France had acted as a revolutionary power, French military actions having reached across Europe as far to the east as Russia. After the defeat of Napoleon in 1814, the Conservative powers (Russia, Austria-Hungary, Prussia,[8] and Britain) and lesser states gathered together in Vienna in 1815 in a Congress hosted by Austrian Prince Metternich. They reconstructed a balance of power accompanied by agreed norms—the "Concert of Europe"—as principal means for sustaining peace and avoiding the scourge of war that had harmed all of them in substantial ways (Kissinger 1957). The general peace lasted for some 99 years until upset by the guns of August in 1914 (Tuchman 1962).

Ideas in the minds of statesmen and other diplomats mattered. Reestablishing a continental balance in the center of Europe required restoring France lest Prussia and Austria become too strong appealed to Viscount Castlereagh and the Duke of Wellington from England and the Russian Tsar Alexander. The principal players thus reconstructed France slightly larger territorially then it had been in 1789—an amazing diplomatic achievement by the French representative, Count Talleyrand.

After all, a defeated France no longer had a military capability to assure a positive outcome. Its fate rested almost entirely on an idea—that restoring a balance of power was in the interest of the other players. This idea of reestablishing a multilateral balance was decisive in driving their deliberations.

---

[6] That each king, duke or other prince could establish the religion of the inhabitants within his territorial domain (*cujus regio, ejus religio*) was core to the emergent concept of sovereignty.

[7] On the Peace of Westphalia, see Kegley and Raymond (2002) and Croxton 2013/2015). On the Thirty Years' War (1618–1648), see Wilson (2011), Wedgwood (2005), and Parker (1984/1987).

[8] Chancellor (Prince) von Hardenberg and the diplomat, Wilhelm Humboldt, represented Prussia, directed by King Frederick William III who was also in Vienna. The Prussian role in these deliberations were decidedly less important than efforts by Metternich, Talleyrand and others.

Their remedy, however, did not stop with the balance of power. The parties also developed norms by which future conflicts might be managed among the great powers of the day. The balance of power and associated norms did not prevent smaller wars as in Crimea (1853–1856) between Russia on the one hand and France, Britain, the Ottoman Empire, and Sardinia on the other. Indeed, there had been some erosion in these consultative norms over the decades prior to the outbreak of war.

Nor did a consultative mechanism prevent war between France and Prussia (1871) but, as in Crimea, it did keep these conflicts from becoming general war on the scale of the Napoleonic period or, earlier, the degree of destruction of lives and property that occurred among the German states prior to the Augsburg and Westphalia settlements.

France had been the leading military power on the European continent until Prussia, to the surprise of most observers, defeated the French in 1871. This defeat was followed by the unification of Germany. Until the 1890s, Otto von Bismarck, the "Iron Chancellor," famously oversaw the development of German military capabilities both on the ground against France and at sea against the British Royal Navy.

By the early twentieth century, the balance of power that had been established in Vienna no longer held sway. The German geopolitical center of Europe had become very strong, France no match for it. The arms race that occurred in the late 19th and early twentieth centuries with Britain and France on one side, trying to counter the military rise of the newly unified Germany, came to a head in the events of 1914.

From a geopolitical view, the center in Europe had again become too strong. It was more than Russia in the east or France and Britain across the channel could balance. Moreover, the norms that kept the parties from going to war in the post-1815 period had eroded completely, fallen by the wayside. The balance of power alone could not keep the peace. Its scales had shifted requiring great powers on the west (France and Britain, later the United States) to ally with Russia in the east to defeat an alliance of central powers—Germany, Austria-Hungary, and the Ottoman Empire.

After the defeat of Germany and the other Central Powers in the "Great War" (World War I), those who met sought to weaken Germany, the geopolitical center of Europe. Economist John Maynard Keynes opposed the terms as too harsh. As he critically put it, no effort was spared further to impoverish the Germans. Beyond disarming Germany, imposition of reparations well above what the recovering German economy could sustain contributed to economic collapse and a political environment in Germany conducive in 1933 to the rise of Hitler.

As the historical record makes clear, in just 20 years a resurgent Germany posed yet again a military challenge to Russia (now the Soviet Union) in the east and France, Britain and, across the Atlantic, the United States in the west. Although a liberal regime had been established in Germany after World War I (the Weimar Republic), it was unable to sustain itself from right-wing assault. The National Socialists under Hitler relied on support by the disenfranchised German working class made to suffer by the imposition of reparations by France and Britain that, in turn, were driven by the American demand that its allies repay their war debts. The Hitler regime quickly formed political alliances with industrialists, the military, agricultural and other interests that composed the fascist state.

The norms needed to sustain peace in the post-World War I period were undermined not just by the reparations and war-debt regime, but also by the United States failure to join the League of Nations that its president, Woodrow Wilson, in cooperation with the victorious allies, had helped craft in 1918. There was enough blame to go round to cover all parties. Once again, not only had there been an erosion of norms—the collective security (collective law-enforcement) norms of the League of Nations Covenant, but also the geopolitical center had become too strong. An "Axis" alliance of Germany, Austria, and Italy now threatened France, Britain, and the United States in the west and the Soviet Union in the east.

The devastation of World War II resulted, yet again in the destruction of German military capabilities. The defeat of Germany was followed by its division between the victorious allies with zones of occupation by the Soviet Union in the east and, in the west, by United States, Britain, and France—the latter's zone of occupation carved out of the American zone opposite the Franco-German disputed Alsace and Lorraine provinces now restored to French control.

Intense in constructing the post-war order, the political leaders and diplomats who met in London, Tehran, Yalta, Potsdam, Washington and San Francisco were painfully aware of the errors that had been made in the post-World War I settlements. Resolved not to repeat them, institutions were constructed to sustain the liberal values seen as conducive to peace.

A decided effort was made to restore liberal values embodied in the rule of law—international law, in particular. Collective security from the League of Nations was restored in the UN Charter, Chapters 7 and 8 in particular—that law-abiding states would coalesce to counter any aggressor states seen as acting illegally. Stronger than the League had provided, Article 42 in Chapter 8 gave authority to the Security Council to authorize the use of force in order to maintain or restore international peace and security in international law-enforcement actions against aggressors.

The UN Charter, however, went well beyond collective security, by recognizing the right of all sovereign states to both individual and collective defense. This addition to collective security as remedy for restoring and maintaining or maintaining the peace was in effect acknowledging the ongoing importance of a balance of power. Collective security norms embedded in a legal regime under the League had proven insufficient to stop Germany and its allies in Europe and Japan in East Asia and the Pacific from invading and occupying other states.

The UN Charter identified peaceful remedies that were collectively to be pursued first (Chapter 7), but when these failed the Security Council could adopt measures to include the use of force to re-establish and maintain international peace and security (Chapter 8). If international law-enforcement (i.e., collective security) failed, states could still act individually or in alliances and other coalitions to challenge aggressors. Put another way, the balance-of-power remedy now also had legal standing under Article 51, which it did not have under the League Covenant. International law, accompanied by other liberal values, thus coexisted with realist understandings of the need for a balance of power.

THE GEOPOLITICS OF THE COLD WAR

The interwar regime (1918–1939) had effectively outlawed secret agreements and alliances because they were understood to have caused World War I. The realist critique was that the absence of alliances meant there was nothing materially to stop a state bent on aggression. Even the League of Nations was precluded from using force. By contrast, the liberal norms established by law and embedded in the UN and other international organizations allowed alliances and other coalitions to form from time to time. Put another way, liberalism accommodated realist geopolitical understandings of the balance of power (Claude 1962; cf. Carr 1939/2016).

Three different images of security emerged in Europe during the Cold War. These images drove the thinking of statesmen and the actions they took. Two of them had realist, geopolitical underpinnings (one East-West and the other keeping Germany in check), the third a liberal or cosmopolitan construct.

East-West Imagery

At the end of World War II, the "Big Four" victorious allies established zones of occupation in Germany and Austria, jointly occupying Berlin and Vienna. The Soviet Union quickly established a buffer zone in the countries it had liberated from German control in World War II. The US, UK, and France solidified their position in the west, their German zones of occupation becoming the Federal Republic of Germany (FRG) in May, 1949. For their part, the Soviets followed suit in October, forming a separate German Democratic Republic (GDR). The Cold War geopolitical lines were in place, thus dividing East and West in a new balance of power on the European continent. As Winston Churchill famously put it:

> From Stettin in the Baltic to Trieste in the Adriatic, an iron curtain has descended across the Continent. Behind that line lie all the capitals of the ancient states of Central and Eastern Europe. Warsaw, Berlin, Prague, Vienna, Budapest, Belgrade, Bucharest and Sofia, all these famous cities and the populations around them lie in what I must call the Soviet sphere, and all are subject in one form or another, not only to Soviet influence but to a very high and, in many cases, increasing measure of control from Moscow.[9]

Keeping Germany in Check

The same territorial lines that divided East from West also effectively divided Germany into two republics. The division of Germany weakened the European center by creating two Germanys. Underscoring recognition of the geopolitical principle of not allowing Germany in the center of Europe from becoming too strong, some Frenchmen—tongues deeply

---

[9]The "Sinews of Peace" or "Iron Curtain Speech" delivered at Westminster College, Fulton, Missouri, March 5, 1946.

embedded in cheeks—commented that the French loved the Germans so much that even two Germanys were not enough, perhaps three, four or even five Germanys would be a better remedy. It was, indeed, a not so subtle reference to an earlier time prior to 1871 when its adversary was still divided into a number of Germanic states.

The Brussels Pact in 1948 established what in 1954 became the West European Union (WEU)—an alliance designed initially to counter any resurgence of German military power—a European balance-of-power remedy pursued by the UK, France, Belgium, Luxembourg, and the Netherlands. One year later the North Atlantic Treaty Organization (NATO) was established. It followed the same balance-of-power remedy as the WEU, strengthened by the admission of the United States. As the first NATO secretary general, British Lord Ismay, put it clearly but rather undiplomatically, the alliance's purpose was "to keep the Russians out, the Americans in, and the Germans down." East-West imagery (keep the Russians out and Americans in) clearly overlapped with keeping Germany-in-check understandings.

For its part, Germany joined both the WEU (1954) and NATO (1955). Rather than balance against Germany, both alliances included the Federal Republic in collective-defense efforts increasingly directed against the Soviet Union and its allies in Central and Eastern Europe that in 1955 became the Warsaw Pact.

As competing alliances, NATO and the Warsaw Pact solidified the division of Europe between East and West. The threat of war, particularly one that could become nuclear, became a stabilizing influence during the Cold War that ended only with the dissolution of the Soviet Union and Warsaw Pact in the early 1990s. For its part, from the outset NATO's focus was not just as an alliance, but also an organization committed to liberal values in general, democracy in particular.

Balance-of-power, collective-defense considerations in Article 5 guarantee that the NATO parties come together to take appropriate action were any member country attacked:

> The Parties agree that an armed attack against one or more of them in Europe or North America shall be considered an attack against them all and consequently they agree that, if such an armed attack occurs, each of them, in exercise of the right of individual or collective self-defence recognised by Article 51 of the Charter of the United Nations, will assist the Party or Parties so attacked by taking forthwith, individually and in concert

with the other Parties, *such action as it deems necessary*[emphasis added], including the use of armed force, to restore and maintain the security of the North Atlantic area.

Moreover, this collective-defense commitment is still under the auspices of the Security Council:

Any such armed attack and all measures taken as a result thereof shall immediately be reported to the Security Council. Such measures shall be terminated when the Security Council has taken the measures necessary to restore and maintain international peace and security.

As a practical matter, of course, the US, British, and French veto power in the Security Council require their concurrence in any initiative for the UN to take over.

Liberal-Institutionalist Imagery

Given Ottawa's advocacy, the so-called Canadian Article 2 of the North Atlantic Treaty goes beyond realist balance-of-power considerations, underscoring commitment to advancing liberal norms seen as essential to maintaining peace:

The Parties will contribute toward the further development of peaceful and friendly international relations by strengthening their free institutions, by bringing about a better understanding of the principles upon which these institutions are founded, and by promoting conditions of stability and well-being. They will seek to eliminate conflict in their international economic policies and will encourage economic collaboration between any or all of them.

These sentiments were fully consistent with efforts in global organizations like the UN and its agencies that advanced human rights, proper treatment of refugees, economic development to advance human welfare—all part of an effort to avoid yet another turn to general war in Europe and globally.

As noted above, US support for Franco-German efforts with each other and Italy, Belgium, the Netherlands, and Luxembourg to form a coal and steel community in 1952 and, six years later, European economic and atomic energy communities were intended to advance peace and security through interdependent and interconnected economic and social links among former adversaries. Although formation of these communities did not address military or security considerations per se, in fact they took them into account.

Franco-German collaboration in the production and trade of coal and steel gave the French a sense of security that they would have sufficient lead time should a resurgent Germany ever use these commodities as part of any rearmament effort. Collaborating with its former enemy also was explicit recognition by France that balancing German power had failed in three wars—the Franco-Prussian and World Wars I and II.

With a clear focus on its own security, French leaders put greater weight on collaboration with the Germans to avoid any future return by them to militarist policies of the past. The success of European integration in succeeding decades, notwithstanding occasional obstacles that had to be overcome, not only accomplished economic and social goals to include the advancement of human rights and other democratic values, but also improved security by reducing the likelihood of major powers in Western Europe returning to the use or threat of force to resolve conflicts.

East-West, European and Atlantic-to-the-Urals Multilateralism

Two multilateral conferences were convened—the Mutual and Balanced Force Reduction Talks (MBFR) in Vienna (1972) and the Conference on Security and Cooperation in Europe (CSCE) in Helsinki (1973). MBFR, following East-West imagery, brought NATO and Warsaw Pact together for arms reduction talks. The CSCE, following liberal, all-inclusive imagery assembled the United States, Canada and all of Europe.

In many respects, the CSCE was a multilateral outgrowth of West German liberal-cosmopolitan thinking. The *Ostpolitik* pursued beginning in 1969 by West German Chancellor Willy Brandt, the former mayor of West Berlin, was a reaction to the East-West division of Europe in general, Germany in particular. Some sixty million people resided in the Federal Republic of Germany—a country roughly the size of the US state of Colorado. Caught in the crosshairs of US-NATO and USSR-Warsaw Pact rivalry, Germany would be the likely battlefield in any East-West war.

Seeking a way out of this security dilemma that also kept Germans in the East separated from those in the West, *Ostpolitik* pursued a liberal-cosmopolitan approach to security. A wall in Berlin and other fortifications separated the FRG from the GDR and other East European countries in the Soviet sphere. The idea driving *Ostpolitik* was to find ways to cross these obstacles by reaching out, crossing these imposed boundaries and bringing peoples together through visits, cultural, economic and other exchanges.

Not surprisingly, the Brandt government pressured the United States to expand the all-inclusive scope of multilateralism in what became the CSCE. Over the next two decades, MBFR talks in Vienna bogged down over the so-called "data problem"—that East and West could not agree on what constituted equivalency in units to be eliminated on both sides. In a deeper sense, the impasse reflected an unwillingness by both sides to alter the *status quo*. By contrast to MBFR, the CSCE made early progress on establishing such confidence and security-building measures (CSBMs) as providing for notification and observers of military exercises and establishing communications among opposing parties. Toward the end of the Cold War, agreements were made that limited military deployments—a regime that effectively reduced the likelihood of war. At the end of the Cold War, the CSCE process was institutionalized in Vienna as the Organization for Cooperation and Security in Europe (OSCE) that now has 57 member states from the Atlantic to the Urals (for a detailed discussion of MBFR and CSCE see Viotti 1990).

THE POST-COLD WAR DECADES

The US-Soviet, NATO-Warsaw Pact arms race in the 1980s contributed directly to the economic collapse and ultimate demise of the Soviet Union and its control of countries in the "Soviet sphere." *Glasnost* (openness), *perestroika* (restructuring of economy and politics) and other policies pursued by Soviet leader, Mikael Gorbachev, precipitated unintended events that effectively altered the East-West balance of power in Europe, leaving the United States and its NATO allies in a position of primacy.

NATO expansion to countries previously in the Soviet sphere (to include the Baltic republics that had since 1940 been incorporated within the USSR) still reflected East-West geopolitical imagery as the West moved further eastward, displacing Russian influence in Central and Eastern Europe. At the same time, the West adopted liberal or cosmopolitan policies designed to include all European parties. NATO also established partnerships with former Soviet republics, but except for the Baltic republics, membership in the alliance excluded the Russian Federation and other former Soviet republics. The East-West division line remained in place, albeit moved further to the East.

For its part, the EC by 1992 had established a common market that allows the free flow of the factors of production—resources, labor, and capital—across national boundaries. Now calling itself the European Union (EU), the parties set the objective of becoming an economic and monetary union by 2000 to include an EU central bank in Frankfurt and construction of a common currency, the euro—the UK abstaining from this monetary integration. Some EU advocates worried at the time that "widening" by admitting more members and associates undermined efforts to deepen the level of integration within the EU.

Quite apart from the widening vs. deepening debate within EU circles, Russia—as noted above—saw "widening" of the EU even as the parties were "deepening" the level of integration as encroachment on its traditional sphere of influence. It was a sphere that, in competition historically with Prussia, later a unified Germany and Austria-Hungary, had been constructed over centuries of Czarist and, in the twentieth century, Soviet politics.

Multilateral efforts in arms control transformed the face of Europe, particularly in the 1990s. Accompanied by elaborate CSBMs—agreed geographic and quantitative limits on military forces within the CSCE process (subsequently institutionalized under the OSCE)—reduced threat levels substantially. Progress also was made on banning and destroying chemical weapons (as earlier had been done with biological weapons) as well as eliminating the residual of nuclear weapons in post-Soviet republics.

LOOKING FORWARD

Multilateralism is itself a norm embedded in institutions—the UN and its many specialized agencies, the European Union, NATO, the Council of Europe, and the OSCE among them. A shift away from multilateralism to bilateralism or unilateralism driven by the political right in various countries undermines the embedded liberalism in the elaborate architecture of multilateral institutions constructed and sustained in the three quarters of a century since the end of World War II.

The American shift away from assuming leadership tasks may be a temporary phenomenon that will be reversed by the changing tides of domestic politics within the United States.[10] Certainly US interests still lie with the liberal institutions and cooperative processes its diplomats so laboriously helped construct over more than seven decades. A central question is whether American allies are willing and able to sustain the liberal project by collaborating with each other and helping these institutions weather the storm that has formed around them. On an optimistic note, if the pendulum of American domestic politics shifts back toward the center, the United States government likely will rejoin these mutually beneficial efforts.

References

Carr, E. H. 1939/2016. *The Twenty Years' Crisis, 1919–1939*. New York: Palgrave Macmillan.

Claude, Inis. 1962. *Power and International Relations*. New York: Random House.

Croxton, Derek. 2013/2015. *The Last Christian Peace: The Congress of Westphalia as a Baroque Event*. New York: Palgrave Macmillan.

Haas, E. B. 1953. "The Balance of Power: Prescription, Concept, or Propaganda?" *World Politics* 5 (4): 442–477.

Haas, E. B. 1964. *Beyond the Nation State*. Stanford, CA: Stanford University Press.

Kegley, Charles W. Jr., and Gregory Raymond. 2002. *Exorcising the Ghost of Westphalia*. Upper Saddle River, NJ: Prentice Hall and Pearson Education.

Kissinger, Henry. 1957. *A World Restored*. London: Weidenfeld & Nicolson.

Lee, Brandy X. 2017. *The Dangerous Case of Donald Trump*. New York: St. Martin's Press.

Montefiore, Simon Sebag. 2017. *The Romanovs, 1613–1918*. New York: Random House and Vintage Books.

Parker, Geoffrey. 1984/1987. *The Thirty Years' War*. New York: Military Heritage Press.

Tuchman, Barbara. 1962. *The Guns of August*. Novato, CA: Presidio Press.

---

[10] At the time of this writing, investigations are still underway by the Special Counsel within the Justice Department of any collusion in 2016 between the Trump campaign and Russia as well as whether efforts have been taken by the president or his agents to impede or obstruct the investigation. Some observers also allege loans made by Russian lenders to (and money laundering by Russian operatives using) Trump business affiliates. The impact of these matters on the November 2018 Congressional elections is unclear. Whether legal findings will be confined to participants in the Trump campaign (some have already been charged) or, more broadly, will engulf the Trump administration remains a central legal and political question.

Viotti, Paul. R. 1990. "Arms Control and Security in Europe." In *American Defense Policy*, 6th edition, edited by Schuyler Foerster and Edward N. Wright. Baltimore: The Johns Hopkins University Press.

Wedgwood, Cicely Veronica. 2005. *The Thirty Years War*. New York: New York Review Books.

Wilson, Peter H. 2011. *The Thirty Years War: Europe's Tragedy*. London: Penguin.

Wolff, Michael. 2018. *Fire and Fury: Inside the Trump White House*. New York: Henry Holt and Company.

CHAPTER 4

Europe May Be Done with Power, but Power Is Not Done with Europe: Europe During an Era of American Unipolarity and of Relative Decline

Paul Van Hooft and Annette Freyberg-Inan

INTRODUCTION

Realism is rejected by many European International Relations scholars. Since the early to mid-1990s, European scholarship has been dominated by liberalism as well as constructivist and poststructural approaches. Here we argue that the rejection of realism is shortsighted, and that realism's dismissal is often based on a simplistic understanding of the theory and its premises. We discuss how realist theory can provide important, if often incomplete, explanations for the phenomena it is often accused of failing to account for: the Cold War and the decades of relative peace that followed, as well as the transformations of actors and interactions

P. Van Hooft (✉)
European University Institute (EUI), Florence, Italy
e-mail: Paul.vanHooft@EUI.eu

A. Freyberg-Inan
University of Amsterdam, Amsterdam, The Netherlands
e-mail: a.freyberginan@uva.nl

© The Author(s) 2019
R. Belloni et al. (eds.), *Fear and Uncertainty in Europe*, Global Issues,
https://doi.org/10.1007/978-3-319-91965-2_4

within the global order during that time. Moreover, we stress the importance of distinguishing between structural and neoclassical realism, and argue that many critics have overlooked useful additions and innovations within the realist canon over the past quarter-century. As has been argued elsewhere (Freyberg-Inan et al. 2009; Rathbun 2008; Van Hooft 2015), neoclassical realism has greater potential than structural realism to remain a broadly useful theoretical approach to understanding world affairs.

However, we also insist that several core insights of structural realism, such as the relevance of offensive capabilities within the system, of uncertainty about intentions, and of apprehension regarding the distribution of power, remain important for helping us to explain and predict states' behavioral patterns and systemic developments in international politics. Structural realism goes a long way—and much further than any of its rivals—towards explaining the boundaries within which states operate and that delimit the range of options and interests they can pursue with any likelihood of success. And it offers a compelling argument for the broad nature of their responses, within those limits. In turn, neoclassical realism, with its attention to unit-level differences as intermediating variables, gives a more accurate of states' behavior.

European policymakers should care about these theoretical arguments, because they condense important historical lessons into axioms that can and should inform their assessments of their national interests, the threats to these interests, and the extent and nature of military investments and diplomatic measures they should consequently consider. A further purpose of our contribution is then to employ realist theoretical insights to promote a better understanding of the contemporary security challenges facing Europe as well as the variety and possible shortcomings of policy responses to them. We show how engaging with realism, in its structural as well as neoclassical variants, puts us in a better position to achieve both those goals.

We thus not only claim that realism has much more to say theoretically than acknowledged, but also illustrate how it works practically. At the core of our empirical argument is a discussion of the role of US power in global affairs over the past decades. While US power is a topic much discussed by American realists, it is largely ignored—or only considered in debates on anti-imperialism—by European scholars. The post-Cold War era has seen a gradual withdrawal of US commitment from Europe, culminating in the uncertainty and contradictions of the Trump presidency's approach to American allies. We employ realist insights to lay out the structural implications of the shifts of power and great power commitment Europe has experienced in the past two decades.

This discussion of European security in the shadow of American power illuminates important and currently underappreciated features present in the realist tradition. In his chapter in this book, Jack Donnelly argues that acknowledgements of anarchy and the distribution of power are generic features of most theories, such as for example neoliberal institutionalism, and that realism is therefore not particularly useful for theorizing those features. We disagree. For one, few contemporary European international relations scholars truly acknowledge—let alone integrate—the constraints and incentives of the distribution of power as a central feature of the international system. Poststructuralists do not even pay them lip service.

In fact, non-realist theories generally fail to acknowledge that the distribution of power precedes other explanatory factors for foreign policy action, because it creates the context that preselects viable options for policymakers. Or that acquiring and maintaining power for its own sake is itself at least one important motive for policymakers, though admittedly not the only one. We posit that realist approaches essentially offer a three-stage argument that, starting from a focus on the international distribution of power, does more explanatory work than other theoretical approaches. First, realism grants centrality to role of the international distribution of power as constraining and incentivizing states, setting the range of options they can pursue, regardless of the motives of policymakers. Second, in its neoclassical variant realism acknowledges the constraining and incentivizing role of the domestic distribution of power, and the extent to which it allows policymakers to pursue their preferred responses to the international distribution of power. And third, realism adds a final set of arguments on how power acts as both a motive as well as the means. Power defines whether policymaking elites can ensure security and regime survival at both the international and the domestic level. However, although the distribution of power constrains and incentivizes policymakers, and policymakers attempt to respond rationally to these constraints and incentives, nothing in realist theory says that they will actually manage to. Arguments on misperceptions or other sources of deviation from realist predictions—driven by limited information, ideology, culture, or historical experiences—are entirely consistent with this approach to explaining state behavior.

The chapter unfolds as follows: in the next section, we review the standard arguments which link historical experiences to the supposed obsolescence of realism as a theoretical framework for policymaking in post-Cold War Europe. In the third section, we demonstrate how structural realist arguments can, contrary to those critical arguments, still help us understand the evolving structural context faced by European decision-makers since the end of the Cold War. In the fourth section, we draw preliminary conclusions for policymakers in Europe and sum up why and how the lessons structural realism can teach them remain, and in fact increasingly reemerge as, relevant. In fifth and final section we then add the theoretical innovations brought to the realist school of thought by its neoclassical variant and explain why doing so is necessary to fully explain the foreign policy behavior of different states facing the same structural context.

How Realism Went Out of Fashion in Europe

Realism went out of fashion for two reasons: the end of the Cold War and the era of "globalization" that followed it. For many critics of the structural realists of the theory's heyday in the 1970s and 1980s it was especially structural realism's failure to anticipate the end of the Cold War (Kratochwil 1993; Risse-Kappen 1994; Lebow 1994) that most revealed its flaws. Realism had overemphasized structural factors affecting foreign policy behavior and outcomes—whether the stability of bipolar systems or the challenges towards hegemons predicted by power transition theory—at the cost of domestic ones, and it had worked from the excessively parsimonious assumption that the state was a unitary actor. However, the end of the Cold War was set in motion when Gorbachev and his inner circle initiated domestic reforms within the Soviet Union and accommodated the US in a series of agreements. These led to the collapse of communism across the Warsaw Pact and the eventual dissolution of the Soviet Union.

Realism did not seem to perform much better in the decade that followed. The rapid development of communication technologies and the deep integration of national markets, the increasing role of non-state actors, the growth in the number of intergovernmental international organizations, transnational elite networks, and civil society—in other words, a whole range of important developments associated with globalization suggested that statism was becoming anachronistic and the borders between states increasingly permeable—meant an outright rejection of key assumptions of the structural realists of the 1970s and 1980s.

These shortcomings of realist theory were perceived in American International Relations (IR) scholarship, but arguably were felt more acutely in Europe. As a region, Europe more directly experienced specific trends associated with the end of the Cold War and growing transnational integration. The relief that the Cold War had ended without another destructive continental war, or—even more horrific to the imagination—the use of nuclear weapons, reinforced an already generally post-military view of the world within a regionally integrating and globalizing Europe. In this view, military force was not, and certainly should not be, the decisive arbiter of political outcomes. In a sense, this was the culmination of the legacy of the Second World War (Calleo 2011; Judt 2006; Sheehan 2009; Van Hooft, in preparation). European states and societies had suffered extensively in the first half of the twentieth century; many had committed or been complicit in genocide, or at least failed to prevent it. The partial surrender of sovereignty to multilateral institutions had appeared to stave off the reemergence of the traditional brutal rivalries that had plagued the continent during its eras of most overt great power politics. The predecessors of the European Union in the 1950s and 1960s, and their integration of the European markets, offered an escape out of this brutal dynamic, first dampening and then apparently obliterating the poisonous rivalry between France and Germany, Western Europe's two major powers. For obvious reasons therefore, nowhere was this desire to escape past dynamics more apparent than in Germany, the continent's largest and most populous economy. More than other Europeans, Germans had reasons to want to escape the continent's most troubled recent past. *Realpolitik*, geopolitics, and also realism, had been tarred with the brush of the violent past attempts at mastery over Europe—from the wars of German unification, via the First World War, to especially the Second World War. But also in the rest of Europe, *Realpolitik* had become a mode of thinking that was guilty by association with the empire-builders, social Darwinists, and fascists of the earlier eras.

All of the above undermined the appeal and credibility of the realist view that states were locked in endless competition—even if not necessarily open conflict—due to the uneven and unstable distribution of power within the system. After the end of the Cold War, an atmosphere of complacency settled in. Europeans no longer felt directly threatened militarily due to the collapse of the Soviet Union. Attention shifted to non-traditional threats—ethnic conflict in the European neighborhood, terrorism, and rogue actors. The latter were generally characterized less as powerful international actors than as dysfunctional, "failed" states, as evidenced by the white papers of that era. For example, the 1998 Strategic Defence Review of the new Labour government underlines the necessity to act because "instability inside Europe as in Bosnia, and now Kosovo, threatens [British] security" (Ministry of Defence 1998: para. 7). Nowhere is this view of systemic change and decrease of major threats clearer than in the German white papers. State threats are here considered largely irrelevant: "The danger of large-scale aggression threatening our existence has been banished" ("Germany. White Paper 1994", n.d.: para. 202). However, regional instability, specifically in Central and Eastern Europe, is perceived as causing *other* states "to think increasingly in the old categories of purely military-oriented security" that may "ultimately escalate into violence" ("Germany. White Paper 1994", n.d.: para. 235). But this was seen as precisely the sort of realist thinking that should be rejected. The 2011 guidelines argue that "the greatest challenges today lie less in the strength of other states than in their weakness" ("The 2011 Defense Policy Guidelines", n.d.: 2): as straightforward a rejection of the contemporary applicability of balance of power theory as one could expect.

Given these developments, realism appeared to be overly simplistic in overlooking the complexity of state behavior and the relevance of domestic factors for explaining foreign policy behavior and outcomes. It appeared to be at a loss at explaining many empirical phenomena that drastically reconfigured international relations in the contemporary era, including what seemed the more pressing current threats. This judgment combined with a period of remarkable optimism regarding the obsoleteness of traditional, inter-state conflict to make realism appear all but completely out of fashion in most of Europe.[1] Its traditional warning that security threats can and regularly do emerge from other states concerned about their relative power and their own security was blown to the wind.

---

[1] It should be noted that realism was never out of fashion in Central and Eastern Europe. Yet voices from there were by and large not taken seriously in the rest of the European scholarly or policy communities.

How Structural Realism Still Explains Much About Post-Cold War International Politics

Benevolent Unipolarity Reigns, But Not Eternally

Europe may have been done with power, but power was not done with Europe. Important lessons of realism were, in this historical context of extraordinary optimism about inter-state relations, too quickly unlearned. IR scholarship had its part in this development, as the criticisms of realism presented by scholars at times failed to accurately reflect the core underlying arguments of the approach, or the variety and utility of more recent developments within it. For example, John Mearsheimer (especially Mearsheimer 1990, 2001) is often used as a strawman by critics of realism, as he offers a heavily pared-down model of international politics that gives precedence to the role of offensive capabilities and uncertainty. However, Mearsheimer's work is not representative of other—let alone all—self-identified realist scholars, and has been criticized by other realists (see our discussion of neoclassical realism). We maintain that even in the age of globalization, much remained to be said in favor of looking at states and their relative power first. The relevance of non-state threats does not contradict realist theory; instead, realism insists that states and the distribution of power among them create the larger parameters within which *all* actors operate.

To illustrate this point, the following pages delineate how the US set those structural parameters for the development of the international system as a whole and the evolution of Europe in particular since the end of World War II. We will argue that what we witnessed after the end of the Cold War was neither a fundamental change in the nature of global politics nor a revelation of its true nature as more cooperative and peaceful than claimed by realists. Instead, the twenty-odd years from the end of the Cold War and its aftermath to the early 2010s and the Russian actions in Ukraine were a brief moment of exceptionality allowed by the unipolar nature of the distribution of power within the system. Realization of the brevity of this moment and of its exceptional nature is afforded by the long-term view taken by realists, but overlooked by other approaches. We now take this view, and in doing so answer some of the key criticisms levied at realism discussed above.

First, realist arguments on the decisive role of material power—military and economic—in fact go a long way towards explaining both the Cold War's end and the stable decades that followed. To begin with, the advantages in material power the US enjoyed in the 1980s created the conditions for the end of the Cold War. Of course, no mono-causal explanation suffices for the complex series of geopolitical changes that took place between 1987 and 1992. But the theoretical rivals were too quick to dismiss realism based on its performance in predicting this change. At the time, in the decade that followed Vietnam, the perception dominated that the US was in decline and lost its confidence. However, this does not mean that the Soviet Union was not facing severe structural pressures. The Soviet Union was outspending the US on its defense budget (relative to GDP) by a factor of three just to keep level with it militarily, and with an economy significantly less robust or innovative (Schweller and Wohlforth 2000; Waltz 2000b). More importantly, it was transparently falling behind in the nascent information technology revolution that promised to have economic as well as military applications. Indeed, the promise of American military technology was borne out in the 1991 Gulf War. Despite its superpower status—its massive conventional and nuclear forces—the Soviet Union in fact had few real grand strategic options left to it in the 1980s, beyond either confrontation with or accommodation of the US. Why it accommodated the US rather than confronted can only be explained by taking on board domestic ideas and institutions, as well as possibly individual-level factors. However, as Schweller and Wohlforth (2000) convincingly show, Gorbachev would likely never have been pushed to the fore as Chairman if the Party leadership had not been fully aware of the Soviet Union's weakening position. In other words, the international distribution of power drove the reshaping of the domestic distribution of power, and thereby the ideas and individuals that domestic order produced.

Second, similarly, the years of relative peace and globalization that followed the Cold War cannot be understood without considering the role that disproportionate US power played for dampening great power and regional power conflict. The key here is that two decades of relative peace do not contradict structural realist expectations that *long-term* changes in the distribution of power will shape systemic outcomes. It is true that realists disagree on whether it is merely capabilities (offensive realists such as (Mearsheimer 2001; Layne 1993, 1997) or capabilities combined with intentions (defensive realists such as (Walt 1987; Kydd 1997; Edelstein 2002; Rosecrance 2006; Tang 2010; Rosato 2015) that shape state responses. Yet, both offensive and defensive realist perspectives have a great deal to say about the historically unique pre-ponderance that the US enjoyed after the end of the Cold War. As Wohlforth (1999) shows, the US led on every significant dimension of power—both classical, industrial-age indicators of power and infor-mation-age indicators—creating a unipolar system, unique in modern (Western) history.[2] Yet, despite its advantages, the US took a smaller peace dividend than the Europeans in the Cold War's aftermath. Instead, the US pursued military "full-spectrum dominance" of all domains: air, land, sea, space, and cyber. This had a clear pay-off: as Posen (Posen 2003) shows, the US military was able to achieve full "command of the commons" during this era, unchallengeable by other powers when it came to conventional warfare. That preponderance was difficult, but also less pressing, to challenge for other states: Wohlforth (1999), Levy and Thompson (2010), and Mearsheimer (2001) argue that it is the unique geographic position the US enjoys that makes it both less of a threat and less easy to threaten by other states. Similarly, while Layne (1993, 2006) argues that unipolarity would eventually trigger challeng-ers, James (in Freyberg-Inan et al. 2009) makes an elaborated structural realist argument for why the power chasm is—perhaps today one would have to say *was*—too great to cross for challengers to US hegemony in the short-term.

The role of disproportionate US power and its advantageous geogra-phy has not been entirely ignored in other perspectives. Liberal scholars have explained the stability of the *Pax America* as deriving from the rel-atively benign nature of US foreign policy, and the values and interests it has shared with its likely competitors—Europe and Japan (for exam-ple, Ikenberry 2002). However, defensive realists have made the similar but more parsimonious argument that for a long time the US simply has been very successful at signaling its intentions to its potential challengers, whether these were allies or potential adversaries (Mastanduno 1997). Until 2001, the US was successful in making made clear that it was will-ing to restrain itself. This is why no significant challengers emerged after the end of the Cold War. It explains why the European Security and Defense Policy (ESDP) was set up as a hedging strategy for European dependence on the US, rather than a balancing strategy for a per-ceived American threat (Posen 2006). American protection diminished

---

[2] See Feng (2009) on China's position in the East Asian order from the 15th to the 19th centuries for a discussion of how globally unique American preeminence was.

the motivation to push European integration beyond the perfunctory (Jones 2007). Moreover, European states preferred NATO and the role the US played in it as an extra-regional pacifier to hedge against each other (Art 1996a, b; Mearsheimer 1990), as they explicitly had during the aftermath of the Second World War (when NATO served not only to "keep the Russians out", but also to "keep the Americans in", in order to "keep the Germans down", as General Lord Ismay, NATO's first secretary famously put it). Mearsheimer's (1990) prediction that conflict among EU members would reemerge, and that some of them would acquire nuclear weapons in the process, has not been born out (so far, as he would say). However, it remains true that neither the shape of European unification, nor its pacification, can be understood without assigning a significant role to the extent and nature of US-American power.

The US did not accidentally find itself in this role: it actively created it for itself. The US explicitly sought to maintain its influence in Europe after the end of the Cold War. It emphasized the importance of NATO and came out strongly against the ESDP initiative, as could be seen in Secretary Albright's famous 3Ds statement: ESDP should not duplicate NATO capabilities, discriminate against non-NATO members, or decouple from NATO.[3] In fact, the US expanded its influence through NATO expansion into former Warsaw Pact territory. The US also actively sought to ensure that perceptions of its power were considered compatible with others' interests and benign: the US actively exported its values across the world during and in the wake of the Cold War, endeavoring to create a world more compatible with its own system of values and interests (Layne 2006). Since these were largely or entirely in line with European preferences, the main transatlantic disputes emerged over differences in weight given to relative approaches—such as force vs. diplomacy—not substance.

American unipolarity shaped the drastic changes in the broader international order as well—whether we call this globalization or transnationalization. These were driven by technological and economic changes (if not revolutions) beyond the scope of realist theory, as its critics rightly note. Yet, again, those changes took place within the structural parameters set by the US-led system, in which it made full use of

---

[3] Madeleine K. Albright, "The Right Balance Will Secure NATO's Future," *Financial Times*, December 7, 1998.

its preponderant power in all dimensions. The multilateral international organizations covering security, trade, finance, human rights, and other policy areas gave the US a strong voice; the transnational civil society with its roots in the transatlantic sphere; the accompanying business and academic elite networks; and other features of a US-led global order—all were drastically expanded in quantity and quality under US aegis. It must be said that, indeed against realist expectations, they transformed the day-to-day workings of the international order, posing significant challenges for traditional realist definitions of power (Freyberg-Inan 2018). But the US took an active role in building these multilateral institutions and transnational networks, first to counter Soviet/Communist influence during the Cold War, and then to shape the perceptions, values, and behavior of its competitors.

In sum, there are two points made here. The first is that it was easy for the Europeans to overlook the larger power-structural context of their situation and its relevance, safe as they were during the post-Cold War period and confident in the superiority of their value and institutional systems. Whether we debate the presence of abundant security in Europe, larger global stability, or the reshaping of the institutional and economic frameworks that make up the lived experience of international relations, none of these can be understood without paying attention to preponderant American power. The second, related but more theoretical, point is that the interpretation of the events of the last quarter century, shaped as it is by the experience of the post-Cold War "golden age" of western hegemony, hardly allows for a fair assessment of the strengths and weaknesses of realist theory.

To recapitulate our theoretical defense of key realist insights up to this point: Compared to its main rivals, liberal or constructivist theories, structural realism is uniquely disposed to thinking about the larger structural context in which states and other actors operate. That being said, structural realism does not deliver explanations for individual state behavior, nor for differences between actors' responses in similar contexts.[4] Systemic structural conditions simply do not provide definite predictions of state behavior, and such predictions therefore remain debated within structural realism: does bipolarity increase stability or does unipolarity; does disproportionate power trigger balancing or accommodation?

---

[4]We will return to this point in the second half of the chapter, when we bring on board neoclassical realist insights.

Such indeterminacy, however, does not diminish the important role played by the distribution of power for setting overall structural parameters and thus defining the boundaries of the day-to-day workings of the order. For example, we can look at the US and the Netherlands and recognize their similarities in regime type (democratic), political economy (capitalist), and political culture (western). However, we cannot deny that the US was obviously the only state of the two that could unilaterally invade Iraq in 2003, while the Netherlands—with however many neoconservatives in government, or whatever political economic interests in the energy sector, or whatever explanation we use for the US—could never have conceived of such a move. In other words, the distribution of power decisively constrained the NL while it enabled the US. On this basis, it might be claimed that neorealism gets us quite a bit of the way towards explaining the invasion of Iraq (Adams 2013). Simply put: the US could consider it, the Netherlands could never. Yet, for a fuller explanation, a neoclassical realist approach that incorporates unit-level differences is superior, though less parsimonious (Taliaferro and Wishart 2013, in Sterling-Folker 2013).

Theoretical approaches can allow for contradictory predictions, while still being coherent intellectual frameworks. Schweller and Wohlforth (2000) and Waltz (2000b) also note the risk of using a single event—the end of the Cold War—to falsify and then reject an entire school of thought, especially when that school of thought is more varied than its critics admit, and is not, as we will see, reducible to theories on the international distribution of power *pur sang*. Structural realism should not be rejected for so-called failings that were not really that, especially while it continues to have meaningful things to say about the ongoing changes in the international order, as we will now illustrate.

COUNTER-BALANCING EMERGES AND EUROPE'S SECURITY UMBRELLA SHOWS TEARS

Aside from shedding more light on the recent past than claimed by its critics, structural realism also helps us understand the nature of the developments and events we are seeing now, and in a manner coherent with its premises as laid out in the preceding section. US preponderance pacified large parts of the system, but it also carried within itself the seeds of its decline. This is a simple enough argument: US unilateral actions since 2001 when the George W. Bush administration came to power have undermined the appeal of its leadership and the appearance of benign intentions. The US appeared less restrained and more aggressive; this provoked balancing behavior by *inter alia* Russia and China. There is irony here: the most assertive period in US foreign policy, following 9/11 and leading to the invasion of Iraq, came about precisely because US power was disproportionately large and deterred all competitors except those groups willing to use asymmetric means, like Al Qaeda. It was also so large that it encouraged excessive self-confidence on the part of US-policymakers during the 1990s and early 2000s.

The 2003 invasion of Iraq is the key turning point where the US both alienated its allies and provoked other powers as well as undermined the material base of its power. However, the Gulf War and the Kosovo War represented steps leading up to this turning point. In both conflicts, the US appeared all-powerful and consequently potentially threatening. Evidence of this is found, e.g., in the "other means of war" doctrine prepared by the Chinese military, which explicitly references the two conflicts. It articulates possible asymmetric solutions to US conventional military dominance by challenging it in other political, economic, financial, and technological domains (Liang and Xiangsui 1999). However, more than absolute US power, it was the uncertainty about US intentions signaled by the use of said power that undermined the security of the US's preponderant position—in the Kosovo War; in the missile shield controversy and the abrogation of the ABM treaty in 2002; in the expansion of NATO eastwards in 1999, 2004, and 2009; and, of course, in Iraq—where the US showed that it not only had the power to do what it wanted, it actually did so. At the 2007 Munich Security Conference President Putin claimed that the world now only had, "One single center of power. One single center of force. One single center of decision making. This is the world of one master, one sovereign". He argued that American military actions were "unilateral" and "illegitimate," and had brought "us to the abyss of one conflict after another". However, despite those warnings, even after the Russian invasion of Georgia in 2008, many Europeans were caught by surprise by the 2014 Russian annexation of the Crimea.

Structural realists had foreseen the Russian and Chinese responses, as seen e.g. in Waltz (2000a) and Mearsheimer (2001) on NATO expansion, or Layne (2006) on China and Russia. The shift in Russian thinking even before Iraq is notable, and it is evident that the Russian motivation to counterbalance US-led power has grown ever since. While the 2000 Russian military doctrine still spoke of a largely secure world, it already referenced "attempts to ignore (infringe on) the Russian Federation's interests in resolving international security problems, and to oppose its strengthening as one influential center in a multipolar world; the creation (buildup) of groups of troops (forces) leading to the violation of the existing balance of forces, close to the Russian Federation's state border and the borders of its allies or on the seas adjoining their territories; the expansion of military blocs and alliances to the detriment of the Russian Federation's military security" ("Russia's 2000 Military Doctrine | NTI" 2000). In comparison, in the 2010 doctrine the main external military dangers are: "the desire to endow the force potential of the North Atlantic Treaty Organization (NATO) with global functions (…) and to move the military infrastructure of NATO member countries closer to the borders of the Russian Federation" ("Text of Newly-Approved Russian Military Doctrine" 2010).

In contrast, most European states were acquiescent to American unipolarity, an issue that realist scholars explained in various ways (Posen 2006; Jones 2007). France was a notable exception: Foreign Minister Hubert Vedrine's used the term *hyperpuissance* to describe American power as so disproportionate as to destabilize the international order.[5] The French apprehensiveness was arguably shaped by the national experience of WWII, where it was abandoned by and then dependent on its allies (Van Hooft 2015). However, apprehensions about American intentions among other European states were only triggered by US unilateralist behavior around the Iraq crisis. At the 2003 "Chocolate Summit" in Tervuren, representatives from France, Germany, Belgium, and Luxembourg met to discuss the establishment of a European alternative to NATO, though little came of it in the years that followed.

Despite their predictions of balancing behaviour on the part of the major states within the system, strong disagreements also existed among structural realists. Clearly, the timing and precise nature of responses to US power remain underdetermined by structural realist theory. However, the growth and use of unrestrained US power—specifically during the early 2000s—goes a long way towards explaining

[5] French foreign Minister Hubert Vedrine referred to the US as a hyperpower in 1999. "To Paris, US Looks Like a 'Hyperpower'," *New York Times*, February 5, 1999.

the changing attitudes of Russia and China towards the US. In turn, the recent, more overt challenging of US interests by both Russia and China—very overtly in the Ukraine, but also the South China Sea— cannot be understood without taking into account the subsequent weakening of the US-position in the aftermath of the wars in Afghanistan and Iraq, and the 2008 financial crisis. While the US military is still the most powerful on the planet, its relative superiority is no longer what it was in the mid-1990s (as captured in Wohlforth 1999). In addition, the Iraq War (and Afghanistan) undermined its ability to domestically mobilize resources and constrained the executive. Meanwhile, its behavior alarmed potential competitors, which were thereby led to improve their own power positions vis-à-vis the US. Then, the 1997 Quadrennial Defense Review (QDR) planned for the US to be able to simultaneously fight and win two major regional contingencies (East Asia and the Gulf); the 2010 QDR was more limited to deterring in one area and winning in another (pp. 42–43); the 2014 QDR aims for the military to "be capable of simultaneously defending the homeland; conducting sustained, distributed counterterrorist operations; and in multiple regions, deterring aggression and assuring allies through forward presence and engagement" (p. 22) ("Quadrennial Defense Review" 2014). This signals a form of retrenchment which, in turn, leaves more room for counterbalancing behavior by other actors previously disturbed by US exertions of power. At the time of writing, we cannot yet fully assess the nature and consequences of Trump's contradictory approach to US allies in Europe. In the following section, we will discuss what this changed situation should mean for policymakers in Europe, thereby illustrating the continuing relevance of structural realist insights.

What This Should Mean
for European Policymakers

European policymakers should pay heed to the developments sketched above. The focused power of the U.S. is still immense, but its relative decline affects particularly its ability to shape or fight in multiple regions simultaneously. This should be a troubling development for Europeans used to the US security umbrella. The consequences of downplaying the relevance of hard military power and other material capabilities and of changes in the distribution of power are very real and potentially disastrous.

Leaders in most European capitals are unprepared to think about military power as an important component of overall national policy—or at least unwilling to publicly discuss it in these terms to legitimate their choices to society. Culturally, military power has wrongly become equated with war. Pew Global Attitudes opinion polls released in 2015 and 2017 showed that public majorities in most European states did not support coming to the aid of a fellow NATO member, even if that state had been attacked (Stokes 2017). Consequently, defense spending has been down across the board, with almost no European NATO member meeting the 2% of GDP spending target and with most of the continent's armed forces undersupplied if not in a state of outright disrepair.

Military force plays a complex political function, beyond only fighting open conflict. Realists are astutely aware of this and point to the "fungible" (Art 1996a, 2013: 1) nature of force. Perceptions of a state's material power and of its willingness to use it shape its ability to change the behavior of other states—whether through the deterrence or coercion of adversaries, or the reassurance of allies. Indeed, most of the Cold War strategies employed by the US were part of a complex game of deterrence of the Soviets and reassurance of European allies that it would not abandon them. The US committed itself to a permanent military presence in Europe to raise its stake in Europe and make its promise of protection credible. Otherwise, why would its European allies not fear the US retreating behind the protection afforded by its position behind two oceans?

Not much has changed in these dynamics until recently. President Obama even termed the deployment in continuous troop rotations of US-based armored brigade combat teams to Europe (Poland and Estonia) the "European *Reassurance* [emphasis ours] Initiative." Nor is it arbitrary that these troops are based in the US, and in continuous rotation: their impermanence is aimed at marginally diminishing Russia's fears of threats building beyond its borders, and ensuring that the US's tiny Baltic allies would not feel so comfortable with American power that they might engage in risky behavior. The political use of military force goes both ways: Poland pursued close relations with the US after the end of the Cold War to ensure American support against a possible resurgent Russian threat. Poland immediately rallied to Washington's side during the Iraq war and even took up command of its own occupation zone along the Tigris River. Similarly, instead of purchasing European fighter jets in 2003, Poland opted for American fighters.[6] Unlike Western European states that were less exposed to the threat of a resurgent Russia, Poland clearly condemned the 2008 invasion of Georgia. In contrast, President Sarkozy (who came to power three months after Putin's 2007 speech at the Munich Security Conference) stated that he did not believe that "modern Russia constitutes a military threat to the European Union and NATO."[7] The response to the 2008 Georgia invasion similarly saw France refusing to take sides.[8] In contrast, Polish exposure to the Russian threat even left policymakers doubting the US commitment.[9]

Leaders in most European capitals are similarly unwilling to accept that larger systemic insecurity due to great power dynamics exists, whether Europeans choose to participate in them or not. Middle and smaller powers have little to no choices in these matters. Neutrality or isolation only works when larger powers are willing to accept it. The idea that they can avoid the inevitable consequences of these global events is mistaken. The Ukraine crisis should have already made this clear, though apparently not decisively to many European leaders. Uncertainty and insecurity are endemic to the system, and increased by the combination of Russian and Chinese responses to US power, combined with the relative decline of US unipolarity.

Developments on the other side of the world will have consequences for Europeans. The rise of China in particular has consequences that they are only just beginning to confront. Not because China is a direct threat to Europe, but because its rise has been drawing the U.S. towards Asia

[6] Jan Puhl, "Poles React: Warsaw Fears Washington Losing Interest in Eastern Allies," *Spiegel*, September 17, 2009.

[7] "'Reset' Sought on Relations with Russia, Biden Says," Craig Whitlock, *Washington Post*, February 8, 2009. French President Nicolas Sarkozy was dismissive of attempts by the U.S. government to expand NATO to include Georgia and Ukraine, which have been major irritants to Russia.

[8] "Six days that broke one country—and reshaped the world order," Ian Traynor, *The Guardian*, August 16, 2008. "Don't ask us who's good and who's bad here," said Bernard Kouchner, the French foreign minister, "We shouldn't make any moral judgments on this war. Stopping the war, that's what we're interested in."

[9] "Report: Polish minister calls US ties worthless," Vanessa Gera and Monika Scislowska, *Associated Press*, June 23, 2014. Recordings of a private conversation in 2014 caught Polish foreign minister Sikorski describing Poland's strong alliance with the US as worthless and "even harmful because it creates a false sense of security."

since the turn of the century (Silove 2016). The US might then not only be less able, but also less willing, to keep the European security umbrella in place than it has been in the past. The Obama Administration's clumsy signaling of the "pacific pivot", later renamed "strategic rebalancing", is revealing. In 2016 it was underlined in an interview Obama gave to the *Atlantic*. But even earlier, in 2011, Defense Secretary Robert Gates' last speech at NATO spoke of a two-speed NATO, and warned of a new generation of policymakers and public in the US less willing to supply Europe with security. For a while, Russian aggression in Ukraine (as well as instability in Turkey and along its southern border) has redirected some attention away from Asia and the Pacific, and back to Europe. Moreover, every four years Europe is vulnerable to sudden policy shifts, depending on who wins the elections, and whether the candidates have different views of what American power should accomplish in Europe and at what costs and compensation. Currently, under the incipient Trump presidency, the worst fears we have expressed in the above paragraphs appear to be borne out. The US security umbrella is increasingly letting through rain, which begs a coordinated response across other NATO and European capitals and suggests that important lessons can be learned from reconsidering structural realist arguments. As we have also argued, however, foreign policy responses to these challenges are underdetermined by structural realist theory. The following sections will show that adding neoclassical realist insights can lead us to an understanding of how those challenges can be, are, or indeed are not faced in states' security strategies and policies—thereby connecting the basic lessons taught by the realist theory family to policy-making realities on the ground.

ADDING THE NEOCLASSICAL REALIST VIEW

Up to here we have argued that the weaknesses of structural realism have been overstated by its critics, when it comes to helping us explain both the end of the Cold War and important events since. However, important explanatory limits to this school of thought remain, as in its structuralist form realism is, as Waltz (e.g. Waltz 1996) himself of course has always admitted, indeterminate when it comes to explaining specific foreign policy decisions in specific times and places. This is *inter alia* due to its state-centrism and the assumption that the state acts as a unitary actor. However, realism has not stopped evolving. Are we willing to sacrifice some of the parsimony which is the key strength of the structuralist variant of realism, and take into account the insights developed by its neoclassical variant? If so, we can expand our understanding of the contemporary security challenges facing Europe, of how different states arrive at different responses to them, and of how, from a realist point of view, those responses might be optimized.

Since the early 1990s neoclassical realists have argued that states indeed respond to the international distribution of power. However, how states translate these pressures into strategy and action is determined by intervening variables at the individual and state level (Howorth and Menon 2009; Toje and Kunz 2012). These intervening variables include nationalism (Zakaria 1999; Snyder 1991), liberal beliefs (Dueck 2008; Layne 2006), experiences with war (Van Hooft 2015), state strength and elite cohesion (Christensen 1996; Zakaria 1999; Schweller 2006; Ripsman et al. 2016), interest groups (Snyder 1991), and civil-military relations (Rynning 2002; Van Hooft 2015).[10] Neoclassical realism has built on the insights from classical realism, organizational and decision-making theories, the literature on civil-military relations, as well as more republican liberal accounts about interest groups pursuing specific policy preferences.

We therefore disagree with Jack Donnelly's view in the introductory chapter that the international distribution of power is moved to the background in neoclassical realism or that it offers no substantive or coherent focus. Neoclassical realism acknowledges the constraints and incentives offered up by the international distribution of power within which policymakers operate. In other words, it still precedes other causes. Moreover, neoclassical realists acknowledge the domestic distribution of power, the institutions that mediate it, and the ideational or cognitive features that affect the understanding of and responses to power. In other words, neoclassical realism is coherently and substantively focused on power. Including the domestic and individual level as well as ideas next to material factors leads away from structural realism, but does not contradict the basic tenets of realism as a broader school of thought. For example, in our earlier discussion of the causes of the end of the Cold War, an explanation that emphasizes the distribution of power between the US and the Soviet Union does not exclude that

[10] Though Jack Snyder might take some issue with being included among the neoclassical realists.

individual politicians with specific ideas, such as Gorbachev, play an important role. Rather, realism suggests the conditions under which they may come to power. As Rathbun (2008) points out, no theoretical perspective can lay exclusive claim to any level of analysis, and it makes little sense for any theoretical perspective aiming to explain political behavior to restrict itself by dogma to any one level. If power matters, it matters all the way down, enabling and constraining actors at every level.

The work of the earlier structural realists already signals that states respond in multiple ways to similar material circumstances. For example, Walt (1987) emphasizes the perception of intentions as well as capabilities, and later defensive realists further developed that insight. Here, emphasis continues to lie on the ability to inflict harm on others and how it drives responses, but the effect of this power to harm is seen as mediated by judgments of the likelihood that this power will actually be used. This substantially weakens the offensive realist prediction that conflict is nearly inevitable, and, more importantly, nuances the role of material circumstances. In other words, paying attention to ideas about threats and power does not inherently contradict structural realism—perceptions and misperceptions of power are obviously crucial in a domain rife with uncertainty.

Contrary to what is sometimes claimed by critics, this acknowledgement is not an ad hoc fix of a faulty theory, as we also noted above. Do its critics really believe realism does not consider the inherently social nature of geopolitical decisions? The notion that states are complex units, the policymakers of which, under conditions of limited information and rationality, might arrive at different or also wrong conclusions, does not undermine the main thrust of the realist argument. Namely, the reality of the distribution of material capabilities constrains and enables, because it also "punishes" mistakes. The policymakers of states that get it too wrong will not see their states thrive or even survive: this is the "socializing" effect of the international system (Waltz 2010: 76–77). Neoclassical realists indeed make use of domestic variables as explanatory variables, but without losing sight of those structural conditions. Without this acknowledgment of the role of the structure that constrains states and thus causally precedes other explanations, we indeed "could not distinguish [neoclassical realism] from liberalism and, in many instances, constructivism" (Rathbun 2008). While liberal critics such as Kevin Narizny might justly criticize neoclassical realist scholars for their internal lack of coherence (Narizny 2017), it is not enough to say that liberal approaches acknowledge structural constraints, simply by taking the competing preferences of other states into account. This is the crux, we argue: any theory that gives central place to those constraints is realist at its core.

The international distribution of power represents a decisive initial sorting stage for states. Put concretely, in reference to our earlier point, the relationship between United States and Netherlands cannot be reduced to one of competing preferences: there is a clear hierarchy that very definitively defines what each can and cannot do. It is to maintain the country's close relationship with the United States that the Dutch force posture emphasizes interoperability with the US and that the Dutch contributed to the Iraq and Afghanistan missions. How Dutch dependence on the US constrained its domestic preferences is clear. The Wikileaks cables show that American appreciation of the Netherlands *does* hinge on these contributions, and that Dutch international missions should therefore be considered coinage to signal its supporter-status.[11] In fact, as soon as the Netherlands withdrew from its participation in the Afghanistan mission, the US withdrew its support for continued Dutch participation in the G20.[12] Liberal approaches understate the massive explanatory power represented by the realist insight that power matters, and they are wrong in reducing it to merely a contextual variable.

Neoclassical realist research focuses on cases where simple structural expectations are not realized in practice. Often this is explained as being due to failures by policymakers to correctly interpret structural conditions. In coming up with such explanations, neoclassical realism actually highlights the importance of the structural distribution of power and is therefore a necessary extension of structural realism. Their attention to balancing behavior can make a substantial contribution by explaining (and perhaps preventing) exactly those cases where states do not correctly interpret and respond to the distribution of threats in the international environment (Rathbun 2008). Schweller (2006), for

[11] US embassy in the Netherlands, "Ambassador's Parting Thoughts on Taking the Dutch to the Next Level," Date: August 22, 2005 (05THEHAGUE2309, Wikileaks 2011).

[12] US embassy in the Netherlands, "Netherlands/Afghanistan: Engaging Labor Party Leader Bos—Part of the 'Getting to Yes' Strategy for Extending Dutch Deployments in Afghanistan Post-2010," Date: September 18, 2009 (09THEHAGUE567, Wikileaks 2011).

example, used elite cohesion and consensus, social cohesion, and regime legitimacy as variables to account for the interwar failure of Britain and France to sufficiently appreciate the threat of Germany, and generate the appropriate responses. Policymakers in both states correctly perceived the threat, but were unable to act due to domestic constraints and perceptions of domestic threats (also noted in Posen 1986; Kier 2017). Similarly, Layne (2006) has used the specific liberal ideas among American elites to explain why the US expanded its commitments after WWII beyond what was strictly necessary to maintain its own survival. These are important examples of why states did too much or too little to ensure their long-term security.

In current-day Europe, France illustrates these neoclassical realist arguments. Unlike Germany, the other major continental state, or the smaller European states, France does not have political and societal constraints on the use of military force. Nor is the executive constrained when it comes to the "reserved domain" of foreign and defense policy. The relative preoccupation with great power politics (compared to other European states) and autonomy in France is further evidenced by the prominent role deterrence retains in post-Cold War strategic thinking, as reflected in the 1994, 2003, 2008, and 2013 white papers and military programming laws. France also remains the only other European power besides the UK with extra-regional ambitions. Indeed, over the past decade-and-a-half, France has used force in Afghanistan, Libya, Mali, and Syria/Iraq. The French executive also did not have to deal with the aftermath of the Iraq War that had caused crises of legitimacy in other allies.[13]

In contrast, Germany has long been ideationally and institutionally constrained (Berger 1998; Duffield 1999; Van Hooft 2015) with regards to the use of military force. As noted, both its leaders and public understated threats to Germany security, and questioned the need for defence spending. However, the uncertainty generated by the Ukraine Crisis, Brexit, and the Trump presidency has triggered changes in German policy. German defence spending has levelled and is slowly increasing. As part of the reassurance initiative, the Bundeswehr now has forces stationed in Lithuania, a country ravaged by German troops during WWII. Moreover, the election of Trump has even changed the debate

---

[13]Anonymous French Ministry of Defense official, interview with one of the authors, February 2016.

on a European deterrent. A foreign policy spokesman for Chancellor Merkel has argued that "if the United States no longer wants to provide this guarantee, Europe still needs nuclear protection for deterrent purposes" (Volpe and Kühn 2017; Kühn et al. 2017). In fact, the German parliament has investigated the legality of a "European" program and concluded German financial support for the stationing of French nuclear weapons on German territory would indeed be legal ("Völkerrechtliche Verpflichtungen Deutschlands Beim Umgang Mit Kernwaffen Deutsche Und Europäische Ko-Finanzierung Ausländischer Nuklearwaffenpotentiale (013/17) — wd2 — Sehrgutachten" 2017).

If we take neoclassical realist insights on board, there is also nothing in current US and European behavior that contradicts realist theory. Both the US and European governments have responded to power distribution and redistribution in ways that can be explained with reference to variables commonly included in neoclassical realist analyses. As structural realism would predict, they have all responded. From structural realism we can also take away the warning about the consequences of their not responding sufficiently, or over-responding. Applying the neoclassical realist lens can then help us explain their specific responses before this backdrop, and offer guidance for adjusting policies to better address Europe's contemporary security environment.

Conclusions

In this chapter, we have argued that realism, in both its structural and neoclassical variants, should not be abandoned, because it still gets us far towards understanding and predicting international politics. We have done so by tracing a path through events from the end of the Cold War to the passing stability and then open-ended transformation of the order that took shape in its aftermath. In contrast to many conventional accounts that reject realism, we have reviewed a wide range of literature from the realist school, and argued that the distribution of power—particularly the disproportionate power the US possessed in the 1990s and 2000s vis-à-vis other great powers—has, as structural realism would predict, had a significant influence on state responses and systemic developments. Once that power declined relative to a rising China and other challengers, and the US was exhausted by the long wars in Iraq and Afghanistan, the economic crises, and a general crisis of legitimacy of political elites, other powers became more comfortable in challenging its power. The current result is an uncomfortable edging towards multipolarity, to which states which have so far lived under the US security umbrella should respond. Indeed, they have responded to different extents and in different ways, as neoclassical realism can explain.

We have made this argument by highlighting the roles of the international distribution of military capabilities and a state's exposure to threats, in line with the structural realist approach. But we have also relied on the additions to the realist canon of the last twenty years, i.e. neoclassical realism, in particular (but not only) the importance of perceptions of intentions. And we have reminded ourselves of the subtler political role force plays in realist thinking beyond simply supporting the use of violence. Our short examples draw attention to the roles of reassurance by the larger ally and of signaling support in the behavior of small and middle powers, in relation to the stronger ally on whom they depend.

European states have been and are strongly affected by the changes in relative power of the US, as well as US policies, because of their traditional dependence on the US for their security. They could be—and in practice were—complacent in the decades after the Cold War, as well as after 9/11, because of the abundant security created by US-led unipolarity. Strong beliefs in most European societies in the redundancy (and moral deficiency) of force matter when explaining transatlantic differences, but European beliefs can also be explained as a consequence of experiences with US protection, and earlier European failures in the two World Wars to create security on the European continent (Van Hooft 2015, in preparation). With the exception of certain particularly exposed Central and Eastern European states, Europeans have overestimated their security. Defense expenditures and military preparedness consequently declined. The military capabilities that the Europeans retained were directed at "new" threats and at the ability to support US-led missions. To be able to effectively signal support to the US, they further shifted their resources to non-conventional capabilities that could be deployed alongside US forces. Then, when exhaustion with intervention and crises of political legitimacy appeared in Europe, they were further impaired in responding to the shifting distribution of power in the system. When Russia reemerged as a threat during the Ukraine Crisis, removing any doubt with its invasion of Crimea except among the most naïve or the most cynical observers, most European states were consequently left largely unprepared and quite unable to react as realism would advise.

What should Europeans take away from this? The primary lesson is that the distribution of power in the international system never stops constructing the context and setting up the parameters of decision-making. It was simply less noticeable, because, for decades, the distribution of power was so heavily weighted in the favor of the Western liberal democracies that it seemed easy to ignore. As long as Europeans are dependent upon the US for their security, they should build their own national, minilateral, and Europe-wide capabilities (Meijer and Wijss 2018). By doing so they will accomplish three essential goals. First, Europeans will be able to effectively signal support to the US, making a US departure from its role as security provider in Europe less likely. Second, becoming less dependent on the US, they will be better able to avoid entanglement in ill-considered US policies, such as those in Iraq. Third, should the US decide to leave Europe, or be forced to by crises in East Asia or elsewhere, Europeans would retain the capabilities with which to maintain their own security. The competition for and through power never ends, although, if the appropriate lessons are learned and applied, it does not always end in catastrophe.

References

Art, Robert J. 1996a. "American Foreign Policy and the Fungibility of Force." *Security Studies* 5 (4): 7–42.

———. 1996b. "Why Western Europe Needs the United States and NATO." *Political Science Quarterly* 111 (1): 1–39.

———. 2013. *A Grand Strategy for America*. Ithaca, NY: Cornell University Press.

Berger, Thomas U. 1998. *Cultures of Antimilitarism: National Security in Germany and Japan*. Baltimore, MD: Johns Hopkins University Press.

Calleo, David P. 2011. *Rethinking Europe's Future*. Princeton, NJ: Princeton University Press.

Christensen, Thomas J. 1996. *Useful Adversaries: Grand Strategy, Domestic Mobilization, and Sino-American Conflict, 1947–1958*. Princeton, NJ: Princeton University Press.

Dueck, Colin. 2008. *Reluctant Crusaders: Power, Culture, and Change in American Grand Strategy*. Princeton, NJ: Princeton University Press.

Duffield, John S. 1999. "Political Culture and State Behavior: Why Germany Confounds Neorealism." *International Organization* 53 (4): 765–803.

Edelstein, David M. 2002. "Managing Uncertainty: Beliefs About Intentions and the Rise of Great Powers." *Security Studies* 12 (1): 1–40.

Feng, Zhang. 2009. "Rethinking the 'Tribute System': Broadening the Conceptual Horizon of Historical East Asian Politics." *The Chinese Journal of International Politics* 2 (4): 545–574.

Freyberg-Inan, Annette. 2018. "Global Governance and the Continuing Relevance of Power." *Forum on Power Politics. International Institutions.*

Freyberg-Inan, Annette, Ewan Harrison, and Patrick James. 2009. *Rethinking Realism in International Relations: Between Tradition and Innovation.* Baltimore, MD: Johns Hopkins University Press.

"Germany. White Paper 1994." n.d. Accessed January 31, 2018. http://www.resdal.org.ar/Archivo/d0000066.htm.

Howorth, Jolyon, and Anand Menon. 2009. "Still Not Pushing Back: Why the European Union Is Not Balancing the United States." *Journal of Conflict Resolution* 53 (5): 727–744.

Ikenberry, G. John. 2002. *America Unrivaled: The Future of the Balance of Power.* Ithaca, NY: Cornell University Press.

Jones, Seth G. 2007. *The Rise of European Security Cooperation.* Cambridge: Cambridge University Press.

Judt, Tony. 2006. *Postwar: A History of Europe Since 1945.* London: Penguin.

Kier, Elizabeth. 2017. *Imagining War: French and British Military Doctrine Between the Wars.* Princeton, NJ: Princeton University Press.

Kratochwil, Friedrich. 1993. "The Embarrassment of Changes: Neo-Realism as the Science of Realpolitik Without Politics." *Review of International Studies* 19 (1): 63–80.

Kühn, Ulrich, Tristan Volpe, and Bert Thompson. 2017. "Tracking the German Nuclear Debate." *Carnegie Endowment for International Peace.* http://carnegieendowment.org/2017/09/07/tracking-german-nuclear-debate-pub-72884.

Kydd, Andrew. 1997. "Sheep in Sheep's Clothing: Why Security Seekers Do Not Fight Each Other." *Security Studies* 7 (1): 114–155.

Layne, Christopher. 1993. "The Unipolar Illusion: Why New Great Powers Will Rise." *International Security* 17 (4): 5–51.

———. 1997. "From Preponderance to Offshore Balancing: America's Future Grand Strategy." *International Security* 22 (1): 86–124.

———. 2006. *The Peace of Illusions: American Grand Strategy from 1940 to the Present.* Ithaca, NY: Cornell University Press.

Lebow, Richard Ned. 1994. "The Long Peace, the End of the Cold War, and the Failure of Realism." *International Organization* 48 (2): 249–277.

Levy, Jack S., and William R. Thompson. 2010. "Balancing on Land and at Sea: Do States Ally Against the Leading Global Power?" *International Security* 35 (1): 7–43.

Liang, Qiao, and Wang Xiangsui. 1999. *Unrestricted Warfare.* Beijing: PLA Literature and Arts Publishing House.

Mastanduno, Michael. 1997. "Preserving the Unipolar Moment: Realist Theories and US Grand Strategy After the Cold War." *International Security* 21 (4): 49–88.

Mearsheimer, John J. 1990. "Back to the Future: Instability in Europe After the Cold War." *International Security* 15 (1): 5–56.

———. 2001. *The Tragedy of Great Power Politics*. New York: W. W. Norton & Company.

Meijer, Hugo, and Marco Wijss, eds. 2018. *The Handbook of European Defence Policies and Armed Forces*. Oxford: Oxford University Press.

Ministry of Defence. 1998. "Strategic Defence Review." HM Government.

Narizny, Kevin. 2017. "On Systemic Paradigms and Domestic Politics: A Critique of the Newest Realism." *International Security* 42 (2): 155–190.

Posen, Barry R. 1986. *The Sources of Military Doctrine: France, Britain, and Germany Between the World Wars*. Ithaca, NY: Cornell University Press.

———. 2003. "Command of the Commons: The Military Foundation of US Hegemony." *International Security* 28 (1): 5–46.

———. 2006. "European Union Security and Defense Policy: Response to Unipolarity?" *Security Studies* 15 (2): 149–186.

"Quadrennial Defense Review." 2014. Accessed February 1, 2018. http://history. defense.gov/Historical-Sources/Quadrennial-Defense-Review/.

Rathbun, Brian. 2008. "A Rose by Any Other Name: Neoclassical Realism as the Logical and Necessary Extension of Structural Realism." *Security Studies* 17 (2): 294–321.

Ripsman, Norrin M., Jeffrey W. Taliaferro, and Steven E. Lobell. 2016. *Neoclassical Realist Theory of International Politics*. Oxford: Oxford University Press.

Risse-Kappen, Thomas. 1994. "Ideas Do Not Float Freely: Transnational Coalitions, Domestic Structures, and the End of the Cold War." *International Organization* 48 (2): 185–214.

Rosato, Sebastian. 2015. "The Inscrutable Intentions of Great Powers." *International Security* 39 (3): 48–88.

Rosecrance, Richard. 2006. "Power and International Relations: The Rise of China and Its Effects." *International Studies Perspectives* 7 (1): 31–35.

"Russia's 2000 Military Doctrine | NTI." 2000. http://www.nti.org/analysis/ articles/russias-2000-military-doctrine/.

Rynning, Sten. 2002. *Changing Military Doctrine: Presidents and Military Power in Fifth Republic France, 1958–2000*. Westport, CT: Greenwood Publishing Group.

Schweller, Randall L. 2006. *Unanswered Threats: Political Constraints on the Balance of Power*. Princeton, NJ: Princeton University Press.

Schweller, Randall L., and William C. Wohlforth. 2000. "Power Test: Evaluating Realism in Response to the End of the Cold War." *Security Studies* 9 (3): 60–107.

Sheehan, James J. 2009. *Where Have All the Soldiers Gone?: The Transformation of Modern Europe*. New York: Houghton Mifflin Harcourt.

Silove, Nina. 2016. "The Pivot Before the Pivot: US Strategy to Preserve the Power Balance in Asia." *International Security* 40 (4): 45–88.

Snyder, Jack. 1991. *Myths of Empire: Domestic Politics and International Ambition*. Ithaca, NY: Cornell University Press.

Sterling-Folker, Jennifer. 2013. Making Sense of International Relations Theory. In *Neoclassical Realism: Domestic Opportunities for Great Power Intervention*, ed. J.W. Taliaferro and R.W. Wishart. Boulder, CO: Lynne Rienner.

Stokes, Bruce. 2017. "NATO's Image Improves on Both Sides of Atlantic." *Pew Research Center's Global Attitudes Project* (blog). May 23, 2017. http://www.pewglobal.org/2017/05/23/natos-image-improves-on-both-sides-of-atlantic/.

Tang, Shiping. 2010. *A Theory of Security Strategy for Our Time: Defensive Realism*. Basingstoke: Springer.

"Text of Newly-Approved Russian Military Doctrine." 2010. http://carnegieendowment.org/2010/02/05/text-of-newly-approved-russian-military-doctrine-pub-40266.

"The 2011 Defense Policy Guidelines." n.d. Accessed January 31, 2018.

Toje, Asle, and Barbara Kunz. 2012. *Neoclassical Realism in European Politics: Bringing Power Back In*. Manchester: Manchester University Press.

Van Hooft, Paul. 2015. "The Future in the Past: Victory, Defeat, and Grand Strategy in the US, UK, France and Germany." Unpublished, University of Amsterdam, Amsterdam.

———. In preparation. *The Future in the Past: Victory, Defeat, and Comparative Grand Strategy*.

"Völkerrechtliche Verpflichtungen Deutschlands Beim Umgang Mit Kernwaffen Deutsche Und Europäische Ko-Finanzierung Ausländischer Nuklearwaffenpotentiale (013/17) — wd2 — Sehrgutachten." 2017. Wissenschaftliche Dienste, Deutscher Bundestag. Accessed January 15, 2018. https://sehrgutachten.de/bt/wd2/013-17-voelkerrechtliche-verpflichtungen-deutschlands-beim-umgang-mit-kernwaffen-deutsche-und-europaeische-ko.

Volpe, Tristan, and Ulrich Kühn. 2017. "Germany's Nuclear Education: Why a Few Elites Are Testing a Taboo." *The Washington Quarterly* 40 (3): 7–27.

Walt, Stephen M. 1987. *The Origins of Alliance*. Ithaca, NY: Cornell University Press.

Waltz, Kenneth N. 1996. "International Politics Is Not Foreign Policy." *Security Studies* 6 (1): 54–57.

———. 2000a. "NATO Expansion: A Realist's View." *Contemporary Security Policy* 21 (2): 23–38.

———. 2000b. "Structural Realism After the Cold War." *International Security* 25 (1): 5–41.

————. 2010. *Theory of International Politics*. Long Grove, IL: Waveland Press.

Wohlforth, William C. 1999. "The Stability of a Unipolar World." *International Security* 24 (1): 5–41.

Zakaria, Fareed. 1999. *From Wealth to Power: The Unusual Origins of America's World Role*. Princeton, NJ: Princeton University Press.

PART II

EU Member States

Germany's Growing Power in EUrope: From Multilateral Collectivism Towards Re-Nationalization and Destabilization?

Alexander Reichwein

GERMANY AND EUROPE—A PUZZLING RELATIONSHIP FOR REALISTS

With the end of the Cold War and German unification, the *German Question*, or the *German problem*, was back on the European agenda. Neighboring states, which had experienced German expansion and occupation in World War I and World War II, again felt a growing uncertainty about Germany's future role and politics within EUrope. Nearly all states shared concerns and fears about a unified Germany that was expected not only to take the lead in European affairs, but also might become again the dominant regional hegemon pursuing its economic and political interests in the post-Cold War Europe at the expense of European integration, cooperation among European states, and stability.

The political and academic debates in the early 1990s in Europe about Germany revolved around three main issues: whether or not

A. Reichwein (✉)
Justus-Liebig-University, Giessen, Germany
e-mail: alexander.reichwein@sowi.uni-giessen.de

© The Author(s) 2019
R. Belloni et al. (eds.), *Fear and Uncertainty in Europe*, Global Issues,
https://doi.org/10.1007/978-3-319-91965-2_5

Europe should fear Germany and why—because "deutschmarks might go much further than panzers in extending German power" (Markovits and Reich 1991: 2); how Europe could tame German power, or, as a best-case scenario, integrate unified Germany into the new institutional architecture of the European Union (EU); and the question about continuity (of *West-integration* and '*Westbindung*') or change (back to the future towards a recurrent Prussian-styled concept of reckless power politics) of German foreign policy in post-Cold War Europe. Peter Katzenstein (1997) captured these fears about a *Germanization of Europe* and an assertive and unilateral foreign policy behavior of a changing Germany and the hopes about an ongoing *Europeanization of Germany*. This meshed with a continuous self-understanding as a *tamed 'Civilian Power'* (Harnisch and Maull 2001a, b) whose non-military and multilateral embedded foreign policy behavior, based on international law and the principles of self-restraint, aimed at a civilization of international affairs, regional stabilization, democracy promotion, human rights protection and peace, driven and shaped by its historical memory (Banchoff 1997), its internalized European socialization and identity (Banchoff 1999), and a norm of a '*Culture of Restraint*' instead of *Total War* (Baumann and Hellmann 2001).

It became obvious during the 1990s that even though the geopolitical context, regional setting and security environment in Europe was changing, and even though unified Germany became more powerful in terms of material capabilities, landmass, and population, Germany did not behave according to structural neo-realist predictions: According to Waltz (1993, 2000), unified Germany was located in an improved geographical position after unification; European anarchy was rather benign; Germany became more and more powerful; it had moderately increased its power. Accordingly, Germany was expected by defensive neo-realists to respond to systemic pressures and constraints in the regional environment (such as evolving security issues in Eastern and Central Europe) by an adaptive behavior, namely: to take the lead within Europe; to pursue strategies of *power balancing* to preserve the post-Cold War status quo of the relative power distribution among states within Europe; to preserve its own beneficial power position by means of increased military power resources and/or bi- and multilateral alliance-building against either France, or Great-Britain, or Russia, or any revisionist state (see also Reichwein 2015: 103–106).

According to Mearsheimer (1990), the distribution of power among European states changed dramatically in 1990 after U.S. dismissal as European pacifier (Joffe 1984). New crises and wars resulting from the

Soviet withdrawal, rising ethnic conflicts and nationalism in the Western Balkans, and mis-management of nuclear proliferation were likely to evolve and increase, as they have. Mearsheimer's nightmare in the early 1990s was a new instability in a rather multipolar structured Europe, comparable to the Concert of Powers in the nineteenth century in Europe, and the interwar period. Offensive realist Mearsheimer argued that in order to escape this dangerous situation in which many European powers are struggling for hegemony, the best case would be if unified Germany become a nuclear power. As a result, the new *regional hegemon* (against whom France and Great-Britain would balance in order to keep Germany in check) would, in the short-term, exploit EU institutions for its own interests and purposes and, in the middle-term, leave these institutions to get more autonomy and maintain a stable post-Cold War order.

But, quite the contrary, Germany, still deeply anchored in the West and its institutions, initiated and created new EU institutions such as: the Common Foreign and Security Policy (CFSP) and the European Security and Defence Policy (ESDP); it continued to pursue a European policy of deepening and widening the EU; and to establish a pan-European security architecture in Central and Eastern Europe. Today, Germany, characterized as 'normal' in terms of national interest-driven (Bulmer and Paterson 2011) and 'grown-up' and 'self-confident' (Hellmann 2011), is playing the decisive role as a *'shaping power'* (*Gestaltungsmacht, Spielmacher*) within a crisis-ridden EUrope (Hellmann 2015, 2016a), and it seems that Germany has resisted the temptation to become Europe's hegemon (Loriaux 1999: 354, 370), and that it has avoided falling into the hegemony trap of overexpansion, isolation and decline (Hellmann 2016a: 9–11).

The chapter aims to discuss the following three questions:

(1) How does German foreign and security policy in the post-Cold War era fit into the realist picture? Which factors drive and shape Germany's European policy?

(2) Did Germany strive for collective action within EU institutions to reach common European interests, and therefore subordinate national interests and transfer sovereignty to promote an ongoing institutionalization in the last three decades? Or did Berlin use its increased power to realize national interests through unilateral actions? In other words: Has the tendency been that Germany moves away from multilateral collectivism as an institutionalized and internalized norm of behavior within EU, towards an assertive, unilateral, self-referred and re-nationalized German foreign

policy? Or is there a third way of German foreign policy *sui generis?*

(3) What are the consequences of a rising Germany? Does EUrope suffer from a new 'German problem'? After decades of diminishing if not overcoming the European security dilemma, does Germany cause new fear, uncertainty and a destabilization of Europe?

The chapter reconstructs the long road from the so called 'Checkbook Diplomacy' during the Second Gulf War via the Balkan wars to EU Enlargement, and from the Iraq War via Libya to the Crimea through neoclassical realist lenses (see Donnelly in this volume; Reichwein 2012). It works out milestones and identifies continuity as well as *turning points* and remarkable *shifts* which help to understand Germany's role and foreign policy within EUrope across the years since 1990. The chapter ends with a brief summary of how to come to terms with German foreign policy in a changing EUrope.

From Gulf War via the Balkan Wars to EU Enlargement

An Uncertain Partner: German Checkbook Diplomacy

Although actively taking part in the deepening of the European integration process from the economic European Community (EC) to the political EU including an Economic and Monetary Union and a CFSP/ESDP as a complementary, not competing, European pillar within North Atlantic Treaty Organization (NATO) (Overhaus 2006; Reichwein 2015) went on in the 1990s, a behavior which was not in line with neo- or structural realist expectations, Germany did not accommodate the demand of the U.S. and other NATO partners in January 1991 to take part in the United Nations (U.N.) mandated Second Gulf War ("Operation Desert Storm") to free Kuwait from Iraqi invasion. There were various reasons for this; one was that at this time, there was no legal clarity about the possibility of German participation in NATO "out of area" operations. Another was that the Bundeswehr was then a defence army, not designed for interventions abroad. Bonn paid 17.9 billion D-Mark to its allies for cost sharing, provided military infrastructure to NATO operation quarters in Turkish Erhac, and supplied Israel with Patriot antimissile defence systems against Iraqi missile strikes. Washington, Paris, London and other members in the coalition against Iraqi dictator Saddam were nevertheless disappointed about the German culture of restraint, and the criticism of Checkbook Diplomacy circulated (Sperling 1994).

Germany's Unprecedented Alleingang in Recognition Policy

The second case of Germany's turning away from multilateral collectivism and joint decision-making within the EC/EU was the unilateral recognition of Slovenia, Croatia and Bosnia. In the context of Germany's postwar history of multilateralism in foreign policy, this was an unprecedented decision, and a case of defection from cooperation (Crawford 1996). From a neoclassical realist perspective, the source of Germany's preference for diplomatic recognition of the former Yugoslavian republics can be traced back to regional constraints, power considerations, domestic pressure and normative and ideational factors (see Donnelly in this volume).

Slovenia and Croatia had declared independence at 25 June 1991, resulting in the outbreak of the Balkan wars on 27 June 1991 when Serbia attacked Slovenia and Croatia. Already in March 1991, the foreign ministers of the EU member states initially agreed in a European Political Cooperation (EPC) meeting in Luxembourg not to recognize but to vote for the preservation of a federal Republic of Yugoslavia under Serbian President Slobodan Milošević in the capital Belgrade, supported by Brussels through financial and economic assistance to start reforms. The reasoning at the time was to prevent the outbreak of war. This was the official EC position during 1991, even though Germany was against this position and tried to make a plan to recognize all former Yugoslavian republics as independent states. During the Intergovernmental Conferences in 1991 to arrange the summit of the member states' Heads of Government in Maastricht at 10 and 11 December 1991 to sign the EU Treaty, a division which was problematic given the principle of unanimity in EPC affairs became more and more obvious: Germany, Belgium and Denmark argued in favour of recognition and a trade embargo against Serbia. The main argument was to prevent or stop displacement, human and minority rights violations, ethnical cleansing, and wars between Croatia and Serbia and in Bosnia and Herzegovina between Serbs, Croats and Muslims, and to internationalize the conflicts in order to enable the international community to react and intervene and stabilize the region. In the German case, the main driving forces behind the pro-recognition position in light of an ongoing escalation of violence in the Croatian-Serbian war and the war in Bosnia were also domestic pressure of media such as the *Frankfurter*

Allgemeine Zeitung (the F.A.Z. reported daily on Serbian atrocities in Croatia and Bosnia), of the Roman Catholic Church, of the Croatian and Slovenian community in Germany, and the vote of the Bundestag and popularity within German population to recognize in order to prevent migration and refugee influx.

Another strong motive was historical responsibility and the idea of compensation, given Nazi war crimes in the Balkans during WW II. Furthermore, the German government under Chancellor Helmut Kohl referred to the Paris Declaration of the Organization of Security and Cooperation in Europe (OSCE) dated from December 1990, in particular the principle of self-determination as prevailing norm for all European states. Defence Minister Volker Rühe announced at a ECP meeting in The Hague at 1 July 1991 to the international media: "We won unification through the right to self-determination. If we Germans now think that everything may remain as it is in Europe, that we may pursue a policy of the status quo without recognizing the right to self-determination of Croatia and Slovenia, we lose our moral and political credibility" (cited according to Maull 1995: 117). But, beyond ideational motives such as credibility, integrity and normative purposes (which are power resources, too) driving and shaping Germany's Balkan policy, it is also plausible to suppose that unified and more powerful Germany wanted to show a capacity to act as a sovereign state with its own interests, in particular vis-à-vis its partners and allies, and that it claimed taking the leadership role in new but unstable EUrope.

As a consequence, Germany became more and more isolated within EPC during 1991. France was undecided and hesitated to choose sides. But United Kingdom (UK), Spain, Italy, Greece and those member states who feared unintended consequences in view of their own minority and secession movements in the Basque region, Catalonia, Northern Ireland, Scotland, Tyrol or Macedonia still positioned themselves against a recognition of former Yugoslavian republics, and these states voted for a common position supporting the preservation of a federal Republic of Yugoslavia. The official argument was to prevent precedents, given the fact that the Soviet Union was the next multi-ethnic state that collapsed into 15 parts all expected to claim for independence. Because of the outbreak and escalation of the Balkan wars, but also because of German diplomatic pressure vis-à-vis some EC member states, things changed at the end of 1991. German foreign minister Hans Dietrich Genscher's threat not to sign the Maastricht Treaty[1] and to rethink the decision

[1] See: Crawford 1996; *Die Welt*, 7 November 1991, "Bonn setzt die EG unter Druck."

to give up the D-Mark in favour of the Euro made an impact. Great-Britain and France's position was not to endanger the political project of the EU just because of the recognition issue. As nearly all member states feared losing credibility given the EU's claim to formulate a *common* foreign and security policy in post-Cold War Europe, the foreign ministers changed the official position on the recognition issue at a EPC meeting at 16 and 17 December 1991. The member states (with the exception of Greece) agreed to recognize Slovenia, Croatia and Macedonia (which had declared its independence in September 1991) through a common decision in 1992 based on reports of the so-called Badinter Commission, established in 1991 in order to define criteria such as rule of law, minority rights and democratic standards which states who wanted to be recognized by the EU had to fulfill. But Germany hurried ahead, recognized Croatia and Slovenia at 23 December 1991 (and the Croatian and the Muslim part of Bosnia in April 1992, directly after the declarations of independence in March 1992), and implemented the decision unilaterally on 15 January 1992 by starting diplomatic relations, followed by Denmark, Belgium and Italy. By the end of January 1992, all other member states[2] had recognized Croatia, Slovenia and Macedonia as a common EU position, and individually.

As Mearsheimer predicted, Germany had exploited the EC/EU as an arena and instrument to pursue its national interests (Mearsheimer 1990). The other member states did follow for a simple reason: "In France's priorities saving the Treaty on the Union came before managing the Yugoslav crisis effectively" (Lucarelli 1995: 28). Former British foreign minister Douglas Hurd justified the decision in the House of Commons at the end of 1991: "There is no prospect of British influence for good in Yugoslavia if it is in rivalry with other EC powers" (cited according to Lucarelli 1995: 28). According to former Italian foreign minister Gianni de Michelis, Kohl and Genscher did threaten with rethinking the German commitment to accept the border between Germany and Poland (*Oder-Neiße-Linie*).[3] The criticism of a unilateral German foreign policy (*'deutscher Alleingang'*), and of the fact

---

[2] All states with the exception of Greece which had a package deal with Germany not to block the recognition, but to elude the decision because of an unsolved Greek-Macedonian dispute concerning a Greek province called Makedonia, and unsolved territorial questions at that time.

[3] Interview with Gianni de Michaelis in *L'espresso*, 4 July 1993, cited according to Lucarelli (1995: 21, footnote 25).

that Germany's recognition policy not only compromised and pressured European partners, but also led to escalation and prolonged wars in Croatia and Bosnia until 1995, circulated in Brussels and other European capitals (see Crawford 2007; Maull 1995).

Transatlantic Multilateral Collectivism as Dominant Modus Operandi—*Including Gradual Shifts*

However, it would be inaccurate to draft the picture of a fundamental change in German foreign policy after the end of the Cold War, and to suggest a general turning away from transatlantic multilateralism, joint decision-making, and collective action within EU institutions towards a re-nationalization of German foreign policy. Rather, reluctance and Checkbook Diplomacy, and attempts of blackmail and unilateralism in German foreign policy prioritising its own national interests over EUropean interests at the expense of EU joint decisions were two *exceptional* cases until then.

Arguably, German behavior conformed to what experts call 'modified continuity' (Harnisch and Maull 2001a) of established patterns of external behavior, namely integration with the West and guiding modus operandi principles such as 'reflexive multilateralism' in an indeed changing European environment (Maull 2006), despite changes such as: a debate on 'normalization' (Gordon 1994) and 'militarization' in terms of a more self-assured and grown-up Germany, and a more assertive and national interest-driven German foreign policy including the use of military force (Baumann and Hellmann 2001; Hellmann 1996; Hyde-Price 2009: 122–131; Staun 2017) in the 1990s; that the Bundeswehr was transformed into an army that took part in NATO-led "out of area" humanitarian or U.N. mandated peace-keeping missions in line with the so called "Petersberg Tasks" (Wagener 2006); the Bundeswehr participation in the U.N. mandated Bosnia War and in the Kosovo War (without an U.N. mandate) leading to a controversial debate about whether Germany is still a Civilian Power (Harnisch and Maull 2001a, b); and an important change in the government in 1998 from a liberal conservative to a left-green one. There were fundamental changes in the regional setting, and gradual shifts in both Germany's self-conception/self-perception and external expectations leading to a more pro-active and offensive German foreign policy pursuing new aims and objectives by using new instruments. But Germany did not aim to acquire nuclear weapons (as Mearsheimer predicted and nearly advised) or leave NATO, nor did it, after the Maastricht conference, ever again question the territorial status quo in Europe, the Euro, or the CFSD/ESDP, nor did it disappoint or compromise its European allies. Quite the contrary, Germany succeeded with a hedging strategy (Art 2004: 184) of strengthening ESDP (together with the St. Malo partners, France and UK) in the 1990s without weakening NATO. The Kohl government as well as the government under Chancellor Gerhard Schröder perceived, and Chancellor Angela Merkel and former foreign minister Frank-Walter Steinmeier also perceive the ESDP (for civil and military missions in Europe) as strengthening the European pillar within NATO and a way of relieving the U.S. (burden-sharing). It is stated in the German Defence Policy Guidelines of 2003 that, "the ESDP is not a substitute for but a necessary complement to NATO". ESDP missions in Bosnia-Herzegovina and Macedonia did not change the primacy of NATO in Germany's foreign and security policy (Reichwein 2015: 109–113).

Also, the participation in the NATO missions to stop the Balkan wars in the 1990s, and in particular the leading role of Germany and the new government under Chancellor Schröder and foreign minister Joseph Fischer during Germany's 1999 EU presidency to legitimate the Kosovo War (see Friis/Murphy 2000), fit into the neoclassical realist picture. Germany's position was driven by three—normative, domestic, strategic—motives: by a humanitarian one to protect human rights; and by a kind of historical legacy and perceived German responsibility to prevent another genocide in Europe *because* of German history, even though the new Republic was represented since the 1998 elections by a younger and much more pragmatic and forward-looking postwar generation which moved from old small Bonn to a pulsating cosmopolitan new capital Berlin. A second motive was domestic, given a widespread public opinion in favour of preventing a refugee influx to Germany. Finally, it can be argued that Germany did also take part for a strategic reason, namely in order to prove that Berlin is a reliable partner within NATO (Overhaus 2006). Altogether, Germany continued its twofold grand strategy to act as a reliable NATO partner and to deepen and widen EUrope in the 1990s, a strategy that was in line with its own but also with U.S. and European interests, but which includes a problem leading to a new and self-inflicted security dilemma with incalculable and on-going consequences.

EU Enlargement—The Road to a New
Security Dilemma in EUrope

The best example for this strategy and dilemma is the Eastern Enlargement of EU and NATO. Enlargement was on the agenda as a high priority issue since 1990 (Garton Ash 1996; Tewes 2002: 92–109), and its ongoing implementation began at the NATO Summit in Madrid 1997 (Tewes 2002: 115–133). EU and NATO enlargement shows continuity in Germany's foreign policy from Kohl/Genscher via Schröder/Fischer to Merkel/Steinmeier. Enlargement was supported by both the U.S. and France from the beginning, and the most convincing argument vis-à-vis France was Germany's promise and guarantee that the Mediterranean area would continue to have high priority in the EU's CFSP/ESDP in the future (Szabo 2006). The support of the U.S. and France was quite important, given the historical postwar constellation that sees Germany having to perform a double balancing act between Washington and Paris, and between West-integration and a new 'Ostpolitik' vis-à-vis Central and Eastern European (CEE) states and Russia (Loriaux 1999: 373).

It can be argued in line with any realist theory that EU and NATO enlargement was a kind of German self-help strategy to respond to new security challenges and threats in a radically changed post-Cold War geopolitical environment in Europe since the 1990s (see Flockhart 1996; Hyde-Price 2009). Germany was forced to deal with three issues: instability in Europe (systemic level), which made a new pan-European security order after the demise of the Soviet Union including institutional patterns of cooperation with Russia and the Ukraine more than ever necessary (see Haslam 1998; Joetze 2006); external expectations such as the demands of the CEE states to become members of the EU and NATO as a kind of ongoing protection against Russia (interstate/regional level); and to pursue German vital national interests and to address domestic pressure groups' preferences (unit/intrastate level). It can be argued from a neoclassical realist perspective that Germany weigh influence and commitments coming along with this (to shape this security order in certain directions) against autonomy (to let other states establish a security architecture without Germany) in favour of the former, and that it used EU institutions, in particular the German EU presidencies in 1994 and 1999, to convince its partners to enlarge the EU and NATO. And it can be argued from a neoclassical realist perspective that EU and NATO enlargement is a very illustrative case of how systemic-, regional- and unit-level variables are linked to each other and can explain the enlargement decision as a rational one (see also Tewes 2002: 138).

Germany's motives and perceived benefits in enlarging the EU and NATO have been multiple: it was "stabilization, democratization, multilateralization" (Tewes 2002: 137)—and the opportunity and ability to (re)shape its security environment. Because of the new post-Cold War European geography and constellation in which Germany was and still is situated, and its geopolitical position as '*Zentralmacht*', unified Germany feared a security vacuum in the proximate neighbourhood between Russia and its Eastern border, as well as instability in Central and Eastern Europe (including failing democratization processes in Poland, Hungary, Czech Republic and other states, and ethnic and territorial disputes and conflicts, and growing nationalism leading to migration and refugee influx). The task was to improve what Stanley Hoffmann calls the 'national situation' of a state defined by its geographical position and security claims, economic resources, political culture and historical legacy (Hoffmann 1968, 1995: 75–76). It was first and foremost systemic pressure in terms of security and stability concerns that drove and shaped Germany's enlargement policy in the 1990s until today, and Germany took (and still takes) the pivotal role of a provider and promoter of regional stability, and mediator between CEE states and Russia. This German role and responsibility was (and still is) expected by its European partners in the future. Free trade, direct investments and new markets, labour force and other economic, commercial interests also played a crucial role. It is exactly here where domestic pressure groups such as labour unions, the agricultural sector, and other key economic players come into the foreign policy decision-making process; in order to address these economic interests from the beginning, the EU started the enlargement process by launching and implementing so called Europe and Association Agreements to integrate the CEE states into the European Market, even without full membership status. Beside these utilitarian calculations and strategic benefits, German governments also argued during the 1990s that this political project of EU and NATO enlargement would finalize the pan-European unification process, and widen a zone of democracies, peace and human and minority rights, prosperity and welfare (Fischer 2000).

Finally, German history and Nazi war crimes in Central and Eastern Europe did play a crucial role. As in 1990, Germany was again expected to take responsibility and to avoid uncertainty, old fears and concern. Accordingly, EU and NATO enlargement was interpreted by advocates as a kind of reconciliation and reparation (Phillips 1998), with a normative purpose (see also Hyde-Price 2009: 182–183). Enlargement, which was also in line with the national security and economic interests of post-Cold War Germany, allowed Berlin to gain influence and to (re)shape and control a new sphere of influence in Central and Eastern Europe.

However, Germany was not able to deal with the deepening- and widening-dilemma coming along with EU and NATO enlargement: "the German proposal was to use enlargement in order to secure institutional deepening" (Tewes 2002: 136). In fact, widening was successful *at the expense* of deepening and of a partnership with Russia. During the Iraq War in 2003, it became very clear that a greater EU with more member states (and candidates) did not develop automatically into a closer EU. As a result of the growing divergences of 'national situations' and national interests between EU member states, and a characteristical 'Logic of Diversity' (Hoffmann 1995: 84) which the EU had already experienced in the beginning of the 1990s at the Balkan, the EU time and time again lacked the capacity to act as a common actor (Toje 2008). A consensus gap, a splitting into advocates and opponents of peace-keeping missions, humanitarian interventions and wars, advocates and allies of the U.S. and those of Russia, and far left-wing/liberal and conservative/far right-wing governments are integral parts of widen but a more and more divided EUrope. Germany began to suffer some of the consequences of EU and NATO enlargement, namely to choose sides in the geopolitical conflicts between CEE states and Russia. Even though Germany was a driving force behind the strategy to integrate Russia into a pan-European security architecture by means of a NATO-Russia Council from the beginning (see Haslam 1998; Joetze 2006), Russia became more and more isolated, and NATO did not keep to its promises not to arm new NATO members Poland, Hungary and Czech Republic with nuclear weapons, and not to make the Baltic states, Georgia or the Ukraine NATO members, which means that NATO territory borders on Russia (Mearsheimer 2014).

Enlargement policy allegedly provoked Russia under Putin to respond to this systemic pressure. In the case of the war with Georgia in 2008 over South-Ossetia and Abkhazia (Allison 2013) as well as in the case of the Crimea annexation, Russia has argued that it feels threatened by NATO and NATO-allied states in its neighbourhood (Smith 2017). In fact, Russia has the same claim and pursues the same goal as Germany and the West do, namely to control a sphere of influence between its and Germany's borders. To keep it in (realist) perspective, actually, EU and

NATO enlargement are the sources of today's conflict between Russia, the Ukraine, and the West. As some claim, Germany has contributed to, or even indirectly and partly caused, the Russo-Georgian and the Russo-Ukrainian war and destabilization in Europe (see Mearsheimer 2014; Smith 2017). For Mearsheimer, there is just one way out from the self-inflicted security dilemma and the liberal illusion-trap: to stop EU and NATO plans to westernize Central and Eastern Europa including Ukraine and Georgia as Western strongholds on Russia's borders, and instead to make Ukraine a neutral (and divided) buffer between Russia and the West, and to leave Georgia stranded.

EU and NATO enlargement, thus, can be identified not only as a milestone in the European integration process, and maybe a big mistake and dangerous endeavour; it was also a first *turning point* in post-Cold War German foreign policy, off from passive and cautious Checkbook Diplomacy and a "Culture of Restraint" towards a more offensive, assertive, national interest-driven foreign policy (that time in line with the common European interests), and defined and formulated by a new generation of foreign policy-makers in the new capitale Berlin characterized by a willingness to articulate and pursue and implement national interests representing a grown-up and self-confident Germany (see also Hyde-Price 2009)—but in retrospect with (un)intended negative consequences for EUrope's stability today. Another *turning point* is a first remarkable rhetorical shift in the late 1990s from Bonn's "Nie wieder Krieg" (as a justification *not* to take part in military interventions abroad because of German history) to Berlin's "Nie wieder Auschwitz" (this was Fischer's justification to take part in the military intervention in Kosovo against Serbia) because of German history (Staun 2017: 34).

From the Iraq War via Libya to the Crimea

Like the end of the Cold war in 1990, the terror attacks of 11 September also caused fundamental changes in international politics. From 2001 on, the EU and its member states had to respond to new systemic constraints and new challenges in security policy, but also to deal with U.S. unilateralism. And from 2008 on until today, the regional setting in Europe again has changed radically (Hellmann 2016a: 3; 2016b: 6), given the fiscal and financial crisis, the rise of revisionist Russia and its geopolitical motivated interventionist foreign policy in its shared neighbourhood, the BREXIT, rising nationalism and populism in Europe, ethnic conflicts and authoritarian governments in power in some CEE states, and the collapse of Iraq and Afghanistan and the war in Syria leading to refugee influx towards EUrope. In particular Germany is challenged by these developments, and from the 2010s on, calls from outside for Germany to take more responsibility and the leading role within a crisis-ridden EUrope became more frequent and louder (Staun 2017: 5–8; Hellmann 2016a).

Getting into a Mess:
Iraq War, Germany's Unexpected Opposition and EU Crisis

During the Iraq War, a real split within the enlarged EU became apparent, and old and new EU member states were forced to choose sides (Mouritzen 2006). Germany and France positioned themselves against the war, and they were in strong opposition to Washington. At an exclusive summit between Germany, France, Luxembourg and Belgium on 29 April 2003 in Tervuren (Belgium), this position was reinforced with the exclusion of the UK, Spain and the new CEE member states (Visegrád Group). Again, the reasons for this have been various: It was the cultural clash between U.S. unilateralism and EU's established multilateralism as a modus operandi in foreign affairs, and different threat perceptions leading to different agendas how to deal with terror, political Islamism, and Islamic states. Some EU member states put the legitimacy of American leadership, as it revealed itself in the Iraq War, into question (Szabo 2006). The Schröder government made the argument that in contrast to the Afghanistan war, in which the Bundeswehr was participating as part of the U.N. mandated NATO "Enduring freedom" mission since 2001, the Iraq War was not in line with international law. Domestic politics also mattered. Schröder was re-elected as Chancellor in 2002 because of his public opposition to war, a view shared by large parts of the German population. But, there was also a new, younger generation of foreign policy-makers and elites in Berlin seeking diplomatic influence and to shape power within EUrope (see Haftendorn 2006; Rudolf 2005).

In this particular case, Berlin and Paris sought diplomatic 'soft balancing' against U.S. coercive hegemony within the transatlantic community, and against the 'special partner' UK. The new CEE member states, however, clearly positioned together with Italy and Spain under the leadership of UK on the side of the U.S. Poland, Hungary or the Czech Republic argued on behalf of the CEE states that the security guarantee against Russia was a matter for the U.S. and NATO, and only possible within the framework of a strong transatlantic alliance ruled by the U.S.

In other words, during the Iraq War, it became quite obvious that some EU member states prefer strategies of bandwagoning with instead of soft balancing against the U.S. (Wivel 2008: 296, 301). From a neoclassical realist perspective, bandwagoning is also a form of rational choice under concrete circumstances: as experienced freeloaders, these CEE states benefit from the protection that is offered by NATO and the U.S. in and for Europe at the expense of an autonomous ESDP pillar within NATO without fearing disadvantages or sanctions. Even though ESDP was already well institutionalized within the EU institutional framework since the late 1990s, and even though there have been civil missions in the Balkans and elsewhere, ESDP is still rather a paper tiger given its lack of common military resources, its dependence on single EU member states and/or NATO military resources, and a lack of political will among EU member states in times of crisis (Reichwein 2015: 112/113; Toje 2008).

As a result, the EU was divided, and lacked credibility for many years in security affairs. Many experts at the time had been rather pessimistic about EU's common foreign, security and defence policy (Crowe 2003; Toje 2008). The U.S. waged and lost the Iraq War and withdrew, leaving a failed state and a destabilized region. And Germany failed, because it misjudged the security concerns of the CEE states, it underestimated the strong tie between Washington and these new EU members, but, in contrast to 1991, Germany could not put pressure on its partners to align with Berlin and Paris. As a medium-term consequence, Berlin did lose instead of gain or maximize its influence within EUrope and it became isolated, uncertain and restrained again in the succeeding years. For some experts, Germany's unexpected opposition to the U.S. was a kind of (failed) assertive foreign policy of a too self-confident power (Hellmann 2011). For others, it was in line with the multilateral embedded foreign policy culture of a Civilian power (Rudolf 2005). Anyway, Iraq, was the third *turning point* in post-Cold War German foreign policy, with remarkable consequences.

Backsliding to the Bonn Tradition?
German Abstention in the Libya Intervention

Germany did not position itself in 2008 when Russia waged war against Georgia. Germany, as a non-permanent member in the U.N. Security Council (SC) at the time, abstained in the vote on UNSC Resolution 1973 on 17 March 2011 to intervene in Libya against the government of Muammar Gadhafi, which was violently suppressing protests by civil society. This is all the more surprising, given that when Germany joined the SC in January 2011, former foreign minister Guido Westerwelle presented a motto that would guide his country through its two-year tenure: "responsibility, reliability and commitment" (see Brockmeier 2013). The decision was one of the most controversial German foreign-policy decisions since unification, and it caused again considerable surprise and irritation among Western allies and partners. With the exception of Franco-German opposition to the U.S. invasion of Iraq in 2003, Berlin's allies had increasingly been able to count on German financial, political and, more recently, military support for interventions in the 1990s and 2000s. In a harsh break from this tradition, Germany joined China, Russia and India in a vote of abstention (Brockmeier 2013). As a consequence, German foreign policy again had come under scrutiny and harsh criticism due this unpredictable decision not to support France, the UK and the U.S. The result as that there was no common EU position towards Libya, and NATO's response to the crisis proved difficult.

What drove and shaped Germany's position? For some neo-realist analysts, the abstention provoked speculation that Germany wanted to shed its supporting role in the U.S.-led Western alliance in favour of the more autonomy and independent, non-aligned and mercantilist-driven positions taken by leading emerging powers. Less alarmist (and rather constructivist inspired) observers saw the abstention as a confirmation that Germany's 'culture of restraint' on military matters as a domestic constraint was still alive and did work. When it comes to decisions on the use of military force, Germans still need time to have a debate at home about the consequences. An alternative explanation was that the abstention was merely a diplomatic accident and mistake resulting from the particular circumstances and time pressures of the Libya crisis (see Brockmeier 2013). According to Miskimmon, German foreign policy was caught between enlarging its claimed influence and role in international crisis management and reserving the right to reject military involvement in operations that do not fit with its national interest. Miskimmon argues in line with neoclassical realism that Germany's decision can be explained by understanding the rational cost-benefit calculations of the German government, being aware of the dilemma of a gap between external expectations on the one hand, and limited military power resources and pressured by the protracted Eurozone crisis on the other hand (Miskimmon 2013).

Germany's Greater Responsibility*—Rhetoric Shifts or Re-Nationalization of Foreign Policy?*

The war in Syria (since 2011), failed states in Iraq and Libya, and the Crimea crisis (2014) caused Germany's response to these challenges based on a new rhetoric of 'leadership' and 'greater responsibility'. This new rhetoric marks the last *turning point* in German foreign policy so far. Again, systemic, domestic and cognitive factors can explain another remarkable shift towards an even more assertive German foreign policy.

In the context of the events in the Ukraine and in the Middle East, German policy-makers started a new debate about a 'new German foreign policy' in 2014 by using a new vocabulary in order to ultimately establish a Berlin tradition in foreign policy and break free from the Bonn legacy. In their speeches at the Munich Security Conference in February 2014, former Federal President Joachim Gauck and former foreign minister Steinmeier introduced a new understanding of Germany's power and responsibility in fragile and crisis-ridden international affairs (see Kappel 2014), and its contribution to the international and regional order. Given external expectations and a new growing self-conception, and keeping its own limited power resources and its capacities, and its national interests in concrete situations in mind, Steinmeier stated that Germany had a greater responsibility to respond to crises and security issues in Europe and the near abroad through a greater engagement as European pacifier and '*Ordnungsmacht*' which also has the task to europeanize Russia, to multilateralize the U.S., and to defend the liberal Western order, as crisis manager, and as an actor in conflict prevention by means of diplomacy, monitoring, mediation, and, if necessary, the use of force.[4] In both speeches, terms such as 'leadership of the central power' ('Führung aus der Mitte') and 'shaping power' ('*Gestaltungsmacht*') (Hellmann 2016a: 4, 11–12) were used. In further speeches, Steinmeier announced that "Germany will seek to play an efficient role as Europe's chief facilitating officer" (cited according to Hellmann 2016a: 7).

The message is clear: There is no longer a Berliner "culture of standing aloof" and "keeping out" of international affairs, but instead

---

[4] Federal President Joachim Gauck's speech Germany's role in the world: Reflections on responsibility, norms and alliances on 31 January 2014 at the opening of the Munich Security Conference (cited according to Hellmann 2015, 2016a, b); Foreign Minister Frank-Walter Steinmeier's speech on 1 February 2014 at the Munich Security Conference (cited according to Hellmann 2015, 2016a, b).

a new culture of *taking* responsibility, and shaping order. Germany is a "reflective power" with a "special responsibility", a "moral duty for peace", and an "increased military role in the world" *because* of its "historical lesson learned". Whereas the understanding of "responsibility" in the Bonn Republic did mean restraint because of both world wars and the Holocaust, it now meant quite contrary Berlin's *engagement to (re) shape* because of German history. In essence, responsibility and power, which had been strictly separated from each other as a suggested dichotomy in Bonn, are in fact inseparable: more power means to take more responsibility, leading to a policy of greater responsibility *as* new (but complementary to EU-institutionally embedded) form of German power politics *sui generis*, which is the opposite of old Prussian-styled aggressive, war-prone foreign policy behavior, because *interests* (such as security and influence) and *moral values* (such as protecting human rights and taking refugees) are combined. However, this self-perception and self-conception of German foreign policy does *not* exclude unilateralism.

New German Foreign Policy in Practice

In order to demonstrate the willingness to engage, and to play a more active role in EUrope, and to take responsibility in line with the new self-conception (Hellmann 2016a: 6–7) and external expectations, the Merkel government made two decisions that had dramatic consequences for EUrope. The first was in summer 2015 with the unilateral and not coordinated decision to let estimated 1.5 million refugees from Syria, Iraq and elsewhere into the EU and Germany, thus violating the Dublin agreement (Hellmann 2016b: 11). As a consequence, the EU is again splitted into Germany, Sweden and a few states taking negotiated numbers of refugees, and the majority of in particular Eastern European states such as Hungary and Poland that refused to do so. The fact that Germany tried to exert pressure on CEE states to take refugees was largely reinforcing the image that Germany was trying once again to mould European institutions, processes and decisions to serve its national interests at the expense of its partners (Hellmann 2016a: 8–9). Germany was neither praised nor followed in the refugee policy, but harshly criticized for breaking the rules of Schengen, Dublin, and the principles of cooperation and multilateral cooperation.

The second decision was in the beginning of 2014 to condemn and to sanction Russia because of the annexation of the Crimea and the intervention in Eastern Ukraine to support Russian separatists fighting against the Ukraine army in the Donbass region, which was judged in Berlin as reckless Russian power politics to destabilize the pan-European order. Berlin didn't hesitate to claim and to play the key role in diplomatic mediation between Russia and the Ukraine in the so-called Minsk negotiations from 2015 on until today. However, it coordinated the sanctions together with its EU partners and the U.S. (Hellmann 2016a: 7; 2016b: 11). What is obvious is that Germany used a clear and offensive language and coercive diplomacy vis-à-vis Russia (Forsberg 2016), making clear that Russia didn't act in line with international law and the rules of the game in Europe (Hellmann 2016a: 13), and that German leadership role was widespread highly praised by EU partners (Hellmann 2016a: 7).

CONCLUSION

Germany's post-Cold War foreign policy can be explained through neo-classical realist lenses by combining systemic (such as constraints because of the anarchical environment and the security dilemma), regional (geopolitics), domestic (domestic pressure groups) and cognitive factors (such as threat perception, or perceived moral obligations) at the systemic-, interstate- and unit-level, and by bringing the state, statesmen (Byman and Pollack 2001) and domestic institutions as key actors in foreign policy, and influence-seeking as the driving force behind a state's foreign and security policy back into the realist framework of analysis.

The empirical findings of this chapter offer a mixed picture. There is continuity and change in terms of multilateral collectivism as well as unilateralism and a more assertive German post-Cold War foreign policy, and there is stabilization and destabilization as a consequence of German foreign and security policy. Continuity means an interest-driven, but multilateral and EU institutional embedded German foreign policy. Germany did pursue its interests within the EU (and NATO) framework, and it will do so in the future—sometimes successful, sometimes less so. And there is continuity in terms of a culture of responsibility, even though the understanding of what is meant by 'responsibility', and what are the consequences of Germany's responsibility, have changed through the last three decades because of a changing understanding of the legacy of German history in terms of a willingness to protect human rights and promote democracy by the use of force (as a last resort), and in terms of a claim to (re)shape the regional pan-European order and promote stability, welfare and peace.

What have changed fundamentally in the last three decades are the systemic parameters and the regional environment/setting in which Germany is situated and embedded, and the pressures and challenges Germany is confronted with coming along with this. And, what has changed is that Germany is expected by its partners to take the lead in EUrope (Hellmann 2016a). All in all, there is neither a reckless Prussian-styled German power politics and return of a German problem, nor a clear tendency to a radical re-nationalization of a still multilateral embedded, but nevertheless moderately changing German foreign policy *sui generis*. Rather, we can assess an ongoing process of *gradual* and *remarkable shifts* since the late 1990s until today in both Germany's self-conception/self-perception (including self-expectations) and external expectations, and in Berlin's rhetoric leading to a changing role, and a more pro-active, offensive, assertive and *shaping* German foreign policy aiming for maximizing influence and pursuing national interests (sometimes, if necessary or unavoidable, at the expense of common European interests, and stability) and new aims by using old (multilateralism, cooperation, restraint) and new patterns of behavior and instruments (in certain cases including unilateral 'Alleingänge' or abstention from collective decision-making, the use of EU institutions as arena, bargaining processes and package deals, civil or military means, soft balancing etc.). The *rhetoric shifts* characterize the more and more self-confident and established Berlin Republic, and a clear development away from a categorial 'Culture of Restraint' and a behavior of standing aloof and keeping out of international politics as moral imperative and core principle of behaviour, towards a 'new responsibility' in European and international affairs (see Hellmann 2016a).

References

Allison, Roy. 2013. *Russia, the West, and Military Intervention*. Oxford: Oxford University Press.

Art, Robert J. 2004. "Europe Hedges Its Security Best." In *Balance of Power: Theory and Practice in the 21st Century*, edited by T. V. Paul, J. J. Wirtz, and M. Fortmann. Stanford: Stanford University Press.

Banchoff, Thomas. 1997. "German Policy Towards the European Union: The Effects of Historical Memory." *German Politics* 6 (1): 60–76.

Banchoff, Thomas. 1999. "German Identity and European Integration." *European Journal of International Relations* 5 (3): 259–289.

Baumann, Rainer, and Gunther Hellmann. 2001. "Germany and the Use of Military Force: 'Total War', the 'Culture of Restraint', and the Quest for Normality." In *New Europe, New Germany, Old Foreign Policy? German Foreign Policy Since Unification*, edited by D. Webber. London: Cass.

Brockmeier, Sarah. 2013. "Germany and the Intervention in Libya." *Survival: Global Politics and Strategy* 55 (6): 63–90.

Bulmer, Simon, and William E. Paterson. 2011. "Germany and the European Union: From 'Tamed Power' to Normalized Power?" *International Affairs* 86 (5): 1051–1073.

Byman, Daniel L., and Kenneth M. Pollack. 2001. "Let Us Now Praise Great Men: Bringing the Statesman Back In." *International Security* 25 (4): 107–146.

Crawford, Beverly. 1996. "Explaining Defection from International Cooperation: Germany's Unilateral Recognition of Croatia." *World Politics* 48 (4): 482–521.

Crawford, Beverly. 2007. *Power and German Foreign Policy: Embedded Hegemony in Europe*. Basingstoke: Palgrave Macmillan.

Crowe, Brian. 2003. "A Common European Foreign Policy After Iraq?" *International Affairs* 79 (3): 533–546.

Fischer, Joseph. 2000. "Vom Staatenverbund zur Föderation – Gedanken über die Finalität der europäischen Integration." Rede an der Humboldt-Universität Berlin, 12 May. https://www.europa.clio-online.de/quelle/id/artikel-3231.

Flockhart, Trine. 1996. "The Dynamics of Expansion: NATO, WEU and EU." *European Security* 5 (2): 196–218.

Forsberg, Tuomas. 2016. "From Ostpolitik to "frostpolitik": Merkel, Putin and German Foreign Policy Towards Russia." *International Affairs* 92 (1): 21–42.

Friis, Lykke, and Anna Murphy. 2000. "Negotiating in a Time of Crisis: The European Union's Response to the Military Conflict in Kosovo." RSC Working Paper No. 2000/20, Florence.

Garton Ash, Timothy. 1996. "Germany's Choice." In *In Search of Germany*, edited by M. Mertes, S. Muller, and H. Winkler. New Brunswick, NJ: Transaction Publishers.

Gordon, Philip H. 1994. "Berlin's Difficulties: The Normalisation of German Foreign Policy." *Orbis* 38 (2): 225–244.

Haftendorn, Helga. 2006. "Epilogue: A New Geometry? A German Perspective." In *The Strategic Triangle: France, Germany, and the United States in the Shaping of the New Europe*, edited by Helga Haftendorn, et al. Washington, DC: Woodrow Wilson Center Press.

Harnisch, Sebastian, and Hanns-Werner Maull. 2001a. "Introduction." In *Germany as a Civilian Power? The Foreign Policy of the Berlin Republic*, edited by Hanns-Werner Maull and Sebastian Harnisch. Manchester: Manchester University Press.

Harnisch, Sebastian, and Hanns-Werner Maull. 2001b. "Learned Its Lesson Well? Germany as a Civilian Power Ten Years After Unification?" In *Germany as a Civilian Power? The Foreign Policy of the Berlin Republic*, edited by Hanns-Werner Maull and Sebastian Harnisch. Manchester: Manchester University Press.

Haslam, Jonathan. 1998. "Russia's Seat at the Table: A Place Denied or a Place Delayed?" *International Affairs* 74 (1): 119–130.

Hellmann, Gunther. 1996. "Goodbye Bismarck? The Foreign Policy of Contemporary Germany." *Mershon International Studies Review* 40 (1): 1–39.

Hellmann, Gunther. 2011. "Normatively Disarmed, But Self-confident. German Foreign Policy 20 Years After Reunification." *Internationale Politik Global Edition* 3: 45–51.

Hellmann, Gunther. 2015. "Im offensiven Mittelfeld: Deutschlands neue Spielmacherrolle in der europäischen Politik." In *"Früher, entschiedener und substantieller"? Die neue Debatte über Deutschlands Außenpolitik*, edited by G. Hellmann, D. Jacobi, and U. Stark Urrestazaru. Wiesbaden: Springer VS.

Hellmann, Gunther. 2016a. "Germany's World: Power and Followership in a Crisis-Ridden Europe." *Global Affairs* 2 (1): 3–20.

Hellmann, Gunther. 2016b. "Zwischen Gestaltungsmacht und Hegemonialfalle. Zur neuesten Debatte über eine 'neue deutsche Außenpolitik'." *Aus Politik und Zeitgeschichte* 28–29: 4–12.

Hoffmann, Stanley. 1968. "Obstinate or Obsolete? The Fate of the Nation-State and the Case of Western Europe." In *Conditions of World Order*, edited by Stanley Hoffmann. Boston: Houghton Mifflin.

Hoffmann, Stanley. 1995. *The European Sisyphus: Essays on Europe, 1964–1994*. Oxford: Westview Press.

Hyde-Price, Adrian. 2009. *Germany and European Order. Enlarging NATO and the EU*. Manchester: Manchester University Press.

Joetze, Günter. 2006. "Pan-European Stability: Still a Key Task?" In *Germany's Uncertain Power: Foreign Policy of the Berlin Republic*, edited by Hanns-Werner Maull. Basingstoke: Palgrave Macmillan.

Joffe, Joseph. 1984. "Europe's American Pacifier." *Foreign Policy* 54: 64–82.

Kappel, Robert. 2014. "Global Power Shifts and Germany's New Foreign Policy Agenda." *Strategic Analysis* 38 (3): 341–352.

Katzenstein, Peter J. 1997. "The Smaller European States, Germany and Europe." In *Tamed Power: Germany in Europe*, edited by Peter J. Katzenstein. Ithaca, NY: Cornell University Press.

Loriaux, Michael. 1999. "Realism and Reconciliation: France, Germany, and the European Union." In *Unipolar Politics. Realism and State Strategies After the Cold War*, edited by Ethan B. Kapstein and Michael Mastanduno. New York: Columbia University Press.

Lucarelli, Sonia. 1995. "The European Response to the Yugoslav Crisis: Story of a Two-Level Constraint." RSC Working Paper No. 95/37, Florence.

Markovits, Andrei, and Simon Reich. 1991. "Should Europe Fear the Germans?" *German Politics and Society* 23: 1–20.

Maull, Hanns-Werner. 1995. "Germany in the Yugoslav Crisis." *Survival* 37 (4): 99–130.

Maull, Hanns-Werner. 2006. "Conclusion: Uncertain Power—German Foreign Policy into the 21th Century." In *Germany's Uncertain Power: Foreign Policy of the Berlin Republic*, edited by Hanns-Werner Maull. Basingstoke: Palgrave Macmillan.

Mearsheimer, John J. 1990. "Back to the Future. Instability in Europe After the Cold War." *International Security* 15 (1): 5–56.

Mearsheimer, John J. 2014. "Why the Ukraine Crisis Is the West's Fault. The Liberal Delusions That Provoked Putin." *Foreign Affairs* 93 (5): 77–89.

Miskimmon, Alastair. 2013. "German Foreign Policy and the Libya Crisis." *German Politics* 21 (4): 392–410.

Mouritzen, Hans. 2006. "Choosing Side in the European Iraq Conflict: A Test for New Geopolitical Theory." *European Security* 15 (2): 137–163.

Overhaus, Marco. 2006. "Civilian Power Under Stress: Germany, NATO and the European Security and Defense Policy." In *Germany's Uncertain Power: Foreign Policy of the Berlin Republic*, edited by Hanns-Werner Maull. Basingstoke: Palgrave Macmillan.

Phillips, Ann L. 1998. "The Politics of Reconciliation: Germany in Central-East Europe." *German Politics* 7 (2): 64–85.

Reichwein, Alexander. 2012. "The Tradition of Neoclassical Realism." In *Neoclassical Realism in European Politics: Bringing Power Back In*, edited by Asle Toje and Barbara Kunz. New York: Palgrave Macmillan.

Reichwein, Alexander. 2015. "Realism and European Foreign Policy: Promises and Shortcomings." In *The SAGE Handbook of European Foreign Policy*, edited by Knud Erik Jørgensen, et al. London: Sage.

Rudolf, Peter. 2005. "The Myth of the "German Way": German Foreign Policy and Transatlantic Relations." *Survival* 47 (1): 133–152.

Schröder, Gerhard. 1999. "Die Grundkoordinaten deutscher Außenpolitik sind unverändert: Frieden und Sicherheit und Stabiles Umfeld für Wohlstand festigen." *Bulletin der Bundesregierung*. Bonn: Presse- und Informationsamt 83/S, 6 December.

Smith, Nicholas R. 2017. "What the West Can Learn from Rationalizing Russia's Action in Ukraine." *Orbis* 61 (3): 354–368.

Sperling, James. 1994. "German Foreign Policy After Reunification: An End of Cheque Book Diplomacy." *West European Politics* 17 (1): 73–97.

Staun, Jorgen M. 2017. *Normal at Last? German Strategic Culture and the Holocaust.* Copenhagen: Royal Danish Defence College, Report October.

Szabo, Stephen F. 2006. "Enlarging NATO: The German-American Design for a New Alliance." In *The Strategic Triangle: France, Germany, and the United States in the Shaping of the New Europe*, edited by Helga Haftendorn, et al. Washington, DC: Woodrow Wilson Center Press.

Tewes, Henning. 2002. *Germany, Civilian Power and the New Europe. Enlarging NATO and the EU.* Basingstoke and Houndmills: Palgrave Macmillan.

Toje, Asle. 2008. "The Consensus-Expectations Gap: Explaining Europe's Ineffective Foreign Policy." *Security Dialogue* 39 (1): 121–141.

Wagener, Martin. 2006. "Normalization in Security Policy? Deployments of Bundeswehr Forces Abroad in the Era Schörder, 1998–2004." In *Germany's Uncertain Power: Foreign Policy of the Berlin Republic*, edited by Hanns-Werner Maull. Basingstoke: Palgrave Macmillan.

Waltz, Kenneth N. 1993. "The Emerging Structure of International Politics." *International Security* 18 (2): 44–79.

———. 2000. "Structural Realism After the Cold War." *International Security* 25 (1): 5–41.

Wivel, Anders. 2008. "Balancing Against Threats or Bandwagoning with Power? Europe and the Transatlantic Relationship After the Cold War." *Cambridge Review of International Affairs* 21 (3): 289–305.

CHAPTER 6

When Power Meets Perception: France's Fight Against Terrorism in the Sahara-Sahel

Benedikt Erforth

Introduction[1]

During François Hollande's presidency (2012–2017), France emerged as one of the principal actors in the "Global War on Terror". By turns, France took on the roles of the defender of liberal values, the "victim of barbarism", and the retaliating power. Beyond its borders, France engaged in the fight against terrorism by launching a large-scale military operation in West Africa and actively supporting the US's efforts against ISIS in the Middle East. These actions surpass the highly institutionalized and norm-based approach that generally characterizes European foreign policy (Kagan 2002) and are the direct result of decisions taken in an unstable environment governed by uncertainty and fear.

At first glance, realism appears to be the obvious theoretical framework to capture France's military activism. Not only does realism focus on the fundamental question of war and peace, it also accounts for fear

[1] All translations are by the author.

B. Erforth (✉)
SciencesPo, Paris, France
e-mail: benedikt.erforth@sciencespo.fr

© The Author(s) 2019   109
R. Belloni et al. (eds.), *Fear and Uncertainty in Europe*, Global Issues,
https://doi.org/10.1007/978-3-319-91965-2_6

and uncertainty as drivers of state action. However, in order for realism to become a suitable framework to explain foreign policy decisions, it also needs to capture the impact of human subjectivity on policy-making processes and the interactions that take place between the different existent levels of analysis.

Explaining decisions made by emotional actors in an inter-subjectively created reality does not come easily to a theoretical tradition that in its quest for parsimony has reduced individuals to single-minded rational like units. In particular, following the success of structural realism, the international system and its ordering principles have been described as the primary explanatory variables of twentieth century realism in IR. In line with Donnelly's contribution, I argue that realism is a complex and multidimensional "thing" (this volume) and its alleged ambition for parsimony is only one possible interpretation—mostly limited to structural realism—that does not constitute the core of this longstanding intellectual tradition. Treating the international system (structure) as the single most powerful explanatory variable is neither distinctively realist nor very useful for analytical purposes. By way of looking at France's military intervention in Mali, the aim of this chapter is to assess realism's actual capability to account for individual actors, their perceptions, and ideas in the concrete case of the French military operation against terrorist forces in Mali and the Sahel. Realism is understood here as a rich "general orientation" (Donnelly 2002: 6) capable not only of encompassing different levels of analysis within its explanatory framework but also of accounting for both material and ideational factors in international affairs. Rather than applying a clear-cut distinction between different levels of analysis (or images) (Waltz 1979: 88–89), I suggest a reading where individual actors, society, and the international system constantly interact with one another. Understanding foreign policy outcomes requires an understanding of these interactions.

The chapter proceeds as follows. The first part sets up a realist framework of French foreign policy. Whilst acknowledging the interaction between Waltz's three levels of analysis—the individual, society, and structure—this section highlights the realist tradition's commitment to treating individuals as the irreducible analytical starting point and the base unit of societies and the system (Lebow 2008: 114). This section also shows realism's ability to account for cultural variables. In the chapter's second part, the discussion shifts from the theoretical to the empirical, explaining the Hollande administration's decision to fight terrorist groups in Mali. The case study illustrates how combining material and ideational factors and cutting across the three levels of analysis produces comprehensive and convincing explanations of foreign policy decision-making. Furthermore, it considers uncertainty and fear as crucial factors during the decision-making process and traces their influence on French decision-makers prior to the deployment of French troops to West Africa in January 2013. Both the theoretical and the empirical discussions make the case for an eclectic foreign policy analysis offering convincing explanations that do not compete with but are rooted in realist thought.

INDIVIDUAL ACTORS AND THEIR MOTIVES

Motives matter when it comes to foreign policy decision-making (Donnelly 2002: 43). This insight is neither new nor foreign to the realist tradition. The acknowledgment that motives as causes of social action are rooted in human attributes such as passion, reason, spirit, and appetite for long has been present in realist thought. By giving *"primary* emphasis to egoistic passions and the 'tragic presence of evil in all political action'" (Morgenthau quoted in Donnelly 2002: 10), realism accounts for certain aspects of human subjectivity and by consequence acknowledges the necessity to understand the complexity of the human mind and its impact on political outcomes.[2] As Morgenthau pointed out:

> Since it is the human mind which mirrors the physical world and which determines the human actions within and with respect to it, the qualities of the mind must in turn be reflected in the picture we have of nature. Thus,

---

[2] At first, this claim seems counterintuitive, given that since the popularization of neo-realism in the late 1970s and 1980s the greater number of authors in the realist tradition in IR has neglected the individual dimension of social action. The assumption that human nature "has not changed since the days of classical antiquity" (Thompson 1985: 17) has made possible the treatment of individuals as one-dimensional like-units. Yet long before the emergence of such a simplified account of human nature, honor and glory as human motivations took on a central position in what is referred to as the realist tradition. Thomas Hobbes argued that people mainly quarrel with one another for the desire of glory (Hobbes 2008: XIII, 7). Likewise, for Machiavelli and Thucydides, honor, glory, and reputation are strong motivational forces and ends in themselves (Donnelly 2002: 66, 68). All three attributes are both internal and external to the individual as they emerge from the transmitters' psyche but also depend on the recognition of one's actions by an approving audience (Price 1977: 591–592).

the physical world, as we are able to know it, bears in a dual sense the imprint of the human mind; it is in a dual sense its product. (Morgenthau 1947: 123)

In line with arguments of early foreign policy analysts, Morgenthau shows that reality is a construct that can only be understood by focusing on "entities capable of experiencing needs, formulating problems, perceiving phenomena by seeing, hearing, and other sensory behaviour" (Sprout and Sprout 1965: 207). The existence of cognitive biases constituted a sufficient cause for Morgenthau to refute the rationalist—or scientific—paradigm in International Relations, which he accused of misrepresenting "the nature of man in that it attributes to man's reason, in its relations to the social world, a power of knowledge and control which reason does not have" (Morgenthau 1947: 145).

In line with Morgenthau's critique of rational choice approaches, Kenneth Waltz posits that "since making foreign policy is such a complicated business, one cannot expect of political leaders the nicely calculated decisions that the word 'rationality' suggests" (Waltz 1986: 330). To reiterate, both Morgenthau and Waltz point to the central role of individual decision-makers in international relations and acknowledge the existence of cognitive biases making humans anything but rational actors. "Flesh-and-blood-human beings" (Sprout and Sprout 1965: 207) are part of their respective frameworks and considered to be the true subjects of social research.[3] In particular, Morgenthau can be read as much a representative of the realist tradition as an advocate of cognitive and decision-making approaches to foreign policy (Allison 1971; Lebow 2008; Snyder et al. 1962).[4]

---

[3] As for Waltz, this claim applies to his earlier work *Man, the State, and War* (1959) and *Foreign Policy and Democratic Politics* (1967) but not to *Theories of International Politics* (1979).

[4] Admittedly, Morgenthau never elaborated on the impact of cognitive biases of decision-making, besides presenting them as the sufficient cause for refuting rational choice analyses. He also remains rather inconsistent when elaborating (or failing to elaborate) on the impact of subjectivity on social action. Whilst opening the possibility for cognitive and ideational analyses of foreign policy decision-making, Morgenthau simultaneously shuts down this avenue of investigation by referring to emotions and interests being pre-determined. In sum, Morgenthau's thought on the relationship between reason and emotions was tainted by inconsistency.

Not only does realism account for human subjectivity, it is quite explicit about the role of individuals as the starting point of all social actions. "The relations between nations", writes Morgenthau, "are not essentially different from the relations between individuals; they are only relations between individuals on a wider scale" (1947: 43). By consequence, the "action of society, of the nation, or of any other collectivity, political or otherwise, as such has no empirical existence at all. What empirically exist [sic] are always the actions of individuals who perform identical or different actions with reference to a common end" (Morgenthau 1947: 161). In sum, both Morgenthau and Waltz, arguably the two most influential twentieth century realists in IR, make room for cognitive biases in their respective analyses, yet fail to provide the necessary tools that would have allowed for translating realist assumptions into empirical accounts of the human mind. Hence, a research agenda that combines a power-centric worldview in the realist tradition acknowledging fear and uncertainty as driving forces of international politics with process oriented empirical foreign policy analysis seems a promising step forward.

By consequence, a realist reading of France's military interventionism needs to take into account individual decision-makers, beginning with those individuals that have the biggest say over the country's foreign and security policy. It is important to note that—as will be shown below—acknowledging the individual as the irreducible starting point of social research does not negate the impact of societal and cultural variables.

Two leadership traditions inhere in the Fifth Republic's political system—personal and parliamentary leadership. Together, these legacies of French history have led to the creation of a semi-presidential system with a dual executive and shared powers between the president and the prime minister (Elgie 2005: 70–72). Notwithstanding the dualistic character of the Fifth Republic, there exists a de facto hierarchical order, which makes the president "the main political actor in the regime" (Gaffney 2010: 5). Presidential authority is particularly prominent in the realms of foreign and defense policy, where policies are inextricably linked to the person and personality of the president.

The presidential dominance in the constitutional design of the Fifth Republic follows from the collapse of the Fourth Republic, which was founded on the parliamentary leadership principle. Strong leadership came to be seen as a necessary condition to unite the country and reinforce France's international standing and grandeur (Elgie 2005: 71–72). Charles de Gaulle, who took office in the course of the Algerian

War to become the Fifth Republic's first president, personified the ideal type of a charismatic and dominant decider. Successive French presidents have referred to de Gaulle and his interpretation of the presidential mandate as their original point of reference. How de Gaulle interpreted and exercised the presidential mandate during the early phase of the Fifth Republic crucially shaped the collective perception of the role of the president and paved the way for his successors. Consequently, French presidents to date have enjoyed a high degree of decisional autonomy in foreign affairs that is unique in Europe.

France's foreign and defense policies constitute the core of presidential exclusiveness (Chipman 1989: 117, 155). The decision to involve France in a military intervention abroad is incumbent on the president alone. As commander-in-chief, the president can take such a decision without the authorization of any other constitutional body.[5] The autonomy of the French president, his undisputed decision-making authority, and his central position at the top of the system removed from party-political quarrels allow for decisions to be taken within the shortest possible time (Cohen 1986: 18). From the moment the president decides to deploy troops to another country, the first rapid deployment forces can be activated within a couple of hours.

In light of its dominant position, the French president deserves to be placed at the heart of any empirical analysis of French military interventionism. Repeatedly François Hollande had been portrayed as a president who decided little or not at all—a maneuverer who waited for crises to ebb away (Biseau 2013). However, during the Malian and the Central-African crises in 2013, François Hollande demonstrated strong leadership by taking considerable political risks. The two crises showed the president quite plainly what *his* country was able to achieve as a global security player. Morgenthau's distinction between the *statesman* [sic] (political leader) and the *politician* seems a fitting description of the two diametrically opposed roles President Hollande personified during his term. The politician is an opportunist who lacks sound judgment and has their eyes on the next election only. In contrast, political

---

[5] Since the constitutional reform of 2008, the government needs to *inform* Parliament within three days after having decided a military intervention. A debate can take place, but the decision is not due for parliamentary approval. Only if a military operation exceeds the duration of four months, parliamentary approval is required (Constitution de la République française, art. 35).

leaders commit themselves to their actions and face difficult choices in an uncertain world. What makes political leaders honorable as opposed to politicians is their firmness and exposure in the light of uncertainty. In the realm of foreign policy, François Hollande the politician turned into François Hollande the political leader. Media, public opinion, and expert commentators alike described a transformed president; a president that demonstrated firmness and strength in an uncertain and brutish world.

FRANCE'S DOMESTIC ENVIRONMENT

Despite their non-negligible idiosyncrasies, human beings are social animals that do not act in isolation but are embedded within a society and networks of friendships and professional relations. By consequence, even in a semi-presidential system that is noted for the dominant role that it accords to the president, decision-making can never be attributed to only one single actor.

Realism acknowledges this premise and understands individual actors within their wider societal context. Prior to the publication of Waltz's, *Theory of International Politics*, realism was mainly concerned with the foreign policies of states and thus per definition attentive to domestic structures and their effects on political action. Realism, in other words, is a social theory (James 1989: 221). "Man's behaviour", writes Waltz in *Man, the State, and War*, "his very nature, which some have taken as cause, is, according to Rousseau, in great a product of society in which he lives" (Waltz 2001: 5). Like others, Waltz is critical of the assumption that any meaningful conclusions about the occurrence of war and peace can be inferred by *only* looking at the individual.[6]

For Morgenthau the content of the concepts of power and interest strongly depend "upon the political and cultural context within which foreign policy is formulated" (Morgenthau 2006: 11). Reason and choice are subject to cultural determinants that structure the psycho-milieu of decision-makers ahead of any calculation or evaluation processes. In other words, political or more specifically strategic culture[7]—as

---

[6] Arguably, Waltz' (2001: 42–80) criticism was mainly directed against the behavioralist's hope to actively change human behaviour through external stimuli.

[7] Strategic culture "provides the lens through which national authorities refract the structural position of the state in the international system; it explains the subjective understanding of objective threats to national security, the instruments relied upon to meet those threats, and the preference for unilateral or multilateral action" (Sperling 2010: 11).

a common mind-set among a group of people—limits the collective attention "to less than the full range of alternative behaviours, problems, and solutions which are logically possible" (Elkins and Simeon 1979: 128). Individual ideas, propositions, and solutions that coincide with the prevailing political culture in a given society are more likely to be accepted and hence to influence the policy-making process (Risse et al. 1999: 157). Options that fall outside the realm of possibilities laid out by the domestic structure will easily be discarded. Socialized within a specific historical and political context, and assisted by their ministers and advisors, presidents are not outliers but representatives of society, which shapes and co-determines them.

Even with the emergence of structural realism and the analytical shift toward the international system, the state (society)-centric focus has not disappeared completely. Epitomized by Putnam's two-level game and elaborated by neo-classical realism (Rose 1998), numerous writers describe a situation of "dual pressure" in which actors respond and adapt to the pressure exerted by the international environment, yet only within the scope of domestic processes that act as "an opaque filter through which assessments, choices, and judgments are being made regarding the international realm" (Sterling-Folker 1997: 19).

At the heart of France's foreign policy lies the idea of projecting "political, economic, and cultural influence beyond the national territory" (Charillon 2002: 916–917). The belief in the universalism of its values as a means to exercise power has made France a particularly active actor as well as vigorous promoter of democracy and human rights on the global stage. The importance French policy-makers attribute to reputational factors such as honor, responsibility, and standing in the international system cannot be overemphasized. A proactive foreign policy is one of the constitutive elements of France's political culture and national identity. Founded during the Algerian War and a decade after the end of WWII, the birth of the Fifth Republic occurred against the backdrop of an environment of extreme political violence. Internal divisions should be overcome through external strength. When considering French

---

Induced by the dominant worldviews of the political elites of a given state, as well as their instrumental and interaction preferences, "strategic culture defines a set of patterns of and for behaviour on war and peace issues" (Booth 2005: 25).

foreign policy-decision, one cannot forget the unique political environment within which opinions are shaped and decisions are made.

Political culture is both fluid and multifaceted, meaning that it cannot be easily captured within one concise and definitive term. However, when trying to understand French foreign policy and its cultural particularities, scholars frequently resorted to the notion of *grandeur* (greatness), which was first employed to describe the "embodiment of General de Gaulle's hopes and aspirations for his beloved France" (Cerny 1980: 3). More recently, decision-makers and scholars alike have replaced the concept of *grandeur* by the less conflictual notion of *puissance d'influence* (influential power). The notion of *puissance d'influence* comes without preconceived ideas of neo-colonialism and anti-Americanism and has become the preferred *élément de langage* (element of speech) of French foreign policy elites. According to former Foreign Minister Laurent Fabius, eight characteristics make France an influential power in the world (Fabius 2012):

1. Its permanent membership in the UN Security Council
2. Its status as a nuclear power
3. Its status as the world's fifth largest economy
4. 200 million French speakers in the world and an estimated 700 million by 2050 (mainly Africans)
5. Cultural *rayonnement*
6. The positive perception of France across the globe
7. The defense of a certain conception of human rights
8. The country's history

These eight aspects can be understood as permanent pillars of French foreign policy. They constitute the boundaries of the political spectrum within which foreign policy is made. Any decision French decision-makers take with regard to the external world takes into account a combination of these characteristics first.[8]

Before turning to the actual case study of France's military intervention in Mali, it is necessary to briefly address the role of the international

---

[8]Among these factors, France's permanent seat in the UN Security Council, its EU membership, and its role as an active player on the African continent stand out as the most important elements of the country's foreign policy identity. A powerful role within these fora is considered as beneficial to the country's national interest.

system, as it is understood here. Whilst enabling and constraining political action, anarchy per se does not explain state motivations; and thus only gives away a part of the story. It simply provides a background condition in which causes (and explanations of behavior or outcomes) may operate (Donnelly this volume). Structural realists that employed Waltz's theory to explain international politics had to rely on additional variables to produce convincing explanations of international politics (Mearsheimer 2001, 2011; Walt 2006).[9] As Donnelly (2002: 51) puts it, "the attempt to circumvent the need for a substantive account of state motivation through an appeal to anarchy—cannot succeed…motives cannot be left out of structural theories." Kenneth Waltz acknowledges this limitation inherent to structuralism when pointing out, "structurally we can describe and understand the pressures states are subject to. We cannot predict how they will react to the pressures without knowledge of their internal dispositions" (Waltz 1979: 71). Consequently, in order to understand the nature and the timing of France's reactions to an external stimulus, it is not enough to examine the existing power distributions that characterize the international system at a given point in time. Instead, individual motives and domestic structure need to be added to the analytical framework. Against this backdrop, the remainder of this chapter illustrates how the interaction between individual decision-making, domestic structure, and the anarchic international environment can help explain the French military intervention in Mali.

War—Operation Serval in Mali

In 2012, the security, political, and humanitarian crises that smoldered in Mali reached new heights. In the midst of succeeding political crises, militant Islamist groups had emerged as new and powerful actors on Mali's territory. The best known of these extremist groups, *Al-Qaeda in Islamic Maghreb* (AQIM), operated across an area that reaches from Sudan in the east to Mauritania in the west. Mali's armed forces were no match for the well-equipped, well-trained, and well-financed fighters that by the end of 2012 had conquered and now controlled the country's

---

[9] Donnelly calls such models "augmented structural realism".

northern part in the name of a global jihadist agenda. The presence of Islamist extremist groups in the north of the country and the fear they induced among the international community and notably France, whose leaders felt particularly close to the events in Mali, transformed a domestic political conflict and regional insurgent movement into an issue with global reach. Within a few years' time, Mali had become the setting of a larger conflict between competing ideologies and differing conceptions of order, the so-called Global War on Terror.

At first, the international response to the deteriorating situation in Mali consisted in supporting the interim government in Bamako and setting up a multilateral intervention force to restore order in the country. In quick succession, the UN Security Council unanimously adopted three resolutions (UN Res. 2056, 2071, and 2085) to enable the deployment of an African-led International Support Mission (AFISMA). Yet, despite these verbal commitments, initially neither the African Union nor the United Nations nor the European Union provided sufficient financial, material, and human resources to set up a robust multilateral force to confront the increasingly powerful Islamist groups that by then controlled the northern part of Mali.

Following an offensive led by *Anṣār ad-Dīn*-led towards the government-controlled south in early January 2013, Mali's interim President Dioncounda Traoré—fearing the collapse of what remained of the Malian state—issued a written request for French military assistance. On 11 January 2013, François Hollande announced that he had given the order to launch a counter-offensive against Islamist fighters and criminal groups that threatened the existence of the Malian state (Hollande 2013b). By early February 2013, 4,500 French troops were taking part in the operation code-named *Serval*.

This decision to intervene resulted from a combination of a permissive structure, a President who recognized himself as an effective and popular commander and who acted within a political culture that legitimizes military intervention in order to uphold specific values, strengthen the country's reputation in the world, and contain security threats. The identification of terrorism in the Sahel region as both the underlying cause of the Malian crisis and its most serious consequence further enhanced the need for a military solution. Fearing the consequences of a failed state on Europe's southern shore, French decision-makers pushed for a timely strike, transcending the rule-based European approach to conflict settlement.

Before and during the intervention, references alluding to Europe's security were driven by the fear that "a state the size of Mali that falls for terrorism is a state that then will prepare attacks thousands of kilometers beyond its borders" (Nadal 2013). As one presidential advisor pointed out, "what is happening in the Sahel region—geographically speaking—is not very far from us. This is our neighbourhood. If the problems are not dealt with on site, in a couple of years they will be here with us [in Europe]" (Interview 2014b).

Decision-makers, ahead of the French military intervention, had been genuinely worried about an escalation of the Malian crisis because of the potential implications such an escalation would have had for the security of France and Europe. A report published by the French Senate in early 2013 stated, "Africa is too close, both in terms of geography as well as population (*en termes de population*), for Europe not to be concerned when observing the multiplication of 'fragile states' in the region" (Sénat 2013: 475).

Similar to the Cold War era domino theory, French actors described an inevitable proliferation of the terrorist threat across the West African region. The Foreign Ministry summarized the situation as follows: "To do nothing means taking the risk that AQIM will contaminate—via spill over—other countries in that region and even more than today become a threat to France, its expatriates, and interests" (Ministère des Affaires Étrangères 2012). When President Hollande later had to weigh the costs and benefits of a unilateral strike, the idea of a proliferation of the terrorist threat clearly supported a military solution.

Frequent references to this perceived fear and the link made between the crisis in Mali and global jihad, also served the more instrumental purpose of convincing France's partners to support a military operation. Over the course of the second half of 2012, statements emphasizing the danger the Malian crisis posed not only to the country itself and the region but also to Europe should encourage other countries to actively participate in the conflict resolution. However, this instrumental dimension of this discourse does not contradict the more constitutive function these references fulfilled, which was endowing an object with a fancy that would give it its meaning.

It should be noted that most of France's European partners did not attribute the same importance to the threat described by the French administration looming on Europe's southern shores.

While some authors explain Europe's reluctance to act by blaming French elites' arrogance and their failure "to produce evidence they claimed to have about the threat Mali represented" (Marchal 2013: 491), French decision-makers themselves held the lack of a common European vision responsible for the general disinterest. In particular, among the military the lack of a common strategic culture is understood as the principal factor preventing successful European military cooperation. Distinctive political cultures, what Morgenthau terms national character, often have "permanent and decisive influence upon the weight a nation is able to put into the scales of international politics" (Morgenthau 2006: 141). Aware of persisting divides among European partners and knowing of the difficulty to change political cultures, French decision-makers soon arrived at the conclusion that, as one civil servant put it rather bluntly, establishing order in Mali will be "first of all a French issue. With the exception of Germany, Italy, Spain, and Belgium, go and try to get the rest of Europe interested in Africa, well good luck. The Poles do not give a toss; neither do the Scandinavians or the rest of Eastern Europe. They do not have the means or the desire" (Interview 2013).

France's proactive stance during the crisis in Mali can be attributed to the country's special historical, linguistic, and cultural ties with the region that until today remain, if not special, so at least different from those relations other European member states entertain with sub-Saharan Africa. Embedded in such an enabling domestic structure a small group of actors took the decision to launch a large-scale military operation on Malian territory.

In reaction to the insurgents' offensive towards the southern part of Mali in early January 2013, France's permanent representative at the UN requested a closed-door meeting of the Security Council on 10 January. On 11 January, François Hollande reunited the restricted Defense Council at the end of which he decided to respond to the request issued by Mali's interim president and to deploy French troops in a veritable counter-offensive that aimed at eradicating as many terrorist fighters as possible (Interview 2014a). In hindsight, Operation Serval qualifies as one of the most successful military operations in the history of the Fifth Republic that boosted France's role as an influential power on the international scene. Yet nothing was less certain than the success of Operation Serval at the time when François Hollande gave the order to intervene.

As Notin points out, "Serval was exceptional in many regards, and its launch was particularly remarkable. France was about to launch its most significant military operation since the Algerian War based not on evidence but an array of presumptions" (Notin 2014: 153).

The notion of responsibility emerged as one of the core elements during both the pre- and post-intervention discourse. Responsibility has a multitude of different meanings, which taken together constitute a core explanatory factor of the French decision. The colonial experience and its heritage made French elites feel more concerned with the Sahel and West Africa than decision-makers in any other country. Notwithstanding the fact that more than half a century had passed since France's former colonies gained independence, French decision-makers acknowledged the impact of their predecessors' practices on the contemporary security state of francophone Africa.

Still more frequently, policy-makers referred to France's role in the UN Security Council. Being one of the five permanent members of this international institution that describes itself as bearing "the primary responsibility for the maintenance of international peace and security" (United Nations 2014) creates certain expectations among French actors and their foreign counterparts. As long as Africa is not represented in the Security Council, France will remain the self-declared defender of African interests in this institution (Collignon 2013).

The perceived responsibility by agents working in the name of a *puissance d'influence* can be considered as one of the principal motivations that led to Operation Serval. The role France intends to play in the international system comes with obligations. As one French colonel put it, "from the moment you are responsible, you take risks. If not, you must not be responsible" (Collignon 2013). Among members of the Hollande administration, it was a widely shared sentiment that the capabilities that allow France to act also oblige France to act. Material capabilities in that sense are more than permissive means of action but in conjunction with decision-makers' perception stir the framing process into a particular direction. There is a fine but important difference between arguing that France did what it did because it could and France did what it did because its decision-makers preferred one solution over another based on their assessment of their country's military capacities. The former explanation assumes a certain automaticity and would limit itself to an evaluation of a given country's military potential whereas the latter takes into account both material and non-material factors when formulating an answer.

The perceived sentiment of responsibility was further enhanced by the fact that, at the very moment of decision, state action became an individual cause of those who were in the position to decide in the name of France. For Hollande, Mali had become a question of personal responsibility, which should turn out to be a crucial factor influencing the French decision to go to war.

> I am responsible, because I am at the head of a country that has a link with Africa, because we [are] connected with this continent, because there are populations that blended by being mobile, by moving: I have a particular responsibility, thus, I am keen that France takes the initiative. (Hollande 2013c)

A strong identification with a certain conception of the French state and its role in the world turned the once hesitating President Hollande into the decisive Commander Hollande (Notin 2014: 177–179), akin to Morgenthau's idea of a political leader. Collective action became a matter of personal prestige (Lindemann 2013: 153).

Finally, references to emotional bounds ran through the French discourse and affected all actors at the heart of the decision-making process. A president who declared himself as being "very much attached" to Africa (Hollande 2012b) was joined by a foreign minister who, when seeking allies across West Africa, declared to 'love Senegal' (Fabius 2012). As a close advisor to Defense Minister Jean-Yves Le Drian stated, "Mali ... is part of us, or at least of our history.... The extremely close ties that persist between Africa and France make us consider ourselves more legitimate than others [to act]. The path we have to cross mentally to imagine rescuing Mali is rather short" (Interview 2013). Bleiker and Hutchison in their study on emotions in world politics, find that "questions of affect play a crucial role in determining how individual and collective identities are constituted, thus also shaping perceptions of the international system and the threats it may pose to states" (Bleiker and Hutchison 2008: 122).

On the one hand, French leaders continue to emphasize France's grandeur, its position in the international system, its dominant role in Africa, and its place in history, on the other they are well aware of the limits of this narrative given the size of France and both its financial and political constraints. This co-occurrence of a proactive foreign policy and a certain number of constraints resulted in a policy that first supported a multilateral problem solution. In the end however, the Hollande administration did not stop short of unilateral action. While the goal of Operation Serval was to save Mali's sovereignty, it just as much served to safeguard France's own identity and its position in the international system. As the president proclaimed on the evening of his decision,

> France is an active and engaged power, which has this ambition of being useful in the world that surrounds it. This ambition is not new, but derives from our history, which makes us hold a series of principles and values, which we have not invented exclusively for ourselves, but which we share with the entire world: democracy, human rights, a balance of power (*une conception équilibrée*), the will to avoid any hegemony or power, and the intention to always resort to international organizations to allow for peace and security. (Hollande 2013a)

The idea of France being a *puissance d'influence* can only be maintained if French actors make national and international audiences believe that France is actually assuming this self-imposed role. The very identity of French actors and thus the French state depends on the acceptance of the narrative of France being an influential power in the world. To maintain this narrative a policy was wanted that would confirm this discourse and put the French role conception into practice. Thus, when intervening in Mali, but also in the CAR and Iraq/Syria, the Hollande administration was not only "saving strangers" and contributing to international stability, but was saving its very identity. For policy-makers in Paris, France exists in the international system as a security actor, as a democracy promoter and human rights defender that does not shy away from using force when it can help defend the values and ideas to which the polity subscribes. Africa remains the first region where France can give proof of its political and military capacities. Accordingly, in January 2013 after all multilateral efforts had failed to materialize and the sovereignty of a state within France's special zone of influence was threatened, a French president, who held that "France is not just any country in Europe and its president not just any head of state in the world [and who] … intends to emphasize France's international ambition" (Hollande 2012a) could not afford to stand and watch but had to act.

Conclusion

This chapter has made a case for an analysis of power politics taking into account both material and non-material factors. The example of French military interventionism in the Sahel demonstrated realism's compatibility with foreign policy analysis and its ability to account for emotions and other human drives that are often missing from structural and institutional analyses of international politics. When facing new and uncertain situations, human beings, rather than relying on bureaucratic and institutional structures, resort to egoistic, passionate, and simplified modes of reasoning, which are captured by the long-standing tradition of realist scholarship.

The empirical analysis broke down the boundaries between three levels of analysis and instead offered a three-dimensional explanatory space within which material and ideational factors interact. Again, this insight is not foreign to realist writers. As Kenneth Waltz put it in the introduction to *Man, the State, and War*, it is "some combination of our three images, rather than any one of them, may be required for an accurate understanding of international politics" (Waltz 2001: 14). For the early Waltz, "The third image describes the framework of world politics, but without the first and the second images there can be no knowledge of the forces that determine policy" (Waltz 2001: 238).

Whilst acknowledging individual passions and societal pressures, empirically speaking, realism fails to elaborate on how exactly different levels of analysis interact with one another.[10] Foreign policy analysis remedies these shortcomings by offering the necessary tools to investigate the role of individual and collective ideas and their impact on policy-making processes. The merger of these two approaches produced a comprehensive and detailed account of France's decision to deploy troops to Mali.

More precisely, the case study described the French decision as the outcome of individual action and collective deliberation within a political and cultural environment that is specific to the French Fifth Republic. Neither the international structure nor material factors alone would have been able to produce the same explanation of the Hollande administration's decision. Such a psychological and culturalist approach is perfectly

---

[10]With the exception of neo-classical realism, which as Donnelly suggests shades into foreign policy analysis (this volume).

in line with classical realism and its commitment to egoistic passions and the "tragic presence of evil in all political action" (Donnelly 2002: 10).

For instance, the shift from a non-interventionist to policy to a quasi-unilateral intervention reflected the constraints of the international environment in conjunction with a pro-interventionist domestic structure. At first, the French intervention was enabled by a challenge to the existing power distribution and a generally permissive international environment. The translation of these systemic incentives into concrete foreign policy decisions, however, took place within the domestic structure and was conducted by individual actors, notably a president who sensed a high degree of responsibility vis-à-vis the Malian state and its people.

Consistent with the realist approach, individual responsibility too, is a product of the surrounding society that encourages certain types of behavior whilst discrediting others. Moreover, responsibility is inherently self-interested and strongly related to the nation's and individual actors' glory on the international stage. Intervening in Mali, did not only help stabilize another state, it also strengthened France's position and role as an influential power in the international system.

Finally, the case study also revealed that the fear of a failing state in Europe's southern neighborhood functioned as a driving force of French action. The presence, respectively absence of this perceived fear, in parts explains the different reactions of European member states towards a political and security crisis in the Sahel region.

Yet, as any solution to a given problem, the comprehensive approach proposed here too suffers from certain downsides. The inclusive conceptualization of realism as a tradition—as opposed to realism as a lean theory—risks establishing a framework that by its very nature of being comprehensive and inclusive loses its explanatory power. If ideas, political culture, and the international environment are part and parcel of realist explanations, what is not? As a solution to this dilemma, I proposed—rather than to discard—to use realism in conjunction with other mid-level theories that allow for translating theoretical groundwork into empirical analysis. Rather than to ask whether or not French interventionism can be described as realist, I posed the question of how can realism help explain the phenomenon at hand. I showed that realism, if understood as a rich intellectual tradition, is far from being obsolete but still should inform foreign policy analyses in a world governed by fear and uncertainty.

REFERENCES

Allison, Graham T. 1971. *Essence of Decision: Explaining the Cuban Missile Crisis.* Boston: Little, Brown and Company.

Biseau, Grégoire. 2013. "François Hollande Est Avant Tout En Cohérence Avec Sa Diplomatie." *Libération*, August 28.

Bleiker, Roland, and Emma Hutchison. 2008. "Fear No More: Emotions and World Politics." *Review of International Studies* 34 (1): 115–135.

Booth, Ken. 2005. "Strategic Culture: Validity and Validation." *The Oxford Journal of Good Governance* 2 (1): 25–29.

Cerny, Philip. 1980. *The Politics of Grandeur: Ideological Aspects of de Gaulle's Foreign Policy.* Cambridge: Cambridge University Press.

Charillon, Frédéric. 2002. "Peut-Il Encore Y Avoir Une Politique Etrangère de La France?" *Politique Étrangère* 67 (4): 915–929.

Chipman, John. 1989. *French Power in Africa.* Oxford: Blackwell.

Cohen, Samy. 1986. *La Monarchie Nucléaire: Les Coulisses de La Politique Etrangère Sous La V. République.* Paris: Hachette.

Collignon, Xavier. 2013. Interview with the Vice-Director of the DAS, August 6. Interview by Author.

Donnelly, Jack. 2002. *Realism and International Relations.* Reprinted. Themes in International Relations. Cambridge: Cambridge University Press.

Elgie, Robert. 2005. "The Political Executive." In *Developments in French Politics 3*, edited by Alistair Cole, Patrick Le Galès, and Jonathan D. Levy, 70–87. Basingstoke: Palgrave Macmillan.

Elkins, David, and Richard Simeon. 1979. "A Cause in Search of Its Effects, or What Does Political Culture Explain?" *Comparative Politics* 11 (2): 127–145.

Fabius, Laurent. 2012. "Déplacement Au Sénégal: Allocution Du Ministre Des Affaires Étrangères, M. Laurent Fabius, Dans Les Locaux Du Mouvement «Y'en a Marre».".

Gaffney, John. 2010. *Political Leadership in France: From Charles de Gaulle to Nicolas Sarkozy.* Basingstoke: Palgrave Macmillan.

Hobbes, Thomas. 2008. *Leviathan.* Translated by J. C. A. Gaskin. Oxford World's Classics. Oxford: Oxford University Press.

Hollande, François. 2012a. "Entretien Du Président de La République Avec Le Site d'information 'Slate.fr.'"

———. 2012b. "Déplacement Aux États-Unis d'Amérique: Conférence de Presse Du Président de La République."

———. 2013a. "Communiqué de Presse: Vœux Du Président de La République Au Corps Diplomatique."

———. 2013b. "Déclaration Du Président de La République Sur La Situation Au Mali."

———. 2013c. "Assemblée Générale Des Nations Unies: Conférence de Presse Du Président de La République, M. François Hollande."

Interview. 2013. Interview with Personal Advisor to the Minister of Defence, September 16.

———. 2014a. Interview with Civil Servant at the Foreign Ministry, 5 February.

———. 2014b. Interview with Personal Advisor to the President, March 16.

James, Alan. 1989. "The Realism of Realism: The State in the Study of International Relations." *Review of International Studies* 15 (3): 215–229.

Kagan, Robert. 2002. "Power and Weakness." *Policy Review*, June/July.

Lebow, Richard Ned. 2008. *A Cultural Theory of International Relations.* Leiden: Cambridge University Press.

Lindemann, Thomas. 2013. The Case for an Empirical and Social Psychological Study of Recognition in International Relations. *International Theory* 5 (1): 150–155.

Marchal, Roland. 2013. "Briefing: Military (Mis)Adventures in Mali." *African Affairs* 112 (448): 486–497.

Mearsheimer, John J. 2001. *The Tragedy of Great Power Politics.* New York: Norton.

———. 2011. *Why Leaders Lie: The Truth About Lying in International Politics.* New York: Oxford University Press.

Ministère des Affaires Étrangères. 2012. "Point de Presse."

Morgenthau, Hans J. 1947. *Scientific Man vs. Power Politics.* London: Latimer House Limited.

———. 2006. *Politics Among Nations: The Struggle for Power and Peace*, 7th ed. Boston: McGraw-Hill Higher Education.

Nadal, Romain. 2013. Interview with the Former Spokesperson of François Hollande, October 7. Interview by Author.

Notin, Jean-Christophe. 2014. *La Guerre de La France Au Mali.* Paris: Tallandier.

Price, Russell. 1977. "The Theme of Gloria in Machiavelli." *Renaissance Quarterly* 30 (4): 588–631.

Risse, Thomas, Daniela Engelmann-Martin, Hans-Joachim Knope, and Klaus Roscher. 1999. To Euro or Not to Euro? The EMU and Identity Politics in the European Union. *European Journal of International Relations* 5 (2): 147–187.

Rose, Gideon. 1998. "Neoclassical Realism and Theories of Foreign Policy." *World Politics* 51 (1): 144–177.

Sénat. 2013. "L'Afrique Notre Avenir. Rapport D'information N 104 Au Nom de La Commission Des Affaires Étrangères, de La Défense et Des Forces Armées Par Le Groupe de Travail Sur La Présence de La France Dans Une Afrique Convoitée: Fait Par Jeanny Lorgeoux et Jean-Marie Bockel."

Snyder, Richard, H. W. Bruck, and Burton Sapin. 1962. *Foreign Policy Decision-Making: An Approach to the Study of International Politics*. New York: The Free Press of Glencoe.

Sperling, James. 2010. "National Security Cultures, Technologies of Public Goods Supply and Security Governance." In *National Security Cultures: Patterns of Global Governance*, edited by Emil Kirchner and James Sperling, 1–18. London: Routledge.

Sprout, Harold, and Margaret Sprout. 1965. *The Ecological Perspective on Human Affairs: With Special Reference to International Politics*. New Jersey: Princetion University Press.

Sterling-Folker, Jennifer. 1997. "Realist Environment, Liberal Process, and Domestic-Level Variables." *International Studies Quarterly* 41 (1): 1–25.

Thompson, Kenneth. 1985. *Moralism and Morality in Politics and Diplomacy*. Lanham: University Press of America.

United Nations. 2014. "The Security Council." http://www.un.org/en/sc/.

Walt, Stephen M. 2006. *Taming American Power: The Global Response to US Primacy*. New York, NY: W.W. Norton & Company.

Waltz, Kenneth N. 1979. *Theory of International Politics*. Reading, MA: Addison-Wesley Publishing Company.

———. 1986. "Reflections on Theory of International Politics: A Response to My Critics." In *Neorealism and Its Critics*, edited by Robert Keohane, 322–345. New York: Columbia University Press.

———. 2001. *Man, the State and War: A Theoretical Analysis*. New York, NY: Columbia University Press.

CHAPTER 7

Unheard Voices: International Relations Theory and Italian Defence Policy

Fabrizio Coticchia

INTRODUCTION

The evolution of Italian defence policy in the post-Cold War era has received scant attention in the literature. Accordingly, the debate about how International Relations (IR) theories explain (or interpret) the transformation of Italian defence has been extremely limited. The reasons for academic—and even public—disinterest are twofold. First, Italy delegated its external security to NATO and allies in the bipolar context. Military dynamism was mostly absent and, consequently, the level of attention towards defence was minimal (Ignazi et al. 2012). Second, Italian political culture (which developed in the shadow of the main political parties, the Christian Democrats and the Communists) was embedded in internationalism and pacifism, and thus tended to avoid the military dimension in the foreign policy debate (Panebianco 1997). In sum, domestic and global bipolar constraints limited attention towards questions about Italian defence.

F. Coticchia (✉)
University of Genoa, Genoa, Italy
e-mail: fabrizio.coticchia@unige.it

© The Author(s) 2019
R. Belloni et al. (eds.), *Fear and Uncertainty in Europe*, Global Issues,
https://doi.org/10.1007/978-3-319-91965-2_7

Despite a significant transformation of Italian defence in the post-Cold War era, defence issues are still marginal to the current debate. Participation in missions abroad represents the most considerable break with practice during the bipolar period. Indeed, since the end of the Cold War, Italian armed forces have been engaged continuously in military operations abroad: since 1989, Italy has participated in more missions than in the previous 40 years combined (Coticchia 2014). Italian troops have been deployed almost everywhere, from Africa to the Balkans, from the Middle East to Afghanistan. In the words of the former President of the Republic Giorgio Napolitano: "the armed forces are today the main instrument of Italian foreign policy" (in Coticchia and Moro 2015: 5). Through its military operations, Italy has enhanced its power projection capabilities. Several crucial reforms of the Italian defence sector have been approved, while public opinion modified the approach towards the armed forces, now considered one of the most appreciated institutions in the country (Battistelli et al. 2012). Yet, despite the significant transformation of post-Cold War Italian defence policy and the considerable military contribution provided by Italian armed forces in multinational operations, the scholarly debate remains limited.

Recent studies have focused on military transformation (Coticchia and Moro 2015, 2016), others have dealt with the interaction among strategic culture, narratives, and missions abroad (Ignazi et al. 2012; Rosa 2014) or with the parties' role in defence policy. However, IR theories have been seldom used to understand or explain Italian defence. While few analyses (Carati and Locatelli 2017) have tested concurrent hypotheses derived from IR paradigms on specific security events, a detailed theoretical and empirical inquiry on Italian defence is still lacking. As stressed by Isernia and Longo (2017), there is still a surprisingly lack of cumulative analyses in theoretical research related to Italian foreign and defence policy. Thus, a comprehensive assessment of the existing debate on IR theories and Italian defence, including both its pitfalls and most promising aspects, is needed.

This chapter aims to fill this gap by providing an exhaustive review—and assessment—of the existing approaches emerged in the literature on Italian defence, relating them to the main IR theories. It is structured as follows. After a discussion of the debate on the drivers of post-Cold War Italian military activism, the paper explores three different theoretical problems of the scholarly discussion—namely, the premature burial of realism, the underestimated role of Foreign Policy Analysis, and the limited interest devoted to domestic institutions—highlighting specific elements that deserve further attention. Then, through official documents, interviews and secondary sources, it examines the most recent Italian military operation (the "Prima Parthica" mission in Iraq against the Islamic State of Iraq and the Levant—ISIL) mainly through the lens of Neoclassical Realism. This analytical framework, which focuses on concepts like alliance values, threats, electoral politics, and prestige, has heuristic value for understanding Italian defence after the end of the Cold War. Finally, the conclusion paves the way for further research on IR theories and Italian defence policy.

The Debate on the Evolution of Italian Defence

A widespread consensus has emerged in the existing literature on the view that there has been a significant transformation of post-Cold War Italian defence policy, focusing on the important role played by international military missions (Croci 2005; Ignazi et al. 2012). This perspective is confirmed both by the new military dynamism and by examining the evolution of the national strategic doctrine. Overall, the participation in military missions abroad represents a strong element of continuity in the Italian post-bipolar defence policy. But why did Italy employ its troops so frequently after the Cold War? Why did it modify its general defence approach, adopting a dynamic attitude towards security issues?

The scholarly debate is still divided over the answers. In fact, several alternative explanations have emerged regarding the driving factors that pushed Italy to employ its forces abroad. International relations paradigms provide the "traditions of thought" (see Donnelly in this volume) for each perspective. On the whole, we can highlight the following (interrelated and not necessarily exclusive) hypotheses regarding the national military dynamism in the post-bipolar era.

First, the post-Cold War strategic adjustment has fostered the new Italian military activism, which aims at confronting growing transnational threats to national security (Coralluzzo 2012). Such interpretations, in line with a realist view of international relations conceived as politics of power and security, are centred on the constraining effects of the international structure on Italian behaviour. Several authors, especially at the beginning of the 1990s (Santoro 1991), shared a realist perspective to explain Italian defence, focusing on "fear and uncertainty" and illustrating how material power represented the crucial means to guarantee survival in the unstable post-Cold War world. Others, drawing from structural realism (Waltz 1979), believe that systematic pressures and the transformation of the global scenario explain the significant evolution of the post-bipolar Italian defence (Coralluzzo 2012).

Second, and partially related with the above-mentioned view, some authors focus on the growing need to protect vital economic interests, such as commercial routes or gas and oil supply, guaranteeing the stability of crucial regions. This viewpoint considers commercial and economic interests as the main reasons behind the post-bipolar Italian military dynamism overseas (Paolicelli and Vignarca 2009). The presence of troops can foster economic ties between the country hosting Italian forces and Rome, advancing the interests of national companies. Accordingly, post-bipolar Italy has "used" the military instrument because decision makers have been pushed by specific domestic interests promoted by relevant national economic and social actors.

Third, another set of scholars also focuses on the domestic political scenario, but they do not interpret domestic factors as something connected to the national interest. Rather, attention is specifically devoted to the influence exerted by the domestic scenario towards Italian international policy. Accordingly, foreign and defence policy issues are closely related to the contingencies of domestic political debate (Carbone 2007). In line with this perspective, the support of the opposition parties to a specific military operation depends more on parliamentary dynamics than on the nature or the aims of the intervention. For instance, Panebianco (1997) illustrated how Italy's socio-political features led to a low-profile foreign policy during the Cold War, aimed at preventing additional divisions in domestic politics. The same occurred also after the collapse of the Berlin Wall when centre-left and centre-right parties maintained a low profile approach on defense issues, avoiding to openly debate military missions in the parliament. Following in the liberal tradition, the types of national institutions, as well as the whole domestic social and political features, are here viewed as the vital factors that explain the evolution of Italian defence policy.

A fourth viewpoint focuses on "prestige", highlighting the national desire to gain international recognition and achieve a positive image to maintain a specific status (Santoro 1991). Italy deploys troops abroad to acquire prestige in terms of social acknowledgment, increasing its relative power (Davidson 2011). By addressing security challenges and contributing to the country's standing in the global system, Italy has enhanced its international reliability. Alliance dependence and alliance value are crucial factors to understand why a country like Italy decides to intervene militarily. This neoclassical realist view (Rose 1998; Taliaferro et al. 2009) develops key foreign policy concepts, such as "rank", "role" and "status for middle powers" (Valigi 2017).

Fifth, from an organizational standpoint, the Italian military option is adopted by decision-makers at the international level because of the particular nature of Italian armed forces that make them a national asset (e.g., police-military forces such as the *Carabinieri*), exportable in multinational interventions. In addition, the operations are crucial "events of learning and adaptation" for the whole Italian military organization, testing interoperability amongst allies and innovations in weapons, tactics and doctrines (Coticchia and Moro 2016: 124). The structure of the Italian forces, as well as their experience, has been portrayed (also in national strategic documents) as perfectly suited to deal with current "complex emergencies". For instance, the skills gained in domestic operations (such as those against organized crime and terrorism) provides troops with adequate training to operate in an urban context typical of contemporary crises characterized by non-military threats.

Sixth, we can highlight a cultural interpretation of the Italian post-Cold War defence policy. Several scholars consider strategic culture essential to understand the evolution of the Italian defence. For instance, Rosa found a "remarkable consistency between the strategic culture and international behaviour of Italy" (2014: 109). The behaviour of foreign policy actors is here viewed as the consequence of the cultural constraints imposed by the given national identity of a country. According to the constructivist approach, norms, ideas and expectations affect the way through which the state pursues the aims of its foreign policy, while the importance of shared norms of appropriateness at the systemic level has been underscored. National culture and national identity shape what are perceived to be the interests of the state (Houghton 2007). Italian foreign and defence policy after the end of the Cold War testifies precisely to the evolution of the national self-perception. The growing involvement in military operations has affirmed the image of Italy as an international peacekeeper, which is fully shared by political and military actors (Ignazi et al. 2012). The lens through which these actors interpret the current security environment are strongly influenced by both shared conceptual frameworks involved in "the peace and humanitarian missions" or "*i soldati di pace*" (soldiers of peace) (Coticchia 2014). Italy considers itself as a security provider, with national defence not limited to the protection of frontiers but aiming to guarantee a border area of stability through deployable armed forces. Strategic culture appears as decisive to understand not only the Italian post-Cold War military activism but also to investigate the nature of this dynamism. Indeed, notwithstanding changes in the international and domestic political system in the early 1990s, an "accommodationist foreign policy" has endured (Rosa 2014: 90). A low profile in military operations, lack of political debate over defence and security issues, and a cautious attitude towards combat missions remain features that define Italian strategic culture (Ignazi et al. 2012). In other words, the persistence of such risk-averse patterns of behaviour over the Cold War and post-Cold War periods suggests that the *way* in which Italy faces its external problems remains stable over time.

Seven, while emphasizing the relevant role of culture, several scholars have focused more on the specific function of norms for better understanding the evolution of Italian defence. In line with the post-Cold War attention in IR to the spread of international norms, other authors emphasize how the sharing of a "responsibility to intervene" attitude to assure peace, human rights and international security has acquired a significant weight for Italy in the post-bipolar era (Pirani 2010). Lombardi (2011) and Miranda (2011) assess the role played by normative considerations and material factors such as trade relations to offer an explanation of the Italian military intervention in Libya. They argue that the employment of the military option to contrast new challenges is strictly linked to the diffusion of global norms, such as the Responsibility to Protect (R2P), that have occasionally led to operations by the international community to protect human rights. As advanced by constructivists (Finnemore and Sikkink 1998), the ways in which the cultural lens interprets global norms is extremely relevant in shaping foreign and defence policy decisions. Global values such as R2P have been adopted by Italian decision-makers to justify the deployment of troops for the protection of the civilian population: from natural disasters to humanitarian assistance in so-called fragile-states. Protecting unarmed populations is a duty of the international community to which Italy is contributing. According to this view, values developed at the global level have been shared and integrated nationally, thus shaping strategic preferences.

Eight, the last perspective on Italian defence relates to the crucial role of multilateral institutions. The commitment to international missions is here interpreted as a direct consequence of participation in multilateral institutions (EU, NATO and UN), whose constraints represent the explaining variables for intervention (Ratti 2011). Looking at defence policy, "NATO's missions have affected the transformation of Italian forces more than any other multilateral framework" (Coticchia and Moro 2015: 72). Thus, multilateralism has been interpreted not only as a guideline for Italian defence and foreign policy but also as a doctrinal, tactical and strategic framework within which Italian forces have been deeply transformed. Some authors (Carati and Locatelli 2017) have more recently developed the concept of "followership" to explain Italian military engagement abroad. "Italy tends to take part to multilateral missions to follow its allies and partners. In this sense, followership is more than just a quest for status. 'Following' the allies can be a strategy to preserve or improve the Italian international status but it is also a deliberate policy that finds its ultimate goal in 'being part' of the international community" (2017: 10).

These eight (not mutually exclusive) interpretations of the supposed key-drivers of Italian military dynamism illustrate the national debate over the most relevant aspects of the post-bipolar national defence policy. The main IR paradigms stand behind some of these hypotheses. As already shown, the "conceptual borders" among those interpretations are extremely thin and flexible. Above all, the lack of a comprehensive analysis of Italian defence and IR theories, as well as the absence of cumulative research, has hindered the proper development of a dialogue among alternatives explanations, hampering the development of possible integrating analyses. The next section highlights both the main elements that have been neglected and the most challenging and promising dimensions in the above-mentioned hypotheses. Then, the paper empirically examines the interpretations provided by the "realist schools" (Donnelly 2000), as well as by the alternative perspectives on the most recent Italian military operation abroad.

PITFALLS, PROMISING ELEMENTS AND UNHEARD VOICES

In light of the scholarly debate reviewed above, this section emphasizes selected factors that deserve further attention because of their problematic methodological and ontological nature or due to the marginal attention they have received thus far.

Marginal Foreign Policy Analysis (FPA)

According to Kaarbo, many IR theories still ignore "decades of research in foreign policy analysis on how domestic political and decision-making factors affect actors' choices and policies" (2015: 189). Also for this reason, Kaarbo and Cantir (2012) focus on integrating Foreign Policy Analysis (FPA) and Role Theory and National Role Conceptions (NRC), stressing how FPA can provide insights into the mass—elite nexus and intra-elite conflicts, while the NRC literature could incorporate the use of ideas and identity in foreign policy-making. Despite significant attention towards the role of Italian national identity and its defence policy, such attempts have been seldom addressed. On the contrary, FPA is still marginal within the theoretical debate, while the few analyses on Italian political actors, parties and security issues (Coticchia and De Simone 2016) have rarely developed theoretical approaches explicitly related to FPA. Recently, Brighi (2013) provided a comprehensive analysis of Italian foreign policy, stressing the role of ideas and discourse in the interplay between "actors" and "strategically selective contexts". Other authors have focused on the role concept that Italy developed in the first years after its reunification (Ignazi et al. 2012), emphasizing its inconsistency and the perverse dynamic between internal weakness and international recognition: to compensate for a weak domestic structure (in terms of economic might, cultural and technical innovative values, etc.) a greater, heavier global role for Italy was required. But this "schizophrenia" of self-image and foreign policy has been rarely analysed with respect to security and defence issues. For instance, very little attention has been devoted to the relationship between political parties, coalitions, foreign and defence policy. Therefore, a greater emphasis on decision makers, which is frequently conceived as the fundamental contribution of FPA to IR, could be extremely relevant for the development of the debate on Italian defence.

The "End of Realism"?

According to Lucarelli and Menotti (2002), Italy has remained for years a "no-constructivist land", where Italian political scientists have tended to adopt an "excessively positivistic" approach to IR. Structural realism has represented for decades the mainstream view of international politics in Italy. As mentioned above, this perspective interpreted the fall of the Berlin Wall as the main cause that altered Italy's reluctance to deploy troops abroad. However, this dominant position has been eroded in the post-Cold War era. The emergence of non-military menaces and the growing threat posed by non-state actors increased the difficulties for structural realism to provide convincing explanations regarding the new Italian defence and foreign policy in the transformed regional and global context. Cultural interpretations, which even recognize the influence of structural factors (such as the end of the bipolar era), gradually emerged within the IR debate in Italy as the main alternative to realism. According to Rosa (2014), several neorealist expectations (i.e., an increase in defence spending, greater assertiveness, a weakening of support for multilateral organisations, unilateral actions, etc. ...) were not confirmed by post-Cold War developments. For Cladi and Webber (2011: 206), realism "seems at first sight ill-suited to address domestic influence".

However, while realism in Italy has been in retreat, the cultural interpretation of the post-Cold War strategic adjustment only partially explained the role of external constraints and their influence over Italian defence.

First, as illustrated by Donnelly in Chapter 2, structural realism is *one* of the realist schools (or approaches), while in the Italian debate it has been usually considered as a synonym for the entire realist tradition. Indeed, the Waltzian structure is quite different from what Donnelly calls "the permissive cause' of a weak and thin institutional-normative structure". Anarchy and the distribution of material capabilities are "universal features of international relations" while their realist effects arise from "a particular institutional-normative structure" that induce fear and uncertainty (see Donnelly in this volume). From this perspective, it is crucial to understand *how* self-interested states face the problems posed by a weak normative-institutional structure, which is different from a conception of anarchy conceived simply as the absence of government.

Second, Waltz (1979) also sees "systematic pressure" a permissive cause rather than a driver of national foreign policy. Italian foreign policy in the bipolar international system was defined by the rivalry between the United States and the Soviet bloc and adapted quickly to it, while the end of the bipolar system allowed states more space to manoeuvre. In this new context, alliances are less rigid and more open to disagreements and more independent foreign policies can be pursued. This does not mean that systemic constraints are absent; it only means that they are weaker and looser, but they are still there.

In addition, despite the growing role played by ideational or cultural interpretations of post-Cold War Italian defence and foreign policy, the national IR debate left little room to types of realism other than the structural one. The supposed explanatory difficulties of structural realism did not lead to the emergence in Italy of other "realist schools" (Donnelly 2000) that focused on the ways through which domestic actors understand and manage fear and uncertainty in the current institutional-normative structure (Taliaferro et al. 2009). The scant attention to neoclassical realism, as well as the limited attempt to examine the complex relations between domestic and international factors, represent the main pitfalls of the current debate. The next paragraph focuses specifically on these shortcomings.

A (Two Level) Game Nobody Plays: Domestic Factors and Neoclassical Realism

As mentioned, "in reaction to the analytical limitations of Waltzian neo-realism" (Cladi and Webber 2011: 207), other scholars have sought to address the importance of domestic variables in order to explain processes of foreign policy adaptation to systemic pressures. Neoclassical realists consider domestic factors the "intervening variable" (Rose 1998) or the "transmission belt" (Taliaferro et al. 2009) between systemic pressures and national constraints, while systemic factors represent the permissive environment for foreign policy. Neoclassical realism treats anarchy and external material power as background conditions that, as it were, set parameters within which decision-makers operate (see Donnelly in this volume). However, neoclassical realism, which confirms the primacy of the variables located at the international level of analysis, aims to explain national diversity vis-à-vis similar structural conditions (Isernia and Longo 2017). As Donnelly suggests in Chapter 2, what makes "neoclassical realist explanations *realist* is the special emphasis placed on external material power as a constraint and a source of fear and uncertainty". The domestic level helps to highlight the different answers provided by single states. This analytical framework seems particularly promising in the case of Italian defence: after the alteration of the structural conditions with the end of the Cold War, Italian domestics actors have played a crucial role in affecting political attitudes, decisions and approaches (Cladi and Webber 2011; Davidson 2011).

Three main aspects should be pointed out concerning neoclassical realism and Italian defence. First, this approach is still marginal within Italian academic debates and an assessment of its explanatory value in the Italian case is mostly lacking. As highlighted above, only the concept of "prestige" has been frequently embraced by analyses of Italian defence and especially its military dynamism (Davidson 2008, 2011). Despite domestic political and financial never-ending crises, Italy has acquired "prestige abroad" thanks to its military post-bipolar contribution to international security.

Second, the "two-level game" approach has been rarely examined from a neoclassical realist perspective in the national debate. However, it could provide significant insights regarding the complex interaction between the two levels in the case of Italy, advancing integrative approaches through the combination of different variables. A deeper investigation of the interaction between the two levels could better explain the transformation of Italy from consumer of security to producer, combining external pressures and domestic reforms to explain the "dual crisis" (i.e. the end of the Cold War and the end of the so-called "First Republic"[1]).

Third, neoclassical realist approaches have rarely taken into account the crucial role played by Parliament in the development of Italian post-Cold War defence policy. Rather, the specific role of parliamentary procedures in the decision to send troops abroad deserves examination. For instance, German decision-making is severely constrained by the need to involve the Parliament (*Bundestag*) in all key decisions relative to interventions, with procedural elements that enhance the prudence of already reluctant decision-makers to start discussions and debates related to military operations abroad (Dyson 2008). On the contrary, in Italy discussions and debates seldom occur in Parliament (Di Camillo and Tessari 2013). Thus, with limited parliamentary oversight the Italian executive is relatively autonomous, reducing audience costs and political accountability. As reported by Biehel et al. (2013: 389): "the issue

---

[1]According to a widespread literature, the transformation of the Italian party system occurred at the beginning of the 1990s caused the birth of a "Second Republic".

of political control of armed forces is often neglected in works on strategic culture", an observation holding true in the case of Italy. In line with a neo-classical realist explanation (Dyson 2008), domestic material power relations are fundamental in explaining divergence between Italy and Germany: more constraints on the executive's power to act in the defence domain in the latter prevented the flexibility that characterized the former. However, the literature has so far ignored this dimension to explain or interpret the evolution of Italian defence.

In sum, neoclassical realism may provide a useful map to understand the evolution of Italian defence policy in the post-Cold War era. For instance, the approach adopted by Davidson (2011) represents one of the few original, theoretically and empirically grounded attempts to explain Italian defence through a neoclassical realist perspective, focusing on concepts like alliance values, threats, prestige and domestic factors. According to this view, the Italian decision to send troops abroad depends on the value attributed to the main ally (traditionally the US), the threat posed to national interest, the maximization of social recognition of the state's relative power (i.e., prestige), and electoral politics (e.g., public opinion is crucial when its support is vital for the government's survival).

The next section will assess the neoclassical perspective, especially Davidson's approach, in the case of the decision to undertake the Prima Parthica mission in Iraq against ISIL. The case has been selected for three reasons. First, this operation represents the most relevant military intervention (in terms of tasks, risks, troops employed, etc.) undertaken by Italian troops in recent years (at least since the end of the ISAF intervention in Afghanistan). Second, Prima Parthica has rarely been examined by the literature on Italian defence and foreign policy. Third, the operation involves both the fight against terrorism and humanitarian issues and it engages allies and (even if indirectly) international organizations. Far from pretending to generalize the finding from a single case, the empirical analysis focused on the decision-making process behind the political decision to send troops in Iraq (August–September 2014), allowing us to compare and confront different approaches and illustrate the relevance of neoclassical realism. The empirical analysis is based on parliamentary debates, official documents, interviews with political leaders (e.g., at the undersecretary level and with members of the Chamber of Deputies) and secondary sources (mainly newspaper articles collected through *Lexis-Nexis*).

A Case Study: Operation Prima Parthica

The military operations abroad represent the most important example of the post-bipolar transformation of Italian defence. Despite significant problems, failures, financial constraints, and casualties related to the Italian involvement in recent missions (from Iraq to Afghanistan and Libya), public support for national military activism has not diminished. This includes the current Italian intervention against ISIL, which is viewed positively by public opinion (IAI-LAPS 2017).

Italy's contribution to the international coalition against ISIL began in late August 2014, sending weapons to the Iraqi and Kurdish forces, while guaranteeing humanitarian assistance. After some weeks, Italy deployed personnel to the Combined Joint Task for training of national and Kurdish troops, creating also a Task Force Air, with drones and warplanes for reconnaissance and surveillance.

Why did Italy provide its military contribution to the multinational efforts to defeat ISIL in Iraq? In line with the neo-classical realist interpretation, we would expect that Italy aimed at emphasizing alliance value, eliminating a perceived vital threat to national interest, and maximizing prestige in a domestic context characterized by the electoral insignificance of (possible) public opposition. The analysis of the decision-making process during August–September 2014 confirms the explanatory value of neoclassical realism.

First, despite the geographical distance from Iraq, Italian leaders considered the threat posed by ISIL as vital for national interests. Thus "fear and uncertainty" have been clearly induced from the expansion of ISIL. Speaking before the UN General Assembly, Prime Minster Renzi affirmed that ISIL was "not solely a terrorist threat in a specific region, but a risk for the entire [international] community."[2] Thus, the fight against Daesh represented "a battle in the heart of Europe rather than in its periphery" (Il Corriere della Sera 2014a). Although the government advocated a long-term strategy against ISIL, involving European society and the Muslim community and combining culture and security, Renzi's cabinet clearly emphasized the national contribution "against terrorism"[3]

---

[2] Renzi, General Debate at the 69th Session of the General Assembly of the United Nations, September 2014.

[3] Author's interview, Undersecretary of the Italian government, Rome, July 17, 2017.

and its radical challenge to the Western world. Within such a battle the need to avoid the risk of Iraq's complete collapse was considered fundamental.[4] Moreover, the Italian ministers highlighted how Italy was a strategic objective of the jihadist terrorists. According to the then Minister of Interior, Angelino Alfano, Italy was "not a secondary target for ISIS" (Il Corriere della Sera 2014b) and, in the words of the former Minister of Foreign Affairs, Federica Mogherini, "the terrorist menace threatens Europe but also Italy" (Trocino 2014).

Second, in terms of the search for alliance value and prestige, which facilitates the achievement of national goals (Davidson 2011: 17), it is worth noticing how Rome visibly linked the Italian military contribution in Iraq to its main strategic priority in foreign and security affairs: an enhanced national role in the Mediterranean. The crisis in the near Middle East represented a risk for Italy but also "an opportunity to put the Mediterranean again at the centre" of its foreign policy.[5] Successive Italian governments worked hard in post-Russian invasion of Crimea to maintain NATO's focus also on the so-called Southern Front. In a sense, the threat posed by ISIL reinforced the Italian aim to strategically "shape the agenda" at EU and NATO levels.[6] Indeed, also thanks to the Italian military contribution in the Middle East, the United States supported a leading role for Italy in the Mediterranean (Mastrolilli 2014). Italy offered its help in Iraq (according to Renzi: "President Obama and the international coalition can count on the support of Italy to eliminate the threat of ISIS"[7]) and Washington from the very beginning appreciated the Italian military engagement. Such "gratefulness towards the Italian availability to fight against Daesh"[8] represented a very relevant issue for the Italian government, which aimed at consolidating its "close relationship with the Obama administration."[9] On the whole, the crisis in Iraq was perceived as the opportunity to "return to play a role in

---

[4] Matteo Renzi, Chamber of Deputies, September 16, 2014.

[5] Matteo Renzi, Chamber of Deputies, September 16, 2014.

[6] Author's interview, Undersecretary of the Italian government, Rome, January 29, 2016.

[7] Renzi, General Debate at the 69th Session of the General Assembly.

[8] Author's interview, MP Democratic Party, Commission Foreign Affairs, Florence, February 15, 2016.

[9] Author's interview, MP Democratic Party, Commission of Foreign Affairs, Rome, January 28, 2016.

international politics."[10] As stated by Renzi: "Our national interest is that of recovering our role in Europe and in the world."[11] The symbolic dimension was crucial to reach this objective. The "Italian political and diplomatic dynamism in European governments' eyes" was remarked by pundits (Rusconi 2014) and was also highlighted by government officials.[12] For instance, Renzi was the first international leader to visit Iraq in August 2014, at the time when Italy also held the presidency of the EU semester.

In sum, Italian leaders emphasized the threat posed by ISIL to national security, linking its military contribution in Iraq to an enhanced strategic role in the Mediterranean, also thanks to crucial US support. Thus, neoclassical realist logic (prestige, threats and alliance value) fits well to explain Italian behaviour in summer 2014. In addition, the particular domestic scenario should be taken into account. Although public opinion at the very beginning of the operation did not support a military engagement in Iraq,[13] the opposition centre-right parties backed the mission. At the same time, Renzi's government had just obtained (spring 2014) a stunning victory at the elections for the EU Parliament, making the risk of suffering electoral consequences of the public disagreement almost irrelevant.

In addition to the variables identified by Davidson, two domestic factors deserve further attention. First, parliamentary oversight was limited. For the then Minister of Foreign Affairs, parliamentary authorization for the military operation in Iraq was not considered "indispensable" (La Stampa 2014) since the decision to send troops had already been approved and Italian troops were expected to provide training to local forces and air-to-air refuelling activities. The opposition defined as "incredible" the decision to adopt these resolutions "without a proper debate in the Parliament."[14] Therefore, the limited parliamentary control of military operations confirms Italian executive autonomy in defence policy. Second, even if not relevant in electoral terms in summer

[10] Matteo Renzi, Chamber of Deputies, September 16, 2014.

[11] Ibid.

[12] Author's interview, Undersecretary of the Italian government, Rome, July 17, 2017.

[13] The 74% of the sample was against the decision to send arms in Iraq, see Ixè poll, August 25, 2014.

[14] A SEL (*Sinistra, Ecologia, Libertà*), MP quoted in Trocino (2014).

2014, the public disagreement, as well the opposition of the Five Star Movement on the national military commitment in Iraq, contributes to explain *how* Italy designed the operation (i.e., excluding air strikes, focusing on culture as an answer to terrorism, etc.) rather than just explaining the decision to provide (or not) a military contribution.

While the neoclassical realist approach is useful to illustrate Italian defence policy towards the Iraqi crisis in 2014, we should still assess if other interpretations ensure the same explanatory capabilities. "Strategic adjustment" does not seem useful to explain such a specific foreign policy outcomes, because the timing of the transformation of international system is not connected with the Italian decision to send troops in Iraq, which occurred just after the evolution of the domestic Iraqi security context. Also in this case, "systemic pressure" cannot be considered a driver of national foreign policy (but at least a permissive cause). Moreover, international institutions play a limited role, because a multinational (rather than multilateral) framework featured the military operation. The economic interests of domestic groups (e.g., the Italian company involved in the reconstruction of the Mosul Dam) seem to be relevant, even if limited, but they could not be easily identified in summer 2014 because they clearly emerged only years later, when the operation evolved on the ground.

By contrast, humanitarianism seems to play an important role. Renzi emphasized that genocide occurred in Mosul in summer 2014, symbolically linking that city with the Srebrenica events in the Balkans two decades earlier. The parliamentary debates in August and September are full of references to humanitarian norms, to the protection of the local population and to the need to win a "battle of civilisation."[15] Also the type of intervention planned in the first week framed humanitarian support as the key-task of the contingent. As confirmed by interviewees, it is worth noticing the constant attempt by political leaders to connect values such as "solidarity and humanitarianism, in line with Catholic values",[16] to the national interest (e.g., defending Italy from terrorism).

In sum, the humanitarian explanation deserves attention and while this view is not mutually exclusive with the neoclassical realist approach,

---

[15] Renzi, General Debate at the 69th Session of the General Assembly.

[16] Author's interview, Undersecretary of the Italian government, telephone interview, June 26, 2017.

few attempts have been made in the literature to combine them in a more comprehensive way, also because "norms compliance" is often considered as the main alternative to "material interests". However, as stated by Gegout in her chapter, realists, even if they consider politics are not merely a "function of ethics", recognize the relevance of ethical norms and the "possibility of leaders having humanitarian motives when agreeing to intervene in a conflict" (see Gegout in this volume).

CONCLUSIONS

Paraphrasing Santoro (1991), defence policy is a "mysterious field of research". The Italian case is particularly puzzling. How did a "middle power such as Italy, with its highly fragmented domestic state structure and different perceptions among decision-makers, manage to pursue an active and distinctive foreign policy in the post-cold war period"? (Cladi and Webber 2011: 217). This chapter has illustrated the different explanations provided by the literature to answer this question, highlighting both the main pitfalls and the unheard voices in the current debate. Specific attention has been devoted to the still limited scholarly focus on the marginal role played by FPA in the current debate, as well as to the scarce interests towards the complex interactions between domestic and international factors. Moreover, the chapter highlights how the post-bipolar "cultural criticism" towards mainstream realism in Italy has often considered structural realism as the unique school of the paradigm. Therefore, neoclassical realist explanations of the post-Cold War Italian foreign and defense policy have been underrated. But the neoclassical realist perspective seems particularly promising in explaining the evolution of Italian defense after 1989, especially by focusing on concepts like alliance values, threats, prestige and domestic factors. Thus, the chapter assessed a neoclassical realist explanation through the case study of the Italian military mission in Iraq (2014). The empirical analysis of the decision-making process occurring during August–September 2014 has confirmed the neo-classical realist expectations: Italy aimed at emphasizing alliance value, contrasting a perceived vital threat to the national interest, and maximizing prestige in a domestic scenario featured by the electoral insignificance of public opposition. It was worth noticing that, while alternative explanations seem not useful in the case of the operation Prima Parthica, humanitarianism played a relevant role.

Further studies may assess different approaches by comparing additional military operations or confronting Italy with other middle powers. Moreover, they could investigate a possible middle ground between FPA and neoclassical realism. Finally, as empirically emerged by the case study, scholars should better scrutinise what Miranda (2011) calls the "striking balance" between ideas and interest, "unpacking" these concepts to carefully evaluate their role.

REFERENCES

Battistelli, Fabrizio, Maria Grazia Galantino, Livia Fay Lucianetti, and Lorenzo Striuli. 2012. *Opinioni sulla Guerra. L'Opinione Pubblica Italiana e Internazionale di Fronte all'Uso della Forza*. Milano: Franco Angeli.

Biehl, Heiko, Bastian Giegerich, and Alexandra Jonas. 2013. *Strategic Cultures in Europe: Security and Defence Policies Across the Continent*. Potsdam: Springer.

Brighi, Elisabetta. 2013. *Foreign Policy, Domestic Politics and International Relations*. New York: Routledge.

Carati, Andrea, and Andrea Locatelli. 2017. "Cui Prodest? Italy's Questionable Involvement in Multilateral Military Operations Amid Ethical Concerns and National Interest." *International Peacekeeping* 24 (1): 86–107.

Carbone, Maurizio. 2007. "The Domestic Foundations of Italy's Foreign and Development Policy." *West European Politics* 30 (4): 903–923.

Cladi Lorenzo, and Mark Webber. 2011. "Italian Foreign Policy in the Post-Cold War Period: A Neoclassical Realist Approach." *European Security* 20 (2): 205–219.

Coralluzzo, Valter. 2012. "Le missioni italiane all'estero, problemi e prospettive, in L'Italia fra nuove politiche di difesa e impegni internazionali," *ISPI Sudies*. Available at http://www.ispionline.it/it/documents/ISPI%20StudiesItalia. htm.

Coticchia, Fabrizio. 2014. *La guerra che non c'era. Opinione pubblica e interventi militari italiani dall'Afghanistan alla Libia*. Milano: UBE Egea.

Coticchia, Fabrizio, and Carolina De Simone. 2016. "The War that Wasn't There: Framing Italy's 'Peace Mission' in Afghanistan." *Foreign Policy Analysis* 12: 24–46.

Coticchia, Fabrizio, and Francesco N. Moro. 2015. *Adapt, Improvise, Overcome? The Transformation of Italian Armed Forces in Comparative Perspective*. London: Ashgate/Routledge.

———. 2016. "Learning from Others? Emulation and Transformation in the Italian Armed Forces Since 2001." *Armed Forces & Society* 42 (4): 696–718.

Croci, Osvaldo. 2005. "Much Ado About Little: The Foreign Policy of the Second Berlusconi Government." *Modern Italy* 10 (1): 59–74.

Davidson, Jason W. 2008. "In and Out of Iraq. A Vote-Seeking Explanation of Berlusconi's Iraq policy." *Modern Italy* 13 (1): 37–50.

———. 2011. *America's Allies and War. Kosovo, Afghanistan, and Iraq.* Houndmills: Palgrave.

Di Camillo, Federica, and Paola Tessari. 2013. "Italian Missions Abroad: National Interests and Procedural Practice." IAI Working Papers, 1307. Roma: IAI.

Donnelly, Jack. 2000. *Realism and International Relations.* Cambridge: Cambridge University Press.

Dyson, Tom. 2008. "Convergence and Divergence in Post-Cold War British, French, and German Military Reforms: Between International Structure and Executive Autonomy." *Security Studies* 17 (4): 725–774.

Finnemore, Martha, and Sikkink Kathryn. 1998. "International Norm Dynamics and Political Change." *International Organization* 52 (4): 887–917.

Houghton, David P. 2007. "Reinvigorating the Study of Foreign Policy Decision Making: Toward a Constructivist Approach." *Foreign Policy Analysis* 3 (1): 24–25.

IAI (Istituto Affari Internazionali) e DISPOC/LAPS (Università di Siena). 2017. *Gli italiani e la politica estera.* Available at http://www.iai.it/sites/default/files/laps-iai_2017.pdf.

Ignazi, Piero, Giampiero Giacomello, and Fabrizio Coticchia. 2012. *Just Don't Call it War. Italian Military Missions Abroad.* Houndmills: Palgrave Macmillan.

Il Corriere della Sera. 2014a. *Renzi: l'Europa sia qui in Iraq.* August 21.

Il Corriere della Sera. 2014b. *Piano di Obama contro l'Isis E Alfano lancia l'allarme: Roma e l'Italia nel mirino.* September 12.

Isernia, Pierangelo, and Francesco Longo. 2017. "The Italian Foreign Policy: Challenges and Continuities." *Italian Political Science Review* 47 (2): 107–124.

Kaarbo, Juliet. 2015. "A Foreign Policy Analysis Perspective on the Domestic Politics Turn in IR Theory." *International Studies Review* 17: 189–216.

Kaarbo, Juliet, and Cristian Cantir. 2012. "Contested Roles and Domestic Politics: Reflections on Role Theory in Foreign Policy Analysis and IR Theory." *Foreign Policy Analysis* 8 (1): 5–24.

La Stampa. 2014. *Renzi: anche noi nella coalizione anti-Isis.* September 24.

Lombardi, Ben. 2011. "The Berlusconi Government and Intervention in Libya." *The International Spectator* 46 (4): 31–44.

Lucarelli, Sonia, and Roberto Menotti. 2002. "No-Constructivists Land. IR Theory in Italy in the 1990s." *Journal of International Relations and Development* 5 (2): 114–142.

Mastrolilli, Paolo. 2014. "Armi ai curdi e fronte libico. Washington promuove l'Italia interventista di Renzi." *La Stampa*, September 6.

Miranda, Valerie V. 2011. "Striking a Balance Between Norms and Interests in Italian Foreign Policy." *IAI Working Papers* 11 (11): 1–21.

Paolicelli, Massimo, and Francesco Vignarca. 2009. *Il caro Armato. Spese, Affari e Sprechi delle Forze Armate Italiane*. Milano: Altraeconomica.

Panebianco, Angelo. 1997. *Guerrieri democratici. Le democrazie e la politica di potenza*. Bologna: Il Mulino.

Pirani, Pietro. 2010. "The Way We Were: The Social Construction of the Italian Defence Policy." *Modern Italy* 15 (2): 217–230.

Ratti, Luca. 2011. "Italy as a Multilateral Actor: The Inescapable Destiny of a Middle Power." In *Italy in the Post Cold War Order*, edited by Maurizio Carbone. Lanham: Lexington Books.

Rosa, Paolo. 2014. "The Accommodationist State: Strategic Culture and Italy's Military Behaviour." *International Relations* 28 (1): 88–115.

Rose, Gideon. 1998. "Neoclassical Realism and Theories of Foreign Policy." *World Politics* 51: 144–172.

Rusconi, Gian Enrico. 2014. "Uno scossone all'impotenza dell'Europa." *La Stampa*, August 21.

Santoro, Carlo Maria. 1991. *La politica estera di una media potenza. L'Italia dall'Unità ad oggi*. Bologna: Il Mulino.

Taliaferro, Jeffrey W., Norrin M. Ripsman, and Steven E. Lobell. 2009. *Neoclassical Realist Theory of International Politics*. Oxford: Oxford University Press.

Trocino, Alessandro. 2014. "Armi ai curdi, l'ampio sì del Parlamento." *Il Corriere della Sera*, August 21.

Valigi, Marco. 2017. *Le medie potenze. Teoria e prassi in politica estera*. Milano: Vita e Pensiero.

Waltz, Kenneth. 1979. *Theory of International Politics*. Reading: Addison-Wesley.

PART III

Non-EU States

CHAPTER 8

From Ontological Insecurity to Counter-Hegemony: Russia's Post-Soviet Engagement with Geopolitics and Eurasianism

Natalia Morozova

Uncertainty with regards to the intentions and actions of other states has been the mainstay of structural realist theory. Generated by a thin international normative-institutional framework, this uncertainty precludes cooperation between states: in an anarchic order states value relative over absolute gains and autonomy over interdependence, lest they should find themselves at the mercy of other, more powerful states (Waltz 1979: 105–107; Mearsheimer 1995). Concomitantly, unlike actors in the domestic realm, states cannot delegate their security provision to any superior agent or institution, so that security, i.e. physical survival, becomes the highest end. In an anarchic context there are no reassurances or guarantees as to the others' motives and intentions, so states are often forced to engage in security-seeking behavior that might

N. Morozova (✉)
National Research University Higher School of Economics,
Moscow, Russia
e-mail: nnmorozova@hse.ru

© The Author(s) 2019
R. Belloni et al. (eds.), *Fear and Uncertainty in Europe*, Global Issues,
https://doi.org/10.1007/978-3-319-91965-2_8

153

be considered threatening by other states. As a result, from a structural realist perspective, states' efforts at self-protection fuelled by uncertainty and mistrust can pave the way to conflict and war.

However, as has been recently pointed out by constructivists, uncertainty regarding one's own goals and actions can just as easily lead to conflict. They argue that actors attempt to impose order on their cognitive environment in order to relate means to ends and realize their sense of agency. In other words, underpinning a state's capacity to act is a stable self-understanding and self-identity, i.e. consistent answers given by foreign policy experts to the questions "for what/whom do we stand?" and "what is our role in world affairs?" (Guzzini 2012: 49–52). By contrast, uncertainty as to one's own and the other's identity means that states do not know how to act and how to support their self-conceptions through practice. Thus, constructivists argue that in addition to physical security states seek ontological security, or "security of the self", security of the sense of being—that hinges on confident expectations about means-ends relationships and the cognitive environment reproducing it (Mitzen 2006: 345–346; Steele 2005: 526). Importantly, ontological security-seeking might lead to conflict as states, wary of the debilitating effects of uncertainty, can opt for the certainty that conflictual relations provide.

Several aspects of the ontological security literature will be relevant for my discussion of Russia's attempts to come to terms with its post-Soviet ontological insecurity. Firstly, although subjective and intrinsically held, identities refer to role positions of states within the international order. As such, they are rooted in and sustained through social relations and need to be reciprocated and recognized by others. In other words, the project of self-identity is "reflexively, *intersubjectively constructed* over time" (Steele 2008: 56, italics in original). Secondly, it is precisely through routinizing their relationships with significant others that states achieve cognitive and behavioural certainty, i.e. the ability to relate self-identity to actions in a meaningful and consistent way (Mitzen 2006: 342). Finally, ontological anxiety, or "uncomfortable disconnect with the self", occurs in critical situations when certitudes provided by a state's institutionalized routines are disrupted (Steele 2008: 12). Thus, an identity crisis might ensue following a momentous international "trigger" event that transformed the social order in which the state's previous role-conception was embedded (Guzzini 2012: 56–57). Or, alternatively, discursive representations can be just as powerful in making a state feel ontologically insecure if other actors attempt to uncover discrepancies between different self-conceptions or between them and specific foreign policies (Steele 2005: 539; Guzzini 2012: 55).

At the same time, using Russia as a case study could potentially feed back into theory and shed light on the on-going debates within the ontological security literature. What is at stake in one such debate is whether ontological anxiety arises from a lack of external recognition or from the self's own introspective sense of incongruence between its actions and its identity narrative. In other words, do states have reflexive agency so that generating a consistent identity narrative is essentially a domestic, internal affair, or are states heavily dependent on their social environment while their identities are mutually constituted, naturalized and objectified through inter-subjectively shared meanings? Steele maintains that the former is the case; he finds the strategy of becoming attached to significant others and losing a sense of agency in the process both counterintuitive and irrational. In fact, actors see certain situations as critical to their sense of self-identity because "we feel anxiety not about things that are outside our control, but about those we perceive to be in the realm of our possible agency" (Steele 2008: 60–61). By contrast, Zarakol argues that historically 'attachment to significant others' has been a strategy of choice for non-Western states such as Russia that attempted and continuously failed to join the Western core (Zarakol 2011). She sees the twists and turns of Russia's post-Soviet foreign policy as stigma-coping strategies resorted to by a stigmatized state in the hope of regaining its status.

Despite this, both Steele and Zarakol, as well as other scholars working within the ontological security perspective agree on the importance of narrative in ensuring the integrity of the state's self and infusing its actions with meanings consistent with its self-identity (Steele 2008; Zarakol 2011; Della Sala 2017; Subotic 2016). Steele takes this agreement one step further by suggesting that discourse analysis methodology should be employed in order to uncover connections between a state's policy choices and its identity narratives (Steele 2008: 12). In Steele's view the focus on discourse, in particular on the often conflicting domestic identity discourses, helps to solve the methodological quandary of where we should look for evidence of ontological insecurity.

This directly relates to yet another debate within the ontological security literature on how best to address the levels-of-analysis problem that arises when treating states as individuals. Mitzen asserts that it is possible to ascribe an individual need for ontological security to states because states routinize inter-state relations in order to ensure the ontological security of its members (Mitzen 2006: 352). Steele, by contrast, takes issue with what he perceives as unwarranted imposition of uniformity and homogenization of individuals within a state. As he puts it, "by reifying ontological security to all members of a society, we miss out on the very interesting political process of self-identity contestation" (Steele 2008, 17). Steele's own solution to the levels-of-analysis problem is to concentrate on the role of state agents in meeting the ontological security needs of the states they lead. Foreign policy elites, state leaders included, have to explain and justify the identity effects of their prospective policies to their domestic audiences and to each other. Thus, the consensus view among ontological security scholars is that policies can significantly contribute to a stable self-understanding by either sustaining or contradicting identities. However, contrary to Mitzen, Steele suggests employing discourse analysis methodology in order to understand how state agents forge a consistent foreign policy-identity link and, simultaneously, forge their respective states' capacity to act.

This chapter examines post-Soviet Russia's attempts to alleviate its ontological anxiety through the lens of discourse analysis. Specifically, the study looks at one instance of discursive innovation that reflected Russian foreign policy elites' inability and unwillingness to rely on the previously established—Soviet and traditional Russian—self-understandings. This discursive innovation was the emergence of the "geopolitics/Eurasianism" constellation in the post-Soviet Russian foreign policy discourse following the dissolution of the Soviet Union. Both "geopolitics" and "Eurasianism" acquired particular relevance amidst the post-Soviet Russian identity crisis because their conceptual history pre-dated and/or was not part of the Soviet experience. Both "Eurasianism" and, in particular, "geopolitics" enjoyed wide appeal across the whole post-Soviet political spectrum as conceptual resources that could help to mitigate and reduce the identity crisis. Therefore, both the liberal recourse to geopolitics in an attempt to attach a veneer of self-evidence and objectivity to democratic transition at home and the national-patriotic 'geopolitics/Eurasianism' coinage meant to underpin the primacy of foreign policy can be construed as Russia discursively realizing its sense of agency. At the same time, in order to produce consistent state identity narratives both discourses relied on excluding other identity narratives and therefore were still curiously caught up in the conceptual logic associated with their discursive 'others'.

Thus, the aim of the chapter is two-fold. Firstly, it seeks to put forward a methodological claim that discourse analysis is particularly well-placed to shed light on how states address their ontological insecurities: it captures the dynamics of states developing or transforming their identity narratives as well as the effects of socio-cognitive constraints delimiting what can be said and done. Two strands of poststructuralist discourse analysis—a layered structural model of national discourses developed by Ole Wæver and a theory of hegemony proposed by Ernesto Laclau and Chantal Mouffe—will be employed to account for the "hegemony-counter-hegemony" dynamics involved in post-Soviet Russia ensuring the integrity of the self. From this perspective, the research presented here is a "case plus study" meant as a medium for further theoretical and methodological elaboration (Hansen 2006: 10). Secondly, the present study provides empirical substantiation of the theoretical claim that hegemonic relations lend themselves to analysis through the prism of discourse, while the concept of hegemony accounts for particular historical experiences of the latecomers to the international society such as Russia and links them to wider International Relations theory (Laclau and Mouffe 1987; Morozov 2015). The chapter will explore the extent to which the conceptual "tools" from the realist toolkit—namely that the international realm as the one in which self-interested "like" units are motivated by fear and uncertainty to ensure their own survival under the conditions of anarchy shapes behavior and outcomes—are relevant in terms of making meaningful the conduct of Russian post-Soviet foreign policy.

The chapter will proceed as follows. The following section will discuss scholarly contributions that look at post-Soviet Russian foreign policy and discourse through the prism of the ontological security argument. A case will be made for doing discourse analysis in order to elucidate how states discursively reduce their ontological insecurities. Specifically, discourse analysis demonstrates how foreign policy elites engage in domestic contestation of hegemonic 'foreign policy-identity' representations and attempt to forge counter-hegemonic articulations of their own. The third section will discuss the post-Soviet revival and rehabilitation of geopolitics and Eurasianism by the liberal and national-patriotic political elites as an example of such domestic identity contestation. Finally, the chapter will offer some concluding remarks on how discourse analysis can help solve methodological problems inherent in the ontological security argument as well as enrich our understanding of hegemonic relations and fine-tune our methodology of studying them.

ONTOLOGICAL SECURITY THEORY MEETS RUSSIAN
POST-SOVIET FOREIGN POLICY

There are two stories about the way Russia's ontological security is affected by the interactions with its "significant other"—Europe/the West. According to the first story, Russia's relations with Europe/the West are a source of ontological security: they provide a stable and predictable cognitive environment for Russia to implement its foreign policy goals and fulfill its identity needs. The second story argues the exact opposite: Russia's relations with Europe/the West have historically been the source of greatest ontological insecurity, soul-searching, status concerns and incentives for change.

The first story is a familiar one. It is firmly within the scope of the ontological security argument and goes like this. In its first independence years Russia was trying to reinvent itself as a modern and civilized nation that achieves security through cooperation with developed Western states and forms part of the liberal democratic community. Having defined its Soviet past as Russia's constitutive "other", the foreign policy elites believed that democratization was the right policy to pursue in the absence of any viable alternatives and that it would facilitate a complete de-Sovietization of Russia (Hansen 2016: 362). However, Russia was feeling inauthentic in its newly assigned role, which found insufficient support with both the developed liberal states of the West as well as with Russia's own population. Therefore, in the mid-2000s Russia reverted to forging its own unique developmental path which provides the Russian population with an uninterrupted historical narrative and, therefore, a stronger sense of the Self. Thus, greater ontological security and a knowable cognitive and behavioural environment that comes together with it are achieved at the expense of embarking on a conflictual and destructive relationship with the West and exacerbating the physical conditions of Russia's existence.

The second story of how the West has historically undermined rather than ensured Russia's ontological security is much less familiar. While employing the ontological security argument, this story places it within a broad range of international relations theories in order to criticize them for neglecting the stratification and differentiation effects of norm socialization. Specifically, Ayşe Zarakol argues that the ambiguous "insider but outsider" place that non-Western states such as Russia, Japan and Turkey occupy in the international system is the underlying cause of their acute sense of ontological insecurity and somewhat erratic foreign policy behaviour (Zarakol 2011: 30). What makes the three cases of Russia, Japan and Turkey stand out is the history of their engagement with the Western core: the entry of these states into the Westphalian state system resulted not from forceful colonization, but from a voluntary decision of the respective foreign policy elites to emulate certain Western practices. Importantly, these states had existed for centuries as pre-modern self-sufficient empires that enjoyed a position of relative power and privilege and produced their own comprehensive normative standards separating "us" from inferior "others". Therefore, initially Europeanization was limited to specific sectors and often amounted to borrowing military technology. However, as the Western European powers evolved into modern, sovereign, rational and bureaucratized states in the course of political reforms and revolutions of the eighteenth and early nineteenth centuries, such selective modernization was no longer possible. Modernity produced a single, comprehensive and universal standard of civilization predicated on seemingly objective assessment criteria and measurements. The European elites' judgment that Russia fell short of the new normative standard was internalized by Russian foreign policy elites to the extent that the overwhelming reaction was a feeling of shame and a perpetual need to overcome backwardness and be accepted as an equal. As Zarakol succinctly puts it, "the flipside of socialization is otherness" (Zarakol 2011: 16). It is precisely this emphasis on the stratifying effects of international norm socialization that is missing in both the ahistorical and deterministic neorealist accounts of socialization and in constructivist accounts that gloss over power disparities and social hierarchies behind norm socialization.

Therefore, the concept of stigma borrowed from the field of social psychology is introduced in order to account for the fact that international norm socialization can adversely affect national identity. Importantly, stigmatization theory helps to bridge the gap between international, system-level and domestic, unit-level explanations of identity formation as long as stigma is conceptualized as a social relationship between the "normals" and the outsiders and represents "as much the internalization of a particular normative standard that defines one's own attributes as discreditable, as it is a label of difference imposed from outside" (Zarakol 2011: 4). Turning to the three case studies, it is argued that there are two commonalities between Russia, Turkey and Japan from the point of view of how their imperial past continues to shape their present: the stigma label attached to these three 'outsider' states at the onset of modern state formation for being developmentally behind and the difficulty of resigning themselves to the loss of empire (Zarakol 2011: 102). Specifically, throughout the course of their relations with the Western core these three non-Western states experienced stigmatization, attempted to overcome stigmatization by engaging the Western states militarily and were stigmatized again after having suffered a military defeat and losing imperial possessions. Stigmatization as a systemic social constraint affecting foreign policy behavior of the stigmatized state makes available only a limited number of options: either to attempt to join the ranks of the "normal" or to embrace stigma and accept one's "outsider" position. Regarding Russia's post-Soviet foreign policy it is argued that "the more powerful and/or prestigious the state before defeat and imperial collapse, the longer it will take to readjust to the new international environment" (Zarakol 2011: 105). The specificity of Russia's historical dealings with the West lies in the fact that, being a non-Western great power, Russia saw its empire unravel due to an assumed rather than real military defeat, while its sphere of influence was not occupied by a former rival as was the case with Turkey and Japan. This makes the strategy of embracing stigma, identifying with other stigmatized states and rejecting prevalent international norms much more credible. Not surprisingly, the corrective strategy of emulating the Western liberalizing and democratizing practices in the immediate post-independence years soon gave way to an increasingly hostile strategy, which can neither present a fully-fledged ideological alternative nor aspire to restore Russia's status as a European great power.

At this point we need to take stock of the argument thus far. Both Hansen and Zarakol convincingly demonstrate Russia's post-Soviet fixation on its position and status within the West-dominated order, which has been well-documented indeed. What makes Zarakol's study innovative and insightful, however, is the way she conceptualizes the origins of ontological insecurity and grounds them in the agents' coming to grips with their subordinate, peripheral position in the social hierarchy inherent in the global political order. However, while successful in terms of elucidating the sources of ontological insecurity, Zarakol's study is less convincing when it comes to mapping out possible strategies of coping with ontological insecurity. To be sure, if one is interested in system-level explanations of the constraints under which particular foreign policy choices are made, such an explanatory framework can hardly be expected to account for each foreign policy decisions. But attaching generic labels such as "stigma-coping strategies" to the various conceptualizations of Russia's relations with the West put forward by Russian foreign policy elites—hardly advances our understanding of the way state identity contestation influences foreign policy choices, which is one of Zarakol's own contentions (Zarakol 2011: 103).

Indeed, psychological approaches concentrate on emotions and therefore obscure the role of socially constructed meanings as discursive preconditions for particular policy choices (Morozov 2015: 62). In fact, psychological metaphors can be used for the sake of brevity or expressivity, but not as part of one's conceptual apparatus if unaccompanied by meticulous discourse analysis. Firstly, proponents of different strategies are likely to attach very different meanings to the notion of "stigma". Secondly, these meanings would depend on how a national conceptual landscape is structured with regards to the state's desired role position and status in the international system, its conception of relations with significant "others" and its construction of the "state-nation" relationship. After all, if we were to take contestation seriously, we should elucidate certain common discursive positions round which contestation revolves. Finally, it is not as if the advocates of the other two positions—Russia acting a bridge between the Western core and the periphery and Russia rejecting West-originated international norms altogether—were silently waiting for the liberalizing 'emulation' strategy to discredit itself in order to step into the limelight. Actors engaged in a domestic debate actively *con*test, i.e. pass judgments on other constructions and positions (Wæver 2002, 38). These dynamics should be taken into account by those researchers who present reducing ontological insecurity as rationale for particular foreign policy choices. In Hansen's study, for example, the failure of the democratization policy of the 1990s to solve the identity crisis is conceptualized in psychological terms as Russia's "agonizing"—as Russia not being fully honest either with itself or with the West (Hansen 2016: 364). However, in order to make a case for the 'sonderweg' policy of the 2000s successfully contesting the democratization policy of the 1990s—and help the researcher avoid the risk of imposing their own interpretation onto a world of meaning (Morozov 2015: 60)—the latter has to be reconstructed *as discourse* and discussed on its own terms rather than by means of psychological metaphors.

How can one conceptualize ontological insecurity in discourse analytical terms and yet avoid "psychologising" discourse analysis? In fact, both Hansen and Zarakol provide important clues when they discuss the role of the past in sustaining uninterrupted and consistent state identity narratives. They do it either by employing the notion of "habitus" to account for the way in which the historical experience of stigmatization still features in Russia's contemporary self-understanding (Zarakol 2011: 100–102) or by demonstrating the importance of World War II commemorative practices and discourses in othering the West (Hansen 2016: 367–368). What is at stake here is the suggestion that certain ideas, narratives and constructions—for example, the West as Russia's "other", be it a dangerous, life-threatening other or a technologically, economically and culturally superior other—are constitutive of the national conceptual landscape to such an extent that they underpin consensus between political opponents and hardly ever become an object of debate, reflection and politicization.

This is one of the premises underlying Wæver's conceptualization of the basic conceptual logic available in society in terms of a layered discursive structure (Wæver 2002: 31). Since Wæver is mainly interested in how national discourses structure debates on European integration, he identifies three layers that make up the domestic discursive structure. To begin with, there is the basic constellation of the concepts of 'state' and 'nation' acting as a constraint on the possible constructions of "Europe" that are hospitable to the state-nation construction and that, in turn, make possible a certain number of European policies, realistic and meaningful within the highly structured national landscape. Of particular importance for our discussion is Wæver's contention that these conceptual layers display various degrees of sedimentation, as more embedded concepts of who we are as a "state" and a "people/nation" relate to less sedimented and more easily politicized geographical and temporal concepts such as "Europe" or "the West", which are then translated into specific policies subject to contestation. This is how we can conceptualize ontological insecurity by staying at the level of discourse: a particular foreign policy is contested for being incongruent with the state's sense of the self and for not articulating a "state-nation-Europe" constellation in an acceptable way. If the policy discourse cannot address the criticisms and be adjusted through "surface changes", pressure will build up in the system causing contestation at deeper levels and making the actor embrace a different discursive construction altogether.

The argument against letting emotions rather than inter-subjectively held meanings do the explanatory work can be extended further. On the one hand, using the notion of "stigma" to account for Russia's internalization of the West-originated normative standard points to the ubiquity of Europe/the West in Russian collective self-understanding so that every single foreign policy-identity linkage that post-Soviet Russia came up with has Europe/the West as its point of departure. This has direct bearing on the debate on the sources of ontological insecurity mentioned above: Russia, as well as other states that found themselves on the periphery of the international society, can only hope to achieve a stable sense of being if they address their subordinate position in the global hierarchical structure. In other words, Russia has to exercise its reflexive agency within externally defined parameters, i.e. within the constraints imposed by the hegemony of the European discourse. On the other hand, one cannot but agree that, "while having to adjust to the Eurocentric hegemonic order is indeed a central fact of modern Russian history, subsuming the entire gamut of responses under the conceptual umbrella of 'stigma' is hardly a step forward" (Morozov 2015: 58). For one thing, the "stigma-coping strategies" available to Russian post-Soviet foreign policy elites that Zarakol has identified do not represent a level playing discursive field. The advocates of a pro-Western stigma-correcting foreign policy stance project the global hegemonic order domestically, so that the proponents of the stigma-embracing alternatives are confronted with the necessity to mount a counter-hegemonic effort. What this means theoretically is that the concept of hegemony "provides the crucial missing link between the general phenomena (stigmatization, othering, ontological insecurity of the outsiders) and the specific circumstances of individual cases" (Morozov 2015: 63).

In order to conduct discourse analysis that is both context-sensitive and generalizable beyond the individual Russian case, this study employs Laclau and Mouffe's discursive theory of hegemony. "Hegemony" is defined by Laclau and Mouffe as a political relationship of hegemonic representation, whereby "a particular social force assumes the representation of the totality radically incommensurable with it" (Laclau and Mouffe 1987: x; see also Morozov 2015: 63–64). A hegemonic representation requires as its first condition of possibility a relationship of social antagonism, which, in turn, is predicated on the notion of discourse understood as a structured totality underpinned by a particular configuration of its elements. This configuration assumes the form of a system of differential positions between objects whose identities are relational and, therefore necessary, because they depend closely upon one another. However, absolute fixity of meanings and identities is impossible because "a discursive totality never exists in the form of a simply given and delimited positivity", while "the relational logic will be incomplete and pierced by contingency" (Laclau and Mouffe 1987: 110). This becomes particularly obvious when the "self" is confronted by an antagonistic "other" that negates the objectivity of the "self" and prevents it from fully constituting him/herself. As a result of this encounter, all the partially fixed positive signs that went into the constitution of a closed and self-referential identity enter into a relation of equivalence and become *floating* signifiers that do not belong to any discursive totality. The presence of a large number of floating signifiers provides the second condition of possibility for a hegemonic articulation: it ensures that the hegemonic subject is partially exterior to what it articulates and can therefore constantly redefine the meaning of floating signifiers through the opposed logics of equivalence and difference.

What unites Laclau and Mouffe's discursive theory of hegemony with Wæver's conceptualization of discourse as a layered structure is a focus on the deeply entrenched and sedimented meanings—nodal points—that "have taken on particular importance as 'vehicles' of identity production" (Wæver 2002: 30). These self-understandings provide a common point of reference for the national foreign policy debate and ensure that foreign policy makers speak the same language when they dispute each other's positions (Guzzini 2012: 53). Or, to translate the above into the language of Laclau and Mouffe's discourse analysis, these privileged nodal points are at the core of the hegemonic discursive struggle. They partially fix the meaning of the social in an organized system of signification and simultaneously exclude alternative articulations that revolve round the same privileged nodal points. These alternative chains of equivalence are confined to the realm of 'otherness', insofar as "every 'society' constitutes its own forms of rationality and intelligibility by dividing itself; that is, by expelling outside itself any surplus of meaning subverting it" (Laclau and Mouffe 1987: 136–137). Thus, the next section will discuss the rise of the 'geopolitics/Eurasianism' constellation in Russian post-Soviet foreign policy discourse as both an attempt to fix identity crisis and, simultaneously, to mount a counter-hegemonic offensive against the liberal engagement with "geopolitics" and "Eurasianism".

FIXING IDENTITY CRISIS, RESISTING HEGEMONY: 'GEOPOLITICS/EURASIANISM' CONSTELLATION IN RUSSIAN POST-SOVIET FOREIGN POLICY DISCOURSE

In what has so far been the most authoritative and comprehensive attempt to account for the resurgence of geopolitical thinking in national foreign policy debates across post-Cold War Europe, Stefano Guzzini identifies one necessary 'trigger' condition and several facilitating conditions making such resurgence possible (Guzzini 2012). The "trigger" condition was foreign policy identity crisis produced by the interpretation of the events of 1989, whereby previously held self-understandings and role positions were openly challenged and undermined, while a country's national interest discourses ran aground and had to be anchored anew. Geopolitical thought with its emphasis on environmental determinism and seemingly objective, material foundations for formulating national interests was particularly well-placed to provide fixture to this ontological insecurity. Russia's foreign policy narrative was closely tied to the Cold War scenario. As a result, following the fall of communism and the dissolution of the Soviet Union not only specific policies, but also both aspects of Russian foreign policy identity—the values it stood for and the role position it occupied—were no longer valid or self-evident. As such, they became a subject of a fierce domestic debate signaling Russia's ontological insecurity because "identity should come naturally; the moment it needs consciously to justify its assumptions, we can say that a crisis has occurred" (Guzzini 2012: 56). The facilitating conditions were also present in the Russian case. Firstly, dissatisfied with the power status and rank that the international community accorded to Russia, its foreign policy elites mobilized geopolitical arguments in order to stake their claims for 'great power' status recognition. Secondly, ideational path dependence, namely a previously existing materialist traditional of political thought, and the institutional setting within which foreign policy expertise takes shape, in particular the dominance of the realist tradition in International Relations teaching and a direct role of the military in knowledge production (Guzzini 2012: 245) also predisposed Russian foreign policy elites to embrace geopolitics. Finally, geopolitical arguments resonated particularly well with politicians of conservative persuasion who couched their nationalist claims in the language of geopolitics.

This last assertion about a close connection between conservative agenda and a post-1989 geopolitical revival requires further elaboration and qualification. In the hot-house political climate of Russian post-independence years even the Westernizing liberals succumbed to the objectivist, neutral and non-partisan appeal of geopolitics. It was in fact Russia's staunchly pro-Western first Foreign Minister Andrei Kozyrev who first hailed geopolitics as a new reference point for Russia's foreign policy when he suggested that, "the geopolitical dimension of our interests is probably one of the most normal criteria for defining a new foreign policy orientation" (Kozyrev 1992: 86). Kozyrev's statements to the effect that Russia was "still a missing component of the democratic pole of the Northern Hemisphere" and that "anyone can see just by looking at the map that the United States is our closest neighbour in the East" (Tsygankov 2008: 96–97) were meant to tap into the symbolic, rhetorical power of geopolitics amidst a heated ideological debate. Most importantly, geopolitical arguments were invoked in order to buttress the self-evidence and inevitability of Russia's democratization and economic liberalization, with foreign policy providing external conditions conducive to domestic reforms.

Faced with a foreign policy identity crisis, Russian foreign policy makers of liberal persuasion attempted to use geopolitics as a conceptual vehicle of national interest formation, so that specific policies could be read directly off the map. As a blueprint for rational, balanced and objective assessment of Russia's national interests, geopolitics was supposed to usher in Russia's new, pragmatic and de-ideologized foreign policy in contrast to Soviet foreign policy that sacrificed the country's national interests for the sake of ideological crusading and imperial overreach. Discursively 'geopolitics' was also well-placed to reinforce a break with the Soviet past insofar as it was considered "ideological rationalization of aggressive imperialist foreign policy" beyond the pale of official Soviet discourse (Tsygankov 1994: 59). Therefore, as a signifier "geopolitics" was easily inscribed within a system of signification underpinning a new post-Soviet hegemonic articulation that established a relation of equivalence between the following key signifiers: geopolitics, pragmatism, pursuit of national interests, de-ideologization of foreign policy, cooperation, democratization and economic modernization. Simultaneously, the recent Soviet past, whose meaning was constituted through an alternative chain of equivalence linking expansionism, messianism, neglect of national interests, confrontation, totalitarianism, socialist economy, came to represent post-Soviet Russia's much maligned "other" (Morozova 2015: 143). Looking outside-in from the vantage point of the West-originated hegemonic order, the Soviet experience was seen by Russian liberal-minded elites as a mistake, an aberration to be admitted and corrected through emulation and normative socialization.

However, while any hegemonic representation works by excluding and silencing alternative articulations in order to constitute meaningful totality, it is equally true that any link between signifiers/identities within such discursive totality is non-essential and therefore subject to subversion and transformation. Despite being the internal projection of global normative hegemony, the liberal hegemonic articulation was no exception: it came under fire from the members of the national-patriotic opposition for neglecting Russia's historical experiences and distinctiveness that would lend substance to the specifically Russian national interests. Proving the point that "one articulation can be undermined by another not through a head-on collision, ...but only at a deeper level" (Morozov 2009: 120), national-patriots invoked Russia's great power status as a deeply ingrained national code and a point of agreement cutting across political divisions. Russia's great power status was the epitome of Russia's indispensability in global politics and its ability to be in control of its international environment; it was a proof that the Russian state possessed a continuous, uninterrupted sense of selfhood and could help its citizens achieve positive freedom (Lo 2002: 53). Most importantly, in their attempt to use great power status as an identity-fixer the opponents of the liberal discourse advocated the primacy of foreign policy as opposed to the primacy of ideological dogmas, either Soviet socialist or post-Soviet liberal (Astrov and Morozova 2012: 107–108).

Not surprisingly, when the liberals in power responded to the challenge and came up with the "normal great power" variation of the theme (Kozyrev 1992: 85; Primakov 1992: 95; Lukin 1992: 93), this discursive borrowing from a rival camp generated enough pressure to destabilize the hegemonic liberal articulation. For one thing, Russian foreign policy makers put forward a pronouncedly liberal understanding of normalcy. Conceptualized as a check on the messianic streak in foreign policy, this particular understanding of 'normalcy' could not but come into conflict with the demand for greatness generated from within the domestic discourse (Astrov and Morozova 2012: 197). The key conceptual parameters of the liberal discourse originated in the West and could not accommodate any domestic, endogenous articulation of Russia's distinctiveness. It was largely for this reason that the concept of Eurasia put forward by some liberal-minded intellectuals as an antidote to dissolving Russia in Europe and as a point of departure for forging a distinctly Russian identity (Neumann 1997: 147) never made any inroads into the foreign policy discourse of the liberal reformers in the early 1990s. In contrast to his earlier attempts to buttress a liberal understanding of Russia's national interests with geopolitical arguments, Kozyrev referred to Russia's Eurasian location as just a fact of geography (Tsygankov 2008: 96). Of particular importance, however, is the fact that attaching "great power" to the chain of equivalence that sustained the hegemonic liberal articulation as one of its nodal points caused the latter to unravel: it generated systemic problems that could not be solved by going "down one more level" (Wæver 2002: 32). Specifically, the liberal embracing of Russia's great power status blurred the inside/outside divide underpinning hegemony, so that the Soviet past could no longer be denigrated as post-Soviet Russia's 'other'.

The liberal Westernizers' subordination of foreign policy goals to the domestic agenda of democratization and economic modernization was fiercely contested in the run-up to the 1993 Duma and 1996 presidential elections, and the 'geopolitics/Eurasianism' constellation was at the center of this contestation. Geopolitics was conceived of as a science "whose object was global politics, i.e. devising an international political strategy" (Zhirinovsky 1997: 12) and a branch of knowledge at the intersection of the civilizational approach, military-strategic research and theories of geographic determinism (Zyuganov 1997: 14) by the leading figures of the national-patriotic opposition. As such, geopolitics was supposed to lend substance to Russian national interests by grounding them in the constants of physical and human geography. It did not take long before such grounding was accomplished by, among others, the leader of the Russian Communists Gennady Zyuganov. He argued that both the Soviet and the liberal ideologues ignored the fact that Russia's vital interests are objectively inscribed within the natural, i.e. defensible borders of the Russian-Eurasian heartland (Zyuganov 1997: 32). It is this insularity, continentality and inaccessibility of the Eurasian heartland that paves the way for interdependence and cross-border interaction and provides the imperative for far-reaching political integration of the post-Soviet space. In a nutshell, geopolitics was the cornerstone of the national-patriotic doctrine asserting the primacy of foreign policy.

However, while recycling familiar themes of classical European inter-war geopolitics, geopolitics displayed "ideological thinness" and therefore required a fixing of its own that would predicate the independence of geopolitics-informed foreign policy on some notion of Russian civilizational distinctiveness (Astrov and Morozova 2012: 196–199). Such fixing came in the form of Eurasianism, which in its post-Soviet neo-Eurasian version had the advantage of couching foreign policy prescriptions in the language that was distinctively Russian-born. Thus, the long-term leader of the Russian Communists, Gennady Zyuganov, asserted that the normative foundations of the Russian civilization—*derzhavnost'* (self-sufficiency), *sobornost'* (communitarianism), patriotism and social justice—had cross-border normative appeal and were embraced by other peoples of wider Eurasia. Situated at the intersection of the European and Asian civilization, Russia therefore constituted the "natural nucleus of Eurasianism" and "personified" the Eurasian civilization (Zyuganov 1995: 13, 21). By contrast, Alexander Dugin, who to outside observers was the face and the voice of neo-Eurasianism and geopolitical revival, tapped into the conceptual resources of classical post-revolutionary Eurasianism in earnest. In his idiosyncratic conceptualization the geopolitics of "Heartland Russia" was fused with Orthodox ideocracy and provided a metaphysical, political and geostrategic "third way" (Morozova 2009). Invariably, however, there was a division of labour between geopolitics and Eurasianism: the former was responsible for conceptualizing the power-political dimension of Russian foreign policy while the latter took care of its normative underpinnings. In the language of discourse analysis, geopolitics and Eurasianism occupied relational but non-identical positions within the chain of equivalence. Geopolitics stood for the primacy of foreign policy and provided a counterpoint to the de-ideologization and "economization" of foreign policy in the liberal conceptualization. Eurasianism as a key signifier represented Russia's civilizational distinctiveness and was juxtaposed to rationalism, individualism, globalization and American exceptionalism/expansionism/unilateralism, i.e. Atlanticism. In other words, geopolitics and Eurasianism were nodal points of the counter-hegemonic discursive articulation.

An in-depth discussion of why in the long run neither geopolitics nor Eurasianism provided the much-needed fixture to Russia's post-Soviet ontological insecurity falls outside the scope of this chapter and has been provided elsewhere (Astrov and Morozova 2012; Morozova 2009).

The point we would like to make is more general and pertains to the level of theory. Presenting the liberal agenda of democratization, de-Sovietization and economic modernization and the oppositional stance predicating sovereignty on civilizational distinctiveness and Russia's current official synthesis of great power status, Orthodoxy and traditional values as "stigma-coping strategies" (Zarakol 2011) obscures the hegemony-counter-hegemony dynamics informing these discourses. As the above analysis demonstrates, both the stigma-erasing and stigma-embracing strategies implemented by post-Soviet Russian foreign policy elites should be more adequately conceptualized as hegemonic articulations underpinning consistent state narratives as a remedy to ontological insecurity.

CONCLUSION

The current research has aimed to show that an exploration of state identity rooted in the ontological security argument will benefit from employing discourse analysis methodology in at least three respects. Firstly, a discourse analysis of the patterns of domestic identity contestation reveals the difference between an individual and state identity and helps to avoid the pitfall of anthropomorthising the state. Secondly, a detailed explication of the dynamics of identity affirmation and dissent helps to solve the methodological quandary inherent in the ontological security argument, i.e. the problem of proving that a state's ontological insecurity is not just a figment of the writer's imagination and can actually be identified through discursive ruptures and novel conceptual resources resorted to by foreign policy elites. Thirdly, discourse analysis, in particular poststructuralist discourse analysis that centers on the notions of sedimentation and hegemony provides important insights into how states develop consistent identity narratives. This is important in view of the fact that "the ability of the narrative to organize the Self is integral to any understanding of ontological security" (Steele 2008: 58).

However, both discourse analysis and ontological security theory have so far not been particularly receptive to the historical experiences of states such as Russia that were latecomers to the international society. Their domestic identity-foreign policy discourses should be more adequately analyzed through the prism of international normative hegemony, which invariably originated in the West and to which domestic foreign policy elites invariably had to respond. Thus, while the layered conception of discursive structure proposed by Wæver captures well the conceptual parameters of the debate on European integration in EU member states, it has to be adjusted to account for Russia's basic conceptual logic in dealing with Europe/the West in one important respect. As pointed out by Neumann, in the Russian case "the depth span of the three levels of Wæver's model – state-nation constellation, structural relations between this constellation and the collective's conceptualizations of Europe, specific European policies – seem to be more shallow, conflated and truncated, than in the German and French cases" (Neumann 2002: 209). What this means is that historically the Russian debate on the core conceptualizations of state and nation has had Europe as its main reference point and has been subjected to hegemonic pressure that the European 'state-nation' constellations underpinning the international system exerted on the rest of the system. In other words, instead of providing room for different combinations of "state-nation" and "Europe", the Russian discourse seems to align itself rather neatly into two articulations, the one that reproduces the European hegemony at home and the one that resists it on the level of foreign policy. These two articulations—a hegemonic and a counter-hegemonic one—coincide with the stigma-correcting and stigma-embracing strategies identified by Zarakol (2011). Therefore, we would do well to agree with Viatcheslav Morozov that the concept of hegemony can provide the missing link between psychological phenomena such as stigmatization and particular historical contexts and connect Russian identity studies to wider International Relations theory (Morozov 2015: 63). After all, it has long been the mainstay of Russian identity studies that, "European discourse has in some key instances been able to tell Russians who they should be, and indeed how they should construct their walls", which seems to be "as good a definition of hegemony as any" (Neumann 1997: 148).

If we were to consider the relevance of contemporary International Relations scholarship for understanding Russian post-Soviet foreign policy further, we would most certainly choose geopolitics and realism as the two most obvious candidates, i.e. as theories that inform the conduct of Russian foreign policy and therefore can be used as explanatory frameworks. After all, as the above analysis shows, Russian foreign policy makers from the ranks of both the liberals and the national-patriots extensively used the rhetoric of geopolitics in order to elucidate the meaning of Russian national interests and makes sense of the world around them. Indeed, there have been attempts to employ geopolitics as a conceptual lens in order to make the apparently irrational mid-1990 Russian foreign policy shift from multilateralism, Westernism and economization of foreign policy to assertiveness and great power posturing intelligible to an outside observer. On this reading, after a brief liberal interlude "the geopolitical strain" understood as a combination of zero-sum mentality, balance-of-power politics and concern with maintaining a sphere of influence once again came to dominate Russian foreign policy thinking (Lo 2002: 98–122). However, discourse analysis undertaken in this study demonstrates that Russian post-Soviet foreign policy makers tapped into the symbolic power of geopolitics in order to make certain identity conceptualizations self-evident and non-debatable and thus to fix a foreign policy identity crisis rather than as an exercise in making rational strategic calculations for the sake of rank maximization.

By the same token, although it might be tempting to see Russian foreign policy elites as realist-minded and to present Russia as a source of fear and uncertainty in present-day Europe, my analysis of the hegemony of the European discourse in Russia's collective self-understanding can hardly be accommodated within realism. To begin with, this chapter draws on the existing literature to claim that the key characteristic of Russia's post-Soviet condition defining the domestic identity debate is Russia's subordinate position within the hierarchical structure of the West-dominated normative order. On the one hand, it is precisely Russia's inferior status within the international social stratification that generates uncertainty—not with regards to others' intentions, but with regards to one's own sense of selfhood and sources of agency. Within the framework focused on inter-subjectively shared meanings rather than psychological phenomena, uncertainty rather than fear seems to be more appropriate as an individual-level conceptualization. On the other hand, we may agree with Zarakol that this uncertainty and ontological insecurity, or, to use her own term, stigmatization is "a more realistic litmus test for deducing the presence of an "international society" than the sense of "we-ness", "common purpose" or the legalistic approaches used in the IR literature" (Zarakol 2011: 19–20). Concomitantly, with the West being "in control of the key points of reference of the global political discourse" and of the Russian identity debate in particular, Russia can hardly be conceptualized as a rational, self-interested actor envisioned by realism (Morozov 2015: 63). Taken together, the existence of a thick but hierarchically organized normative order within which Russia and other latecomers to the international society are placed on the receiving end of European and transatlantic politics is at variance with the realist conceptualization of the international realm as the one in which self-interested "like" units are motivated by fear and uncertainty to ensure their own survival under the conditions of anarchy.

How would such normative rather than material systemic constraints translate into a meaning attached to the other two key realist concepts— security and power? The much-discussed "securitization of identity" (Morozov 2009: 346–358) as part of Russia's present-day hegemonic articulation is captured better by the ontological security rather than by the realist argument. Similarly, power has been reconsidered along normative lines in the Russian foreign policy discourse, so that being a "separate civilization" (Curanović 2017: 98) or a "state-civilization" (Tsygankov 2016) is considered an indispensable attribute of being a major power. After all, the status of a civilization is strategically important because these are civilizations rather than states that are the main contenders in the global rivalry in the twenty-first century (Curanović 2017: 98). In practical political terms this means being able to express Russia's civilizational distinctiveness in the language of traditional/ Orthodox values that, at least superficially, have native Russian rather than European origins in order to "attack and revise the core of Western 'soft power' – the human rights doctrine" (Suslov 2017: 65). All in all, as the above discussion shows, conceptual tools from the realist toolkit are either irrelevant or have been imbued with different meanings in the Russian foreign policy discourse.

Subsequently, applying a poststructuralist understanding of hegemony to the analysis of Russian post-Soviet foreign policy discourse appears to be a more promising venue of research because it can shed new light on Russia's perennial oscillation throughout its history between Westernization and anti-Westernism, between identification with and alienation from the West. A possible answer would be that both positions easily assume the form of hegemonic articulations that denigrate and oust from collective memory particular historical experiences that can be considered formative for states such as Russia that were socialized into the European normative hegemony relatively late. Thus, the liberal-minded foreign policy elites would regard their state's imperial past as its 'other' that has to be confessed and left behind. The patriotic opposition, by contrast, would confine to the realm of otherness the many failed attempts at Westernization that the country has undertaken. In a nutshell, the national conceptual landscape would converge around the two—liberal hegemonic and national-patriotic counter-hegemonic—positions because they provide a solution, no matter how superficial or short-lived, to the problems of political order and ontological security.

REFERENCES

Astrov, Alexander, and Natalia Morozova. 2012. "Russia: Geopolitics from the Heartland." In *The Return of Geopolitics in Europe? Social Mechanisms and Foreign Policy Identity Crises*, edited by Stefano Guzzini. Cambridge: Cambridge University Press.

Curanović, Alicja. 2017. "Religion and Human Rights in Russia's Foreign Policy." In *Shifting Power and Human Rights Diplomacy: Russia*, edited by Doutje Lettinga and Lars van Troost. Amsterdam: Amnesty International.

Della Sala, Vincent. 2017. "Homeland Security: Territorial Myths and Ontological Security in the European Union." *Journal of European Integration* 39 (5): 545–558.

Guzzini, Stefano. 2012. "The Framework of Analysis: Geopolitics Meets Foreign Policy Identity Crises." In *The Return of Geopolitics in Europe? Social Mechanisms and Foreign Policy Identity Crises*, edited by Stefano Guzzini. Cambridge: Cambridge University Press.

Hansen, Flemming S. 2016. "Russia's Relations with the West: Ontological Security Through Conflict." *Contemporary Politics* 22 (3): 359–375.

Hansen, Lene. 2006. *Security as Practice: Discourse Analysis and the Bosnian War*. London and New York: Routledge.

Kozyrev, Andrei. 1992. "A Transformed Russia in a New World." *International Affairs (Moscow)* 38 (4): 85–91.

Laclau, Ernesto, and Chantal Mouffe. 1987. *Hegemony and Socialist Strategy: Towards a Radical Democratic Politics*, 2nd ed. London and New York: Verso.

Lo, Bobo. 2002. *Russian Foreign Policy in the Post-Soviet Era: Reality, Illusion and Mythmaking*. London: Palgrave Macmillan.

Lukin, Vladimir. 1992. "A Transformed Russia in a New World." *International Affairs (Moscow)* 38 (4): 91–94.

Mearsheimer, John. 1995. "The False Promise of International Institutions." *International Security* 19 (3): 5–49.

Mitzen, Jennifer. 2006. "Ontological Security in World Politics: State Identity and the Security Dilemma." *European Journal of International Relations* 12 (3): 341–370.

Morozova, Natalia. 2009. "Geopolitics, Eurasianism and Russian Foreign Policy Under Putin." *Geopolitics* 14 (4): 667–686.

———. 2015. "Vneshnyaia Politika kak Diskursivnaia Praktika: K Voprosu o Konstruirovanii Politicheskogo Soobschestva [Foreign Policy as a Discursive Practice: On the Question of the Constitution of a Political Community]." *Politicheskaia Lingvistika* 53 (3): 140–147.

Morozov, Viatcheslav. 2009. *Rossiya i Drugie: Identichnost' i Granitsy Politicheskogo Soobschestva* [Russia and Its Others: Identity and the Boundaries of a Political Community]. Moscow: Novoe Literaturnoe Obozrenie.

———. 2015. *Russia's Postcolonial Identity: A Subaltern Empire in a Eurocentric World*. London: Palgrave Macmillan.

Neumann, Iver B. 1997. "The Geopolitics of Delineating 'Russia' and 'Europe': The Creation of the 'Other' in the European and Russian Tradition." In *Geopolitics in Post-Wall Europe: Security, Territory and Identity*, edited by Ola Tunander, Pavel Baev, and Victoria Ingrid Einagel. London: Sage.

———. 2002. "From the USSR to Gorbachev to Putin: Perestroika as a Failed Excursion from the 'West' to 'Europe' in Russian Discourse." In *The Meaning of Europe: Variety and Contention Within and Among Nations*, edited by Mikael Malmborg and Bö Strath. Oxford and New York: Berg.

Primakov, Yvgeny. 1992. "A Transformed Russia in a New World." *International Affairs (Moscow)* 38 (4): 94–98.

Steele, Brent J. 2005. "Ontological Security and the Power of Self-identity: British Neutrality and the American Civil War." *Review of International Studies* 31 (3): 519–540.

———. 2008. *Ontological Security in International Relations: Self-Identity and the IR State*. London and New York: Routledge.

Subotic, Jelena. 2016. "Narrative, Ontological Security, and Foreign Policy Change." *Foreign Policy Analysis* 12: 610–627.

Suslov, Mikhail. 2017. "Framing and Foreign Policy: Russian Media Control and Human Rights." In *Shifting Power and Human Rights Diplomacy: Russia*, edited by Doutje Lettinga and Lars van Troost. Amsterdam: Amnesty International.

Tsygankov, Andrei. 2008. *Vneshnyaia Politika Rossii ot Gorbacheva do Putina: Formirovanie Natsional'nogo Interesa* [Russian Foreign Policy from Gorbachev to Putin: The Formation of National Interest]. Moscow: Nauchnaia Kniga.

———. 2016. "Crafting the State-Civilization: Vladimir Putin's Turn to Distinct Values." *Problems of Post-Communism* 63 (3): 1–13.

Tsygankov, Pavel. 1994. "Geopolitika: Poslednee Pribezhische Razuma? [Geopolitics: The Last Resort of Reason?]." *Voprosy Filosofii* 7–8: 59–71.

Waltz, Kenneth. 1979. *Theory of International Politics*. New York: McGraw-Hill.

Wæver, Ole. 2002. "Identity, Communities and Foreign Policy: Discourse Analysis as Foreign Policy Theory." In *European Integration and National Identity*, edited by Lene Hansen and Ole Wæver, 20–49. London: Routledge.

Zarakol, Ayşe. 2011. *After Defeat: How the East Learned to Live With the West*. Cambridge: Cambridge University Press.

Zhirinovsky, Vladimir. 1997. *Ocherki po Geopolitike* [Essays on Geopolitics]. Moscow and Pskov: Liberal'no-Demokraticheskaia Partiia.

Zyuganov, Gennady. 1995. *Rossiia i Sovremenniy Mir* [Russia and Today's World]. Moscow: Informpechat'.

———. 1997. *Geografiia Pobedy: Osnovy Rossiiskoi Geopolitiki* [Geography of Victory: The Fundamentals of Russian Geopolitics]. Moscow: Partiinaia Pechat' KPRF.

CHAPTER 9

Man vs. the System: Turkish Foreign Policy After the Arab Uprisings

Özgür Özdamar and Balkan Devlen

This chapter examines Turkish foreign policy toward the Arab uprisings during the 2011–2015 period from a neoclassical realist approach.[1] Turkey's foreign policy towards the Middle East during this period can be characterized as an ambitious attempt to establish itself as a regional hegemon and, as explained below, be the "order-maker" in the region. It represents an important discontinuity with the traditional Turkish policy of moderation towards the region, both in terms of means and ends, that emphasizes collaboration with regional and global powers, opposing

---

[1] For neoclassical realism as an approach rather than a theory, see Donnelly in this volume.

Ö. Özdamar (✉)
Bilkent University, Ankara, Turkey
e-mail: ozgur@bilkent.edu.tr

B. Devlen
University of Copenhagen, Copenhagen, Denmark
e-mail: balkan.devlen@ifs.ku.dk

© The Author(s) 2019   177
R. Belloni et al. (eds.), *Fear and Uncertainty in Europe*, Global Issues,
https://doi.org/10.1007/978-3-319-91965-2_9

separatism, irredentism, and regime change and emphasizing territorial integrity and regime stability in the region. Turkey has been a status quo power in the Middle East since the establishment of the Republic in 1923. This was true for the Justice and Development Party's (AKP) initial tenure from 2002 up until mid-2009, when Ahmet Davutoğlu became Foreign Minister as well. Starting from late 2009, Turkish foreign policy became more assertive and active with an eye towards reshaping the regional order and, with the start of Syrian uprising in 2011, the transformation of Turkish foreign policy became clear. Turkey's military and economic power did not change in any meaningful way during this period, nor did the regional balance of power shift significantly. In other words, structural factors cannot explain this significant discontinuity in Turkish foreign policy. A neoclassical realist approach that brings in the individual and domestic variables into the analysis, on the other hand, can help us explain this puzzle.

Neoclassical realism (NCR) assumes that the leaders' beliefs about the international system, domestic political calculations, and domestic political institutions have a significant role in shaping states' foreign policies. While they acknowledge neorealism's assumptions that systemic pressures constrain actors in world politics, neoclassical realists argue that it is necessary to examine the impact of political, institutional, and bureaucratic factors within states and cognitive processes of decision makers in order to understand foreign policy. In this sense, neoclassical realism bridges the gap between International Relations (IR) and foreign policy analysis (FPA) along with decision-making theories. As Turkey is a middle power in the international system, it is important to understand individual (perceptions, beliefs, heuristics, analogies, cultural references) and domestic (public opinion, electoral processes, and Turkey's own ethno-religious structure) variables in order to grasp Turkish decision makers' policy toward the region. It is impossible to explain tensions derived from the asymmetries between the roles and motivations prescribed by the state's leaders and the state's actual capabilities by examining only systemic factors. In this context, explanations regarding domestic politics and beliefs of leadership become important. Examining how Turkish decision makers reach specific decisions through interpreting structural pressures and their state's role in the region, and how they synthesize these elements, with the necessities of domestic politics, will contribute to an explanation of the decisions that seem unintelligible at a first glance.

Neoclassical Realism and Foreign Policy[2]

Gideon Rose, who coined the term "neoclassical realism" in a 1998 *World Politics* article, argues that neoclassical realism:

> [E]xplicitly incorporates both external and internal variables, updating and systematizing certain insights drawn from classical realist thought. Its adherents argue that the scope and ambition of a country's foreign policy is driven first and foremost by its place in the international system and specifically by its relative material power capabilities. This is why they are realist. They argue further, however, that the impact of such power capabilities on foreign policy is indirect and complex, because systemic pressures must be translated through intervening variables at the unit level. This is why they are neoclassical. (Rose 1998: 152)

Neoclassical realists thus aim to analyze the workings of systemic pressures and unit-level variables such as domestic political structures and decision makers' perceptions as influences on a nation's foreign policy. Works by Randall Schweller (1998, 2004), Fareed Zakaria (1998), Thomas Christensen (1996), Jack Snyder (1993), William Wohlforth (1993), and Aaron Friedberg (1988) all posit that, "systemic pressures are filtered through intervening domestic variables to produce foreign policy behavior" (Schweller 2004: 164). Thus, neoclassical realism provides a comprehensive framework to analyze the foreign policy behavior of states. However, as a general approach it is underspecified for purposes of applied analysis, particularly as to: (1) how the ideas of leaders affect their behavior; (2) how these ideas can be operationalized; and (3) which domestic factors affect leaders' assessments of foreign policy challenges. In addition, although in the long run relative power capabilities may determine foreign policy outcomes, foreign policy behavior may not reflect those underlying structural constraints in the short term. As a result, relative power may not be a good predictor of foreign policy behavior in the short to medium term. To address this problem, role theory (Holsti 1970) will be used as a systematic way of analyzing the relevant ideas of political leaders since it argues that the way leaders perceive the position of both their own states and other states and the roles they ascribe to their states are highly influential in their foreign policy behavior.

---

[2] Adapted from Devlen and Ozdamar (2009).

Our argument is based on neoclassical realist foundations in the following three ways. First, as an explanation of foreign policy behavior, it clearly falls outside the purview of structural theorizing (e.g., Waltzian neorealism, offensive realism), which concerns itself with "pattern[s] of outcomes of state interactions" (Rose 1998: 145). Waltz (1979; Keohane and Waltz 1986) clearly posits that his theory is not (and indeed cannot be) a theory of foreign policy. By contrast, much neoclassical realist theorizing is explicitly concerned with how states respond to changes in their relative power positions (Rose 1998: 154). Thus, neoclassical realism explicitly theorizes foreign policy behavior and enters into the realm of foreign policy analysis. Second, as pointed out by Rose (1998) and Schweller (2004), neoclassical realism brings the political leader back in. The neoclassical realist focus on the perceptions of political elites regarding the international system places agency squarely in the center of analysis, in contrast to structural theories in which such a focus on agency is consciously omitted. Our argument centers on the political leader and the leader's beliefs about the international system and domestic political calculations. In this sense, it makes the neoclassical realist choice of bringing the state leaders back in more explicit. Lastly, neoclassical realism, in contrast with structural versions of realism, takes seriously the impact of domestic structures in explaining foreign policy choices. We emphasize that political leaders are constrained by both domestic political concerns and their leadership roles and styles when choosing among different policy options during crises.

In line with neoclassical realist theorizing (Rose 1998: 147), we suggest that the position of the state in the international system defines the boundaries of the possible range of policies it can adopt in the long term. States' relative power constrains what they can do. Their placement within the distribution of power also shapes, in the long run, the interests and aspirations of states; for example, ascending states have different aims than declining states. During system transitions, when polarity changes, states try to adjust themselves to the newly emerging structure. Revisionist states might try to exploit the uncertain nature of the distribution of power or the distraction of the great powers during such times. While system-wide changes, such as one in system polarity, are occurring, it becomes more difficult to gauge "objective" systemic constraints. Therefore, leaders in these situations are more likely to rely on their beliefs about systemic effects, which may or may not reflect the actual distribution of power within the international system and the availability of a great-power patron or regional ally. The leader's perceptions of the international system and the nature of the adversary can distort the picture presented by the objective distribution of power.

Furthermore, the existence (or lack) of domestic political constraints also shapes how the leader chooses to respond to systemic pressures. If these individual- and unit-level factors lead to policy choices that are not in line with the actual capabilities of the state, then the systemic pressures could eventually result in a corrective reaction that would bring the foreign policy back in line with the necessities of the distribution of power. In other words, while the individual- and unit-level factors can lead to foreign policy *behaviour* that is not in line with systemic imperatives in the short to medium term, power—particularly the distribution of material power—will eventually determine the foreign policy *outcome*.

Turkish Foreign Policy Towards the Arab Uprisings

In this section we examine Turkish foreign policy towards the Arab uprisings, focusing on two important variables: the leadership's role conceptions and domestic political constraints. We argue that the neoclassical realist perspective gives us insight to understand both the reasons behind Turkey's "ambitious" foreign policy between 2011 and 2015 and why these policies were not as effective as hoped. At the outset of the Arab uprisings, Turkey attempted to behave like a classical middle power, particularly at the level of discourse. For instance, in the Libyan case in early 2011, it first adopted a cautious policy and expressed reservations about an international military intervention, but later changed tact and supported the NATO operation. Similarly, at the beginning of the so-called Arab Spring, Turkey leaned towards regime change in Tunisia and Egypt but soon after, faced by a quickly evolving regional political confrontation, it took responsibility for both Syria's regime change and the political survival of the Muslim Brotherhood in Egypt, while seeking to preserve and continue its bumpy relations with Israel, Iraq, and Iran.

Why did Turkey abandon its initial cautious foreign policy and seek to play a more assertive role in the Middle East? We argue that two variables (role conceptions of the leadership and domestic politics) provide insights for understanding how and why Turkey adopted this particular foreign policy approach during this period, which has since then been criticized for not being practical and pragmatic enough. With respect to role conceptions, Turkey during Ahmet Davutoğlu's Foreign Ministry

(2009–2014) sought to go beyond its material capacity (including military and intelligence). Davutoğlu criticized previous foreign ministers for not using Turkey's capacity in full while claiming that he was the first political leader to do so (Zaman 2011; Milliyet 2010). As a middle power in the international system, Turkey's claim to be the "central country" and "regional leader" and adopting policies according to these roles were two obvious signs of this self-perception (Özdamar 2014). In other words, Turkish leadership during the period after 2011 overestimated Turkey's capacity, capabilities, and position within the international system and that had significant consequences for Turkish foreign policy.

The second variable is the *lack* of domestic political constraints. In this respect, the unusual freedom of movement the AKP enjoyed in terms of foreign policy and national security and the absence of an effective domestic political opposition contributed to the non-traditional, ambitious foreign policy. The power of the bureaucracy was highly restricted as a result of the AKP's long reign since 2002. The impact of bureaucratic groups, which were traditionally involved in Turkish foreign policy making and imposed their own preferences on civil officials, has been to a large extent reduced. The AKP and its leader Recep Tayyip Erdoğan's uninterrupted and overwhelming successes in elections, unprecedented in the history of the Turkish Republic, have practically eliminated the impact of opposition parties on foreign policy. Turkey's involvement in the Arab uprising and regional politics has been possible thanks to the marginalization of bureaucratic groups such as the National Security Council (NSC) and the Foreign Ministry, which used to have direct impact on foreign policy, as well as the incompetence of opposition parties.

From "Mediator" to "Rule Maker"[3]

The AKP was more or less committed to Turkey's traditional global and regional roles during the 2002–2009 period (Onis and Yilmaz 2005, 2009; Onis 2011). From the perspective of role theory, in this period Turkish foreign policy adopted the roles of "global and regional

---

[3] This discussion has been adapted from Özdamar (2014) and Özdamar et al. (2014).

collaborator" and "balancer".[4] Moreover, it is remarkable that it also adopted the roles of "mediator" and "bridge between Islam and Christian civilizations" (Özdamar 2014).[5] With its moderate approach, Turkish foreign policy was widely appreciated by Middle Eastern and North African (MENA) governments, the European Union, and the United States. Foreign policy during this period was also generally supported by the domestic public and it was not a divisive issue in domestic politics. This foreign policy approach gradually changed after Israel's "Operation Cast Lead" against targets in Gaza, which started in December 2008 and after which Turkey's relations with several regional actors visibly began to deteriorate (Onis 2011).

When AKP's decision makers started to criticize Israel's Gaza operations in December 2008, they had been in power on their own for more than six years. Within this period, the party adopted a moderate and domestically endorsed foreign policy in order to gain legitimacy as a new party. Internationally, it gained popularity by developing relations with MENA countries, re-vitalizing prospective EU membership and maintaining friendly relations with the US and NATO. On balance, Turkish foreign policy during the AKP period had been globally appreciated as a rather successful example of a middle power being influential on both regional and global levels. Although some analysts argued that the party did not abandon its Islamic roots in foreign and domestic politics, other observers pointed out that the AKP's foreign policy was not ideological during the 2002–2009 period (Özdamar et al. 2014).

In this period, in addition to maintaining its traditional role as a "collaborator" and a "balancer" (Özdamar 2014), the AKP's leadership was interested in developing Turkey's ties with Middle Eastern countries and to adopt a leadership role in the region. However, in contrast to continuing traditional roles with little domestic opposition, some of the AKP's new roles in the MENA region provoked a reaction from institutions

---

[4]We use Holsti's (1970) descriptions for foreign policy roles such as "balancer" and "global and regional collaborator" unless otherwise stated. "Balancer" for example refers to states that aim to maintain regional or global balance of power. "Global and regional collaborator" refers to "far-reaching commitments to cooperative efforts with other states to build wider communities, or to cross-cutting subsystems..." (Holsti 1970: 266).

[5]In general, "bridge" role refers to "acting as a 'translator' or conveyor of messages and information between peoples of different culture" (Holsti 1970: 267). For Turkey as a bridge between different civilizations and faiths see Yanik (2009).

such as the National Security Council, where military officers influence foreign policy decisions and the judicial order. In other words, during the first years of their tenure the AKP leadership wanted to develop closer relations with Muslim-majority states and adopt a leadership role in the Middle East. However its adoption of these roles had been limited until 2009 due to opposition from state institutions such as the military and the foreign ministry bureaucracy. Until 2008, Turkey was quite successful in having close cooperative relations with Israel, Iran, Syria, Egypt, Libya, Tunisia, and Saudi Arabia. Considering the regional problems and historical relations and animosities, this was an unprecedented situation and success. Five years later, Turkey, seeking to assert its leadership role and having assumed a controversial position regarding the Arab Spring, cut diplomatic relations with Israel, Syria, and Egypt and it encountered critical problems with Saudi Arabia and Iran. This significant change in Turkish foreign policy was made possible by the gradual disappearance of local resistance towards the AKP's newly adopted roles during the 2002–2009 period which, in turn, empowered decision makers to adopt new roles.

A turning point in Turkish foreign policy occurred with Turkey's harsh criticisms towards Israel's Gaza attacks. The AKP government had previously maintained friendly relations with Israel, which continued until "Operation Cast Lead" started in December 2008. This was after the Israeli President, Shimon Peres, gave a speech in the Turkish parliament the previous month, the first given by an Israeli president in the parliament of a Muslim majority country. Prime Minister Erdoğan also maintained friendly relations with the Jewish community in the United States and in 2005 earned a prestigious prize from the Anti-Defamation League in New York.

As a part of its mediator role, Turkey sought to continue negotiations between Israel and Syria regarding the Golan Heights. Israel's attacks on civilian targets in Gaza were harshly criticized by the AKP government at precisely the peak of the negotiations (and, according to Turkish officials, while they were about to reach a solution on the Golan question). Prime Minister Erdoğan's dispute with the Israeli president about the Gaza attacks became public in front of the international press at World Economic Forum in Davos in 2009 and relations deteriorated further. In May 2010, Turkish-Israeli relations came to the breaking point after an Israeli commando raided the Gaza flotilla organized by international activists whose majority were Turks and which led to the killing of nine

Turkish citizens, leading to an unprecedented decline in Turkish-Israeli relations. Turkish decision makers, in competition in many areas with Israel, sought to adopt a new role and identified Turkey as the "protector of the oppressed" in the region (Özdamar 2014). Prime Minister Erdoğan and Foreign Minister Ahmet Davutoğlu reemphasized Turkey's mission to protect Palestinians against Israeli attacks and stated that, in addition to protecting Palestinians, Turkey would also protect all oppressed people in the region.

Turkey's escalating disputes with Israel increased Prime Minister Erdoğan's popularity and the Turkish government in the Arab world. Turkey's popularity in the region reached its peak during the 2009–2012 period. For instance, an opinion poll conducted by TESEV in 2012 demonstrates that Turkey was the most popular country in the MENA region garnering 78% positive responses from participants from 16 countries (TESEV 2012). However, simultaneously, the AKP officers, who achieved popularity in the region, lost their good relations with several regional countries after the outbreak of the Arab uprisings in 2011 and onwards.

Turkey was caught unprepared by the Arab uprisings and Ankara initially maintained a low profile about the events. This initial stance quickly evolved towards a more assertive foreign policy stance. For example, Turkey was initially opposed to NATO's Libya operation (BBC 2011), but then it changed its attitude and adopted an active role in the 2011 NATO operation that aimed at bringing about regime change to Libya. Turkey also supported regime changes in Egypt, Tunisia, and Syria.

At the outset of the Syrian civil war in 2011, the Turkish government sought to use its influence on Syrian President Assad to find a peaceful solution to the uprisings. Once these efforts proved futile and the civil war escalated, the Turkish government supported the rebels in Syria as a part of its ambition to affirm Turkey's "regional leader" role. After autumn 2011, Turkey gave political and diplomatic support to the rebels and openly adopted a position against the Assad regime. Many independent sources have claimed that Turkey also provided economic and military support to some opposition groups (Taşpınar 2012; Ayata 2014). During an interview with the Japanese newspaper *Nikkei*, the then president Abdullah Gül stated that Turkey's course of action in the region was compatible with Turkey's "regional leadership" role (Gül 2011). Regarding Turkey's support of regime change, Turkish officials identified this support as part of expectations derived from the country's "protector of the oppressed" role, which was also invoked in its relation with Israel. Similarly, another new role, the "leader of Muslim world", required Turkey to take action against persecution of Muslims in Syria (Özdamar 2014). For instance, during his presidential campaign in 2014, Erdoğan repeatedly stated that Turkey had a duty to take sides with the oppressed people of the Middle East, by which he referred to the people of Iraq, Syria, and Gaza (Erdoğan 2014).

When the main opposition party asked whether Turkey had really the mission to protect Syrian people against their government, Foreign Minister Ahmet Davutoğlu claimed that the question showed a lack of understanding of Turkey's "rule maker" and "central/pivotal country" roles in the region (Özdamar 2014). The claim of being "rule maker" in the region was reemphasized within the context of the Arab uprisings during Davutoğlu's visit to Brussels for the NATO summit in 2012 and his visit to Paris for the meeting of Friends of Syria Group (*24Haber* 2012). Davutoğlu's willingness for Turkey to this role in the region was confirmed by his active efforts to organize the first meeting of Friends of Syria Group in Istanbul.

Similarly, Turkey's critical position vis-à-vis the military coup in Egypt that overthrew President Mohammed Morsi in 2013 can be explained by its newly adopted roles. After the cases of Tunisia and Libya where regime change easily took place, the AKP believed that the Arab uprisings and subsequent regime change could create more friendly governments in the MENA region. Indeed, in several MENA countries political parties like the Muslim Brotherhood of Egypt, who were ideologically close to the AKP, were the most influential alternative to existing regimes. Even though the AKP located itself in the center right of the political spectrum, the main founders of the party are political Islamists who are ideologically close to the Muslim Brotherhood. The AKP, seeing the Arab uprisings as an opportunity to create friendlier MENA states, operated to bring Mohammed Morsi and the Muslim Brotherhood back to power. Prime Minister Erdoğan and Foreign Minister Davutoğlu harshly criticized the subsequent military coup in Egypt. During the summer 2013 they took action to start large-scale protest movements against the coup and criticized the hypocrisy of the West regarding Egypt. Similar to the Syrian case, the government stated that Turkey's involvement in the events was derived from its "regional leader" role that created a specific responsibility to protect oppressed Muslims and its "central country" role (Özdamar 2014).

Turkey's relations with other neighbors quickly worsened. Its dealings with Iran deteriorated due to Turkey's anti-Assad stance; relations with the central government of Iraq suffered due to Turkey's close cooperation with the Kurdistan regional government in the oil sector; the Turkey-Lebanon interactions worsened due to Turkey's involvement in the Syrian civil war; and its relations with Saudi Arabia deteriorated due to Turkey's major support to the Muslim Brotherhood in Egypt. In a nutshell, the only actors with whom Turkey had friendly relations by 2015 were Qatar, Gaza Strip leaders, and the Kurdish regional government. Turkey's relatively successful foreign policy in 2009 was transformed into "precious loneliness" by 2015 (Gardner 2015).

Accordingly, Turkey's policies towards the MENA states in the aftermath of the Arab Spring deviated from neorealism's expectation about a middle power's behavior in the international system. From this perspective, Turkey was supposed to pursue a moderate foreign policy and instead, despite its limited material power, pursued a maximalist policy. The underlying causes of this policy, as explained above, were found in the leaders' role conceptions regarding their country such as the "central country", "regional leader", "leader of Islamic world", and "protector of the oppressed" (Özdamar 2014). With respect to these roles, the leadership in Turkey identified a power-vacuum in the international system and aimed to fill it. Turkey's attitude in the Arab uprisings reflected its self-perception as a country that deemed itself suitable for leadership and ready to fill the gap created by the EU, US, and Russia. This attracted criticism, both domestic and foreign, since it was argued that Turkey sought to perform the tasks that it could not actually accomplish as a middle power (Özdamar 2014). It also demonstrated that countries do not always adopt policies that are compatible with their real position in the international system, especially in the short term. In sum, Turkey's attitude regarding the Arab uprisings was directly related to Turkey's expected leadership roles, which exceeded its material capacity and the political, economic, military constraints that emerge during the realization of these roles.

Domestic Debates About Turkey's MENA Policy

The AKP's relative autonomy in domestic politics brought about both foreign policy freedom and contestation over the policy regarding the Arab uprisings. More precisely, Turkey's deteriorating relations in the region led to acrimonious debates in the country, since domestic disagreement regarding the country's roles in the region became increasingly pronounced. It would not be wrong to say that foreign policy debates during the Arab uprisings represented one of the greatest debates—perhaps the greatest one—regarding foreign policy in Turkey's history. In the past, especially during the Cold War period, many foreign policy issues in Turkey led, to a great extent, to consistency and consensus in the country. Even the most contentious issues, such as the situation in Cyprus, did not cause such a polarization and escalation at the discoursive level. Turkey's foreign policy and related debates regarding its roles in the region became daily political material in the country during the 2011–2015 period. However, all of this domestic contestation failed to constrain or limit the AKP's foreign policy ambitions (Özdamar 2016).

Why did Turkey's foreign policy decision making, which used to be associated with consensus and moderation, experience such a radical change? In order to find the answer to this question, it is crucial to examine domestic political developments in the last decade. The AKP's arrival to power at the end of 2002 was an unprecedented success story for Turkey. The AKP benefited from the weakening of secular parties and economic and political crises that had occurred in 2000–2001 and gained almost two-thirds of the seats in parliament. However, its election success did not immediately allow the AKP to pursue its agenda unrestrained by other political forces. The AKP's first years in power are identified as a conflictual period with Turkey's old order. New elected officials had difficulties while applying their own preferences to foreign policy. From time to time, the Turkish Armed Forces (TAF) interfered in foreign policy and became influential via the National Security Council. The Ministry of Foreign Affairs continued to have its pro-Western foreign policy stance guide policy (Özdamar 2016).

The change in the National Security Council's legal status made it easier for the AKP to pursue its independent agenda derived from non-traditional foreign policy roles for Turkey. By the 2000s, Turkey had formally put into effect many EU harmonization packages, including regulations about the TAF's position in the political system (Onis and Yilmaz 2005). In particular, the seventh harmonization package, which came into effect in June 2003, changed the NSC's formation in such a way that the number of civilian members would exceed the number of military members (Tocci 2005; Secretary General of EU Relations 2007). From 2003 to 2007, the effect of the TAF on the political system decreased due to many reforms. This period also witnessed domestic contention and debate about several issues including secularism and civil-military relations. After 2009, many members of the military were imprisoned on the grounds that they planned a "coup against the government", which had been an untried offence in Turkey. In 2010, the government changed the constitution by winning 58% of the votes in the referendum and, after this date, the judiciary has been increasingly under the influence of the executive power. In the 2011 elections, the AKP won 49.95% of the votes cast, becoming the first party to be in power for three electoral mandates. National and international observers have since claimed that the situation with respect to many democratic standards, including judicial independence, freedom of expression and political rights, has worsened. From the perspective of the AKP, constitutional reforms ensured that two traditional and powerful rivals, the TAF and the judiciary, had come under democratic control as in Western liberal democracies (Özdamar 2016).

During this period, other traditional power centers sided with the AKP. President Abdullah Gül, one of the oldest founders of the AKP, had worked in great harmony with Prime Minister Erdoğan from the time of the party's founding. Gül never objected to any of the government's foreign policy initiatives during his seven-year presidency. In addition, intra-party opposition to the governing leadership of a party has always been weak in post-1980 Turkish political life, with all of the political parties under the control of very powerful party leaders. However, there were always debates within parties regarding critical issues that mostly took place among influential party members behind closed doors. After senior government officials (including Cemil Çiçek, Abdüllatif Şener, and Dengir Fırat) quit the AKP, alternative voices to the top-level leadership's preferences were gone. For this reason, foreign policy had no strong opposition within the AKP itself.

All of these domestic developments demonstrate that while changing its MENA policy, the Turkish government restrained the influence of almost all domestic actors who were previously politically and legally powerful on foreign policy. As of the beginning of 2010, all actors who traditionally had an impact on foreign policy issues had been replaced by the AKP's leadership. Apart from the advisers in the inner circle of the Prime Minister, other actors could not seriously affect foreign policy. The full hegemony of the AKP, which has been achieved in Turkish political life, paved the way for Turkey's foreign policy initiatives in the

MENA region. The AKP has created the necessary conditions to adopt a set of new roles regarding foreign policy in a political environment where none of the traditional agents (including the bureaucracy of the Foreign Ministry, the TAF, the NSC, judiciary, media, business organizations, and universities) were powerful enough to express their concerns.

The greatest opposition to the AKP's foreign policy in this period came from three opposition parties: the Republican People's Party (CHP), the Nationalist Action Party (MHP), and the Peace and Democracy Party (BDP) (Özdamar 2016). However, their influence on foreign policy remained limited and did not have a significant impact. The AKP did not have difficulty in passing the law related to the use of force against Syria from 2013 to 2014, since it held a majority in the parliament.

The three opposition parties criticized Turkey's foreign policy in the MENA region during the 2010–2014 period. Despite their ideological differences, the CHP, MHP and BDP vigorously rejected Turkey's "regional leader" or "central country" roles (Radikal 2014). The leaders of the three opposition parties argued that these assertive roles exceeded Turkey's capacity and put Turkey in a difficult position since they were related with the Syrian civil war and the Arab uprisings. Furthermore, all members of these opposition parties rejected the roles of the "protector of the oppressed" or "leader of Muslim world" and they claimed that the AKP used these roles to support ideologically close Islamist parties such as the Muslim Brotherhood, etc. At the elite level, the roles of "central country" and "regional leader" have been most contested among all the roles that were discussed in this period (Özdamar 2016). The consequences of role struggles regarding Turkey's foreign policy in the MENA region were minimal due to the specific domestic conditions mentioned above. In other words, the executive power has been so overwhelming that any tangible impact of opposition parties on the foreign policy was impossible.

Prime Minister Erdoğan and the ruling elite used the foreign policy discourse as an effective domestic policy tool. In other words, the discourse aiming to constitute strong roles in foreign policy was also addressed to the local audience that preferred to have a higher profile and more active foreign policy. According to Onis (2011: 49), "there is no doubt that the new-style foreign policy activism has helped enhance the popularity of the [AKP] in domestic politics". Considering Erdoğan's emphasis on foreign policy issues during the presidential election campaigns in August 2014, it can be said that the roles of "regional leader" or "central country" helped enhance the his popularity among conservative constituents. The surveys conducted throughout Turkey demonstrate that while the majority of AKP voters confirmed their backing of the AKP's foreign policy, supporters of the three opposition parties, despite their ideological differences, did not deem Turkey's foreign policy as a success.

Foreign actors were the only powerful actors that could have an impact on Turkey's top leadership regarding the Syrian civil war. After the Obama administration decided not to intervene militarily in Syria in 2013 despite its initial consensus with Turkey on overthrowing Assad, the Turkish government was reported to experience a big disappointment. In the summer of 2013 then Prime Minister Erdoğan was in favor of an extensive military operation against the Assad government similar to the Kosovo intervention, rather than a limited operation (*Hürriyet Daily News* 2013). It is likely that strong opposition from Russia and the United States prevented a Turkish military operation against Assad in 2013 and 2014.

The possibility of pursuing a more active policy in the whole Middle Eastern region and of working with ideologically close governments has transformed Turkey's cautious policies, which were observed at the beginning of the Arab uprisings and has led to riskier moves after 2011. In this period, the country's role in the region, which was envisioned by the leadership, reached its peak and, accordingly, foreign policy moves became increasingly more daring and costly. After friendly regimes started to lose power in Egypt and Syria, the Turkish government initially double downed but by mid-2015 it became obvious that the roles Turkey had adopted for itself failed to produce the desired outcomes in the region.

Conclusion

Turkey's foreign policy towards the Arab uprisings cannot be understood without comprehending the revolutionary changes in Turkish domestic politics that occurred since the early 2000s. The AKP, which defeated its traditional rivals in domestic politics, found a suitable environment for pursuing a bold foreign policy and imposing its own preferences. Accordingly, it adopted an overly ambitious foreign policy beyond its material capacity in order to realize the foreign policy roles of a "central country" and "regional leader". Even though there has been domestic contestation, AKP was able to project its preferences onto the foreign policy realm. Thus, in contrast to neorealism's expectation about the policies of a middle power in the international system, Turkey's policy towards the Arab Spring can be explained with neoclassical realism, which shows the importance of how decision makers perceive their country's position in the international balance of power and to what extent domestic factors can be highly influential in the realization of the roles determined by the country's position.

In this chapter we focused on foreign policy *behaviour*, rather than foreign policy *outcomes*. Neoclassical realism enables us to understand and explain the choices made by Turkish foreign policy makers both on the eve of the Arab uprisings and immediately after these events as it stresses the impact of domestic politics and individual level factors on foreign policy. But neoclassical realists also point out that in the long run, foreign policy outcomes are largely determined by structural factors. In other words, in the short to medium term domestic politics and leaders' beliefs might shape and determine the choices made by foreign policy makers but the outcome of those choices in the long term will be a function of structural factors, particularly the distribution of power. Foreign policy behavior that does not reflect the actual capabilities and distribution of power are unlikely to produce the desired outcomes. States that do not follow structural imperatives are generally punished and forced to bring their policies in line with the realities of distribution of power.

Systemic factors prevailed after the five-year-long autonomous foreign policy period and Turkey inevitably had to return to its earlier middle-power policies. This did not happen because domestic political constraints re-emerged. If anything, since the constitutional referendum in April 2017 that paved the way for a presidential system, the government is even more unencumbered and unconstrained by domestic politics. The perception of key Turkish policymakers regarding Turkey's role in the region did not change significantly either. What has changed is the ability of Turkey to continue a policy that does not align with its power capabilities. Extra-regional great powers re-asserted themselves in the region. After Russia intervened in Syria to defend the Assad regime in September 2015 and the US-Russian cease-fire agreement in 2017, the chances of Turkey benefitting from the US military power and toppling Assad regime faded away. Failing to gain their support for its policy against the Assad regime and unable to change the power dynamics on the ground, Turkey had to return to a more limited foreign policy abandoning its over-ambitious policy of reshaping the region.

Acknowledgements This research was made possible by a TUBITAK (The Scientific and Technological Research Council of Turkey) grant (Number 112K169).

REFERENCES

Ayata, Bilgin. 2014. "Turkish Foreign Policy in a Changing Arab World: Rise and Fall of a Regional Actor?" *Journal of European Integration* 37 (1): 95–112.

Çakmak, Haydar. 2008. *Türk dış politikası, 1919–2008*. Ankara: Platin.

Christensen, Thomas J. 1996. *Useful Adversaries: Grand Strategy, Domestic Mobilization, and Sino-American Conflict, 1947–1958*. Princeton: Princeton University Press.

Davutoğlu, Ahmet. 2003. *Stratejik derinlik: Türkiye'nin uluslararası konumu*. Istanbul: Küre Yayınları.

"Davutoğlu: Masaya ilişenlerden değil kuranlardan olacağız." 2010. *Milliyet*, 21 May. http://www.milliyet.com.tr/davutoglu-masaya-ilisenlerden-degil-kuranlardan-olacagiz/siyaset/siyasetdetay/21.05.2010/1240909/default.htm. Accessed 10 September 2014.

"Davutoğlu: Türkiye Artık Yükselen Ilımlı Bir Güç." 2011. *Zaman*, 6 March. http://www.zaman.com.tr/ekonomi_davutoglu-turkiye-artik-yukselen-ilimli-bir-guc_1103284.html. Accessed 7 December 2014.

Devlen, Balkan, and Ozgur Ozdamar. 2009. "Neoclassical Realism and Foreign Policy Crises." In *Rethinking Realism in International Relations: Between Tradition and Innovation*, edited by Annette Freyberg-Inan, Ewan Harrison, and Patrick James. Baltimore, MD: John Hopkins University Press.

Erdoğan, Recep Tayyip. 2014. "Mazlumların Yanında Duruyoruz.-7 Ağustos 2014." *AK Parti Resmi İnternet Sayfası*. http://www.akparti.org.tr/mobil/haberler/tek-yurek-halinde-mazlumlarin-yanindayiz/65882. Accessed 9 September 2014.

Friedberg, Aaron L. 1988. *The Weary Titan: Britain and the Experience of Relative Decline, 1895–1905*. Princeton, NJ: Princeton University Press.

Gardner, David. 2015. "Turkey's Foreign Policy of 'Precious Loneliness'." *Financial Times*, 16 November. https://www.ft.com/content/69662b36–7752-11e5-a95a-27d368e1ddf7.

Gül, Abdullah. 2011. "Türkiye Bölgesel Lider Olarak Hareket Etmektedir." *Türkiye Cumhuriyeti Cumhurbaşkanlığı*, 8 August. http://www.tccb.gov.tr/

haberler/170/80436/turkiye-bolgesel-lider-olarak-hareket-etmektedir.html. Accessed 10 September 2014.

Holsti, K.J. 1970. "National Role Conceptions in the Study of Foreign Policy." *International Studies Quarterly* 14 (3): 233–309.

Keohane, Robert O., and Kenneth Waltz. 1986. *Neorealism and Its Critics.* New York: Columbia University Press.

"Libya: Turkey's Trouble with NATO and No-Fly Zone." 2011. *BBC,* 25 March. http://www.bbc.co.uk/news/world-africa-12864742. Accessed 5 September 2014.

"Mecliste Gergin Suriye Oturumu." *Radikal.* http://www.radikal.com.tr/politika/mecliste/gergin/suriye/oturumu-1086125. Accessed 7 December 2014.

Onis, Ziya. 2011. "Multiple Faces of 'New' Turkish Foreign Policy: Underlying Dynamics and Critique." *Insight Turkey* 13 (1): 47–65.

Onis, Ziya, and Suhnaz Yilmaz. 2005. "The Turkey-EU-US Triangle in Perspective: Transformation or Continuity?" *The Middle East Journal* 59 (2): 265–284.

Onis, Ziya, and Suhnaz Yilmaz. 2009. "Between Europeanization and Euro-Asianism: Foreign Policy Activism in Turkey During the AKP Era." *Turkish Studies* 10 (1): 7–24.

"Oyun kurucu olarak Türkiye." 2012. *24Haber Portalı,* 21 April. http://www.yirmidorthaber.com/yazar/Oyun_kurucu_olarak_Turkiye/haber-548888. Accessed 10 September 2014.

Özdamar, Özgür. 2014. "Türkiye'nin Dış Politika Rolleri: Ampirik Bir Yaklaşım." TÜBİTAK SOBAG Proje No: 112K163, Bitirme Raporu.

Özdamar, Özgür. 2016. "Domestic Sources of Changing Turkish Foreign Policy towards the MENA During 2010s: A Role Theoretic Approach." In *Domestic Role Contestation, Foreign Policy, and International Relations,* edited by Christian Cantir and Juliet Kaarbo. New York and London: Routledge.

Özdamar, Özgür, B. Toygar Halistoprak, and İ. Erkam Sula. 2014. "From Good Neighbor to Model: Turkey's Changing Roles in the Middle East in the Aftermath of the Arab Spring." *Uluslararası İlişkiler* 11 (42): 93–113.

Rose, Gideon. 1998. "Neoclassical Realism and Theories of Foreign Policy." *World Politics* 51 (1): 144–172.

Schweller, Randall L. 1998. *Deadly Imbalances: Tripolarity and Hitler's Strategy of World Conquest.* New York: Columbia University Press.

Schweller, Randall L. 2004. "Unanswered Threats: A Neoclassical Realist Theory of Underbalancing." *International Security* 29 (2): 159–201.

Secretariat General for EU Affairs. 2007. *Political Reforms in Turkey.* Ankara: M&B Tanıtım Hizmetleri ve Tic. Ltd.

Snyder, Jack. 1993. *Myths of Empire: Domestic Politics and International Ambition.* Ithaca, NY: Cornell University Press.

Taşpınar, Ömer. 2012. "Turkey's Strategic Vision and Syria." *The Washington Quarterly* 35 (3): 127–140.

TESEV. 2012. "Ortadoğu'da Türkiye Algısı 2012." TESEV Foreign Policy Programme report prepared by M. Akgün and S.S. Gündoğar. Istanbul: TESEV Publications.

Tocci, Natalie. 2005. "Europeanization in Turkey: Trigger or Anchor for Reform?" *South European Society and Politics* 10 (1): 73–83.

"Turkish PM Says Limited Action Against Syria Won't Be Enough, Calls for Kosovo-Like Intervention." 2013. *Hürriyet Daily News*, 13 August. http://www.hurriyetdailynews.com/turkish-pm-says-limited-action-against-syria-wont-be-enough-calls-for-kosovo-like-intervention.aspx?pageID=238&nid=53586. Accessed 10 September 2014.

Waltz, Kenneth N. 1979. *Theory of International Politics.* Reading, MA: Addison-Wesley.

Wohlforth, William C. 1993. *The Elusive Balance: Power and Perceptions During the Cold War.* Ithaca, NY: Cornell University Press.

Yanık, Lerna K. 2009. "The Metamorphosis of Metaphors of Vision: "Bridging" Turkey's Location, Role and Identity After the End of the Cold War." *Geopolitics* 14 (3): 531–549.

Zakaria, Fareed. 1998. *From Wealth to Power: The Unusual Origins of America's World Role.* Princeton, NJ: Princeton University Press.

CHAPTER 10

British Foreign Policy in the Context of Brexit: Realism or Irrationality?

Pauline Schnapper

Among the changes and uncertainties of the post-post Cold War period in Europe, the British vote to leave the European Union on 23 June 2016 (or Brexit) probably stands out as one of the most unexpected and potentially far-reaching developments for the future of the continent. The process of actually leaving the EU promises to be extremely complex and lengthy, and the nature of the relations between the UK and the continent is still unknown. Similarly, in strategic terms, and especially as far as the future of British foreign policy is concerned, most questions remain unanswered. What role will Britain play in Europe and the world? Is economic and therefore political decline inevitable, at least in the short term? Can the dream of the supporters of leaving the EU, a "Global Britain", be achieved?

Bearing in mind the distinction between a realist interpretation of events and an interpretation consistent with realism that Jack Donnelly suggests, we may safely assert that realist theory is helpful to understand post-1945 British foreign policy if we understand it in the neo-classical sense, where rational actors are constrained by the structure in which

P. Schnapper (✉)
University of Paris Sorbonne Nouvelle, Paris, France
e-mail: Pauline.Schnapper@univ-paris3.fr

© The Author(s) 2019
R. Belloni et al. (eds.), *Fear and Uncertainty in Europe*, Global Issues,
https://doi.org/10.1007/978-3-319-91965-2_10

they find themselves and adjust their behaviour to their limited margin of manoeuvre. British foreign policy was informed throughout the Cold War by a classical realist perspective, itself inherited from the nineteenth century, whereby power politics, the defence of national interests and maintaining the global balance of power, here between East and West, were the policy-makers' utmost priorities. The pursuit of power was mitigated by a realization of the UK's reduced capabilities and therefore bigger reliance on the alliance with the USA. British leaders had a cautious approach towards idealism and international law, although they were keen to take part in a number of multilateral international organisations—all relying on American post-war hegemony, which enabled the stability of an otherwise chaotic system.

Although this approach was much qualified after the end of the Cold War, and especially under Tony Blair, it is fascinating to see in the new environment created by the referendum on Brexit that, at first sight at least, the Brexiters' view looks like a return to a traditional nationalist, power-based foreign policy. Their rethoric turns its back on more than forty years of multilateral rules-based cooperation in Europe in favour of global free trade agreements reminiscent of the UK's glorious imperial past, with a case-by-case approach to cooperation and alliances. This points to a return to the realist tradition in British foreign policy, away from entanglements on the European continent and rather based on bilateral deals, even though on security issues the multilateral (NATO) framework would remain.

Whether this is consistent with the reality of globalisation and economic interdependence is debatable, which raises the question of whether this renewed 'realism' is actually realistic. And this is where we, as observers this time, can also adopt a constructivist lens, focussing on identity and representations about foreign policy among British elites and public opinion since 1945. It can be also useful to understand the power of emotions, especially nostalgia and a sense of exceptionalism, in the Brexit vote. Indeed foreign policy is inseparable from a conception of national identity, which is both about self-perception and giving oneself "roles" on the world scene (Wallace 1991, Gaskarth 2013, 2014). National identity informs the definition of national interests and the rationale behind foreign policy choices (Hadfield-Amkhan 2010). This is especially true of a country like Britain, which has a long history of ambitious foreign policy and world leadership, in particular through its empire and continues to see itself as exceptional. We start, therefore, from the premise that national traditions in foreign policy remain extremely potent and may explain elements of delusion present in the narrative of Brexit.

In order to examine recent changes in British foreign policy and what the Brexit vote tells us about a possible neo-realist turn, I will first look at the realist tradition (the latter understood in the social constructivist sense of the word) before and during the Cold War and then at the relative "liberal" turn of the 1990s and 2000s, which was followed by a backlash against intervention. I will then briefly look at the domestic reasons for the Brexit vote before discussing whether Brexit is a sign of a return to a possibly out-of-date Realism among British foreign policy actors, informed by nostalgia rather than rationality.

Britain's Realist Tradition

Britain's eighteenth and nineteenth century foreign policy was clearly inspired by what we now call realism, with its emphasis on sustaining British power and national interest. The Empire dominated the agenda, but in Europe the priority was to maintain a balance of power between different countries, by which no continental power could be so strong that it threatened others, while keeping an overall policy of "Splendid Isolation". The UK would therefore build alliances against the current threat, whether it was Spain, France or later Germany, on a case-by-case basis. Palmerston's famous assertion in the House of Commons on 7 August 1844 that, 'We have no eternal allies, and we have no perpetual enemies. Our interests are eternal and perpetual, and those interests it is our duty to follow', summed up this approach. The national interest was not always explicitly defined, but referred to economic prosperity, national security and reputation. This approach remained broadly unchanged until the First World War. The failure of the League of Nations and appeasement in the 1930s and the eventually successful war against Germany and its allies in the Second World War confirmed the benefits of this approach to many British eyes.

Hence a realist frame clearly dominated the thinking of British policymakers during this whole period, interests—however defined—being the priority rather than values. An exception to this tradition was Gladstone's defence of intervention to help the Christian Bulgarians who were rising against the occupying Turks in 1876. But he was in opposition then, not in power, which made such appeals easier. This nevertheless showed that realism was never the only reference and that more liberal ideas were sometimes debated—another tradition in which Tony Blair was able to tap over a century later in his 1999 Chicago speech. He also referred explicitly to the Liberal leader in his Memoirs:

> [a] traditional foreign policy view, based on a narrow analysis of national interest and an indifference unless that interest is directly engaged, is flawed and out of date. I happen to think as Gladstone did that it is also immoral: but even if I didn't, I am sure that in the early twenty-first century, it doesn't work. (Blair 2010: 225)

Gladstone also referred to a more permanent set of multilateral agreements, the "concert of nations", by which collective security would be maintained, an element of the British tradition which was potent after 1945 (Sanders and Houghton 2017: 37).

THE COLD WAR

The context for British foreign policy changed dramatically after 1945 but the realist tradition survived. The Cold War and the confrontation with the Soviet Union kept issues of power and security at the front of British policy-makers' minds even though the economic power of their country had been much weakened by the war—in addition to its long-term decline since 1914. There was no real questioning and reassessment of the traditional diplomatic principles, but they were adjusted to the new situation. In policy terms, the tradition was translated into a few guiding principles summed up by Øivind Bratberg:

> [a] privilege for Anglo-American relations, with NATO as corollary; insular reserve towards the European continent; a maintained global presence with special preference for the Commonwealth; a policy based on pragmatism rather than principle; and, finally, a liberal belief in international trade (2011: 331).

The idea of short-term alliances was jettisoned for a new permanent Western Alliance centred on the United States. The UK enjoyed a "special relationship" with Washington which was crucial to anchor American interests with European ones and also helped maintain the UK's status as a global power, or at least the illusion of it. Anchoring the US to Europe was also, of course, a necessity to maintain the security of Western Europe and a priority which was all the more crucial as Congress had terminated the Lend-Lease Act in 1945 and passed the McMahon Act forbidding nuclear cooperation with foreign countries in 1946.

Churchill summed up the British leaders' view that their country could still play a major role in spite of its reduced circumstances thanks to its privileged position at the centre of "three circles": Western Europe, the Atlantic community and the Empire/Commonwealth, the latter two reinforcing each other as British possessions overseas became one aspect of the global containment strategy towards the USSR. This image enabled British policy-makers to dodge reexamining previous attitudes and priorities and extended the idea of British exceptionalism, even though the Empire was on the wane. The Suez crisis of 1956, which was a huge setback to Britain's still global ambitions, reinforced the feeling that a close link with the US was the only way to remain influential beyond Europe.

Military overseas commitments remained large until 1967, when the Wilson government finally took the difficult decision to shut all military bases to the East of Suez. Being a permanent member of the new UN Security Council and, from 1952 onwards, one of the five nuclear powers helped sustain and justify the UK's ambition to remain, as far as possible, a power in the world. Margaret Thatcher, Prime Minister between 1979 and 1990 was obsessed with the idea of stopping the British economic and strategic decline and reasserting its world role. Her close relationship with US president Ronald Reagan and, especially, the Falklands War against Argentina in 1982 were ways to show that UK was back, to use an image now in vogue. Ideas of rank and power therefore remained central to British self-perception even if the Cold War was also an ideological struggle and therefore about defending the values of liberal democracy, and not just a collection of national interests.

Another way for British elites to manage their country's decline and retain a seat at the top table was to contribute to the post-war liberal order. The UK was committed to the new multilateral institutions set up after 1945, such as the UN, NATO, the World Bank, and the IMF (with Sterling a reserve currency). But issues of national sovereignty always came first and explained Britain's reluctance to take part in the first steps of European integration in the 1950s. It eventually joined the EEC in 1973, after two failed attempts due to French opposition, for mostly economic reasons and in view of the declining level of trade with Commonwealth countries. In foreign policy terms, Britain was then happy to cooperate with other EC member states but only as long as it coincided with its own policy choices and national interests. Successive governments resisted any effort at further integration, whether economic, monetary or in foreign policy, especially at the time of the Maastricht treaty in 1991.

Realpolitik, deterrence of the Soviet block and the defence of the national interest therefore remained the cornerstones of UK foreign policy throughout the Cold War, which in British minds left little space for other views than the realist one. But this tradition was never absolute and was combined with some liberal principles such as a rejection of appeasement and a recognition of the usefulness of multilateralism in an interdependent world. This is what Oliver Daddow and I referred to as "bounded liberalism" (Daddow and Schnapper 2013). The end of the Cold War opened new opportunities for a further reassertion of the liberal tradition.

THE END OF THE COLD TAR—THE END OF REALISM?

With the collapse of the Soviet Union and the end of the Cold War, the foundations of British foreign policy since 1945 were questioned as the world was no longer bipolar, making Britain's niche on the international scene as a nuclear power, the US's first ally and a European power no longer certain. At first, realism continued to prevail with Britain's successful attempt to maintain an enlarged NATO as the prime security organisation in Europe in spite of the demise (at least for a while) of its original *raison d'être*. The first Gulf war in 1990–1991, when Iraq invaded Kuwait, was also in the continuity of a classical realist state vs state conflict where hard military power was the dominant factor determining the outcome of the crisis.

But the first challenge to realism came with the wars in ex-Yugoslavia which started in 1991–1992. John Major was then the Prime Minister and his first reaction to the civil wars in Slovenia, Croatia and especially Bosnia (1992–1995) was to stick to a traditional worldview by which none of Britain's vital interests were at stake in the Balkans and therefore the UK should not commit to full military intervention. 800 troops were nevertheless sent to protect aid convoys in November 1992 under UN auspices but Major rejected the American proposal to lift the arms embargo and ruled out the use of ground forces. Douglas Hurd, his Foreign Secretary, summed up this vision when he asserted in Parliament that:

It is a British interest to make a reasoned contribution towards a more orderly and decent world. But it is not a British interest, and it would only be a pretence, to suppose that we can intervene and sort out every tragedy which captures people's attention and sympathy. I have never found the phrase "something must be done" to be a phrase which carries any convictions in the places such as the House or the government where people have to take decisions.[1]

The Major government's reluctance to intervene until 1995 was widely criticised in Britain as the war dragged on, the number of civilian casualties dramatically increased to a quarter million and Serbian troops were accused of ethnic cleansing and genocide. The foreign policy thinking of Tony Blair, leader of the opposition Labour Party from 1994 onwards, was heavily influenced by that fateful experience.

Indeed, the collective European and national failure to stop the war for three years led to a partial revisiting among British circles of the realist principle of a narrow defence of the national interest and non-intervention abroad when the national interest was not under threat. Tony Blair, first as leader of the Labour Party then as Prime Minister from 1997 onwards, became the main proponent of such a vision. Although he made much, in a very traditional way, of Britain as a "bridge" between Europe and the US, he and his first Foreign Secretary, Robin Cook, also insisted on an "ethical" turn in their foreign policy, which included no longer selling weapons to autocratic regimes and supporting humanitarian intervention. This was articulated in his Chicago speech in April 1999. As the Kosovo crisis was unravelling, he justified Western (in this case NATO) intervention against Serbia:

This is a just war, based not on any territorial ambitions but on values. We cannot let the evil of ethnic cleansing stand. We must not rest until it is reversed. We have learned twice before in this century that appeasement does not work. If we let an evil dictator range unchallenged, we will have to spill infinitely more blood and treasure to stop him later. (Blair 1999)

In his mind, defending civilians against aggression was part of the British national interest because in the new globalised world, interdependence made the security of one country inseparable from that of others. Opposing *realpolitik* to liberalism was therefore meaningless:

[1] Douglas Hurd, *House of Commons Parliamentary Debates*, April 29, 1993, Col. 1176.

> We are all internationalists now, whether we like it or not. We cannot refuse to participate in global markets if we want to prosper. We cannot ignore new political ideas in other countries if we want to innovate. We cannot turn our backs on conflicts and the violation of human rights within other countries if we want still to be secure… We are witnessing the beginnings of a new doctrine of international community. By this I mean the explicit recognition that today more than ever before we are mutually dependent, that national interest is to a significant extent governed by international collaboration and that we need a clear and coherent debate as to the direction this doctrine takes us in each field of international endeavour. (Blair 1999)

This doctrine justified intervention in Kosovo and Sierra Leone earlier (1998) but was also used to convince the British public from 2001 onwards of the case to take part in the war against Al Qaida and the Taliban in Afghanistan and to invade Iraq in 2003. Blair's commitment to the US-led invasion was based on the moral premise that Saddam Hussein was in possession of weapons of mass destruction and was a threat both to regional security and to his own people. Indeed the Iraqi president had been mentioned in his Chicago speech in parallel with Slobodan Milosevic, the Serbian Premier, as "two dangerous and ruthless men". But the humanitarian case for intervention in Iraq was much less solid than in the case of Kosovo and the Iraq war proved, to say the least, politically controversial in the UK, especially when it appeared that Iraq had harboured no weapons of mass destruction and the invasion itself was followed by years of civil war and chaos. In 2012, 58% of respondents to the British Social Attitudes survey opposed the military intervention in Iraq against 28% who supported it (Gribble et al. 2012).

It was not just that Tony Blair lost his popularity over the war but the whole case for international liberalism was undermined in the UK. The Iraq fiasco led the Conservative party in opposition, and especially its leader from 2005, David Cameron and William Hague, who became Foreign Secretary in 2010, to distance themselves from Blair's messianism, and to claim to pursue national interests more pragmatically and cautiously (Gilmore 2014). Hague stated that "we understand that idealism in foreign policy always needs to be tempered with realism" (Hague 2010). In defining their own "liberal conservatism" they talked about "engagement" with the world rather than "intervention" and pledged to never intervene without the endorsement of the UN Security Council. But they, like Blair before them, continued to argue that interests and values were inseparable. The 2010 Strategic Defence and Security Review stated that:

Our national interest requires us to stand up for the values our country believes in – the rule of law, democracy, free speech, tolerance and human rights... To do so requires us to project power and to use our unique network of alliances and relationships – principally with the United States of America, but also as a member of the European Union and NATO, and a permanent member of the UN Security Council. We must also maintain the capability to act well beyond our shores and work with our allies to have a strategic presence wherever we need it. (HM Government 2010)

In 2011, at the start of the Arab Spring, Cameron decided to send British troops to Libya to stop what was then seen as a potential massacre of civilians in Benghazi by the Gaddafi regime. This operation, conducted with France, showed a degree of continuity with the Blair years (Daddow and Schnapper 2013) in spite of the more restrictive conditions for intervention that Cameron had articulated in a speech in 2006:

First, that we should understand fully the threat we face. Second, that democracy cannot quickly be imposed from outside. Third, that our strategy needs to go far beyond military action. Fourth, that we need a new multilateralism to tackle the new global challenges we face. And fifth, that we must strive to act with moral authority. (Cameron 2006)

The backlash against liberal interventionism in Britain therefore took place not so much in the transition between Blair/Brown and Cameron as after the Franco-British military operation in Libya, which destroyed the regime but failed to establish stability in the country. Wariness towards intervention became apparent after the repression of opposition in Syria was followed by a civil war starting in 2011. David Cameron endorsed President Obama's "red lines" in 2012, which threatened the Assad regime with foreign military intervention should he use chemical weapons against his own people. When this actually happened, in August 2013, the Prime Minister recalled Parliament to debate intervention and was defeated, with 224 Labour MPs and 30 Conservatives voting against his motion. This vote echoed a then widespread opposition to intervention in the British public opinion.[2] It led to President Obama himself withdrawing his threat when Russia suggested the decommissioning of the Syrian chemical arsenal.

[2] 'Poll finds 60% of British public oppose UK military action against Syria', *The Guardian*, August 31, 2013.

A year later, on 26 September 2014, another vote on military intervention took place in the House of Commons, this time not about attacking the Syrian regime but the ISIL terrorist organisation in Iraq, following the killing of several British nationals and in a context of fears about terrorist attacks in Europe. This time the outcome of the vote was positive, but on a very limited mandate, with only a dozen aircraft being sent to Iraq (it was extended to Syria in a further vote on 2 December 2015, following the Paris terror attacks and the attack against a hotel in Sousse (Tunisia) where 30 British citizens were killed).

By 2015, therefore, the coalition government had effectively retreated from its predecessors' broad liberal interventionism, in deed if not in words. This took place in the backdrop of a widespread feeling that the UK had gone too far under Blair and of a financial/economic crisis which led to deep cuts in the defence budget. So an evolution towards a less ambitious foreign policy had started even before the vote on Brexit on 23 June 2016, which shook the very foundations of British foreign policy.

BREXIT AND BEYOND

The vote to leave the European Union was the result of a process originating both at the European and domestic levels. The European Union had faced multiple crises since the start of the financial crash in 2008 which had lowered its already limited popularity in the UK. The right-wing eurosceptic press had regularly announced the demise of the single currency and the collapse of the European project following the Greek debt crisis in 2011–2012. The migrant crisis in the summer of 2015 reinforced a widespread feeling in Britain that the EU was not just economically feeble but also could not control its borders. Nigel Farage, leader of UKIP, made much use of the argument that the EU meant an uncontrolled flow of migrants into the UK, conflating refugees from the Middle-East, Turkey becoming a member in the future and the free circulation of EU citizens. The fear of immigration, together with concerns about the loss of sovereignty, played a major part in the *Leave* voters' decisions.

The Brexit vote was not just a foreign policy decision though, and as much a result of domestic developments as European ones. The effects of the economic crisis and years of austerity imposed by the Conservative/Liberal Democrat coalition were to undermine the economic argument that leaving the EU would be costly, at least for the part of the population which lived in relative poverty or felt "left behind" by globalisation and the central government (Ford and Goodwin 2014; Evans and Menon 2017).

Analyses of the vote saw several new divides that had been previously ignored by political parties (Uberoi 2016). The first one was between young and old, where the older generation tended to favour Brexit (and voted more) whereas under-35s wanted to remain (but voted less). The second was between cities, which tended to vote to stay, and rural or small town areas, which voted to leave. The third one was related to education, whereby people with higher education levels tended to vote to stay in the EU, whereas people who only had secondary education voted to leave. This points to socio-economic issues in Britain, which had little to do with the EU as such but obviously will impact on Britain's position on the world scene (Ford and Goodwin 2017).

The Brexit vote opened a period of uncertainty concerning the future of British foreign policy. Although foreign policy did not feature much in the referendum campaign, Brexit was presented by *Leavers* as not a retreat from the continent, but on the contrary as an opportunity to return to the UK tradition of open trade with the world and renewing old ties with important countries such as the US or emerging economies such as China and India, freed from the "shackles" of the EU. The Vote Leave campaign argued that, "A leave vote means the opposite of isolation—it means regaining a voice in global bodies that will be increasingly important as the EU shrinks in importance."[3] They referred to the "Anglosphere" to which Britain should return. David Davis wrote during the campaign that Brexit would be:

[a]n opportunity to renew our strong relationships with Commonwealth and Anglosphere countries. These parts of the world are growing faster than Europe. We share history, culture and language. We have family ties. We even share similar legal systems. The usual barriers to trade are largely absent'. (quoted in Wellings 2017)

When she became Prime Minister, a newly Brexiter Theresa May expanded on what the future of British foreign policy would be like once it had left the EU in her 2016 Conservative party conference speech:

---

[3] 'What happens when we vote leave', Vote Leave Campaign. http://www.voteleavetakecontrol.org/briefing_newdeal.html. Accessed October 16, 2017.

And that Britain – the Britain we build after Brexit – is going to be a Global Britain. Because while we are leaving the European Union, we will not leave the continent of Europe. We will not abandon our friends and allies abroad. And we will not retreat from the world. In fact, now is the time to forge a bold, new, confident role for ourselves on the world stage. Keeping our promises to the poorest people in the world. Providing humanitarian support for refugees in need. Taking the lead on cracking down on modern slavery wherever it is found. Ratifying the Paris Agreement on Climate Change. Always acting as the strongest and most passionate advocate for free trade right across the globe. And always committed to a strong national defence and supporting the finest Armed Forces known to man. (May 2016)

There would be no strategic retreat, but an ambitious global foreign policy, rather than regional integration, which would pursue British interests. So Brexit was a reassertion of national sovereignty in the classical sense, where the government would be able to choose freely bilateral or multilateral *ad hoc* cooperation with other states, including separate EU member states, as well as rejuvenate old alliances such as the special relationship with the US and the Commonwealth countries.

Theresa May reverted to the classical celebration of the three circles, although the term was not used, in a speech to the Republican Party on 26 January 2017:

We are a European country – and proud of our shared European heritage – but we are also a country that has always looked beyond Europe to the wider world. We have ties of family, kinship and history to countries like India, Pakistan, Bangladesh, Australia, Canada, New Zealand, and countries across Africa, the Pacific and Caribbean. And of course, we have ties of kinship, language and culture to these United States too. As Churchill put it, we "speak the same language, kneel at the same altars and, to a very large extent, pursue the same ideals". And, today, increasingly we have strong economic, commercial, defence and political relationships as well. (May 2017)

Britain's commitment to NATO and to spending 2% of its budget on defence was confirmed, as a sort of implicit compensation to leaving the EU. The May government committed troops to Estonia and RAF jets to Romania as part of the Forward Presence programme in the aftermath of Russia's invasion of Crimea. The UK also took command of NATO's response force in 2017. Similarly, a September 2017 paper on the future of foreign and defence policy after Brexit insisted that the UK "will also continue to ensure that NATO remains the cornerstone of our defence, be a champion of the UN and multilateralism, and be active in other international organisations" while pledging to continue cooperation with EU countries in these fields (HM Government 2017). Yet there were already questions as to whether the UK would be able to keep the military position of Deputy Supreme Allied Commander of NATO.

The whole rhetoric of Global Britain, which became ubiquitous, therefore had clear post-imperial realist undertones, with implicit references to the "bounded liberalism" tradition in May's speech. In his first speech as Foreign Secretary at the Conservative conference in October 2016, Boris Johnson also asserted in his characteristic tone:

I also believe we should have absolutely no shame or embarrassment in championing our ideals around the world and in this era of dithering and dubitation. This should be the message of global Britain to the world: that we stick up for free markets as vigorously as we stick up for democracy and human rights and when all is said and done, my friends – and I know that not everyone will agree with this, but what the hell – I believe that vote on June 23 was for economic freedom and political freedom as well. (Johnson 2016)

This return to a sort of historical realism, not far from Churchill's image of the three circles which dominated the post-1945 period, is characterised by limited foreign interventions, a focus on bilateral or multilateral security cooperation and new global trade partnerships. It relies on the permanent features of British power, such as nuclear power, and a seat on the UN Security Council. It is supposedly based on a rational assessment of the budgetary constraints faced by the UK since the 2008 crash and of the new opportunities brought about by Brexit, notwithstanding the domestic and emotional reasons for this vote in the first place. But there are a number of reasons why we may doubt its feasibility or, indeed, realism.

Leavers refer to the UK's identity as a trading nation, but it may seem paradoxical for Britain to leave the European Union, which is not just its first trading partner, with 44% of British exports and 53% of its imports, but also the biggest free-trade area in the world, ahead of the USA.[4]

---

[4]http://ec.europa.eu/trade/policy/eu-position-in-world-trade/. Accessed October 18, 2017.

Moreover the EU economies are now so interlocked, with spare parts moving from one country to the other in supply chains, that disentangling exports and imports has actually become much more complex and it makes little economic sense to leave the single market. If Britain leaves the EU without a trade deal, tariffs would be imposed, disrupting the whole economy in the UK—and, to a lesser extent, the EU. The Brexiters' argument that Europe has shrunk as a percentage of the world economy, while technically right, ignores these facts.

The second limitation to a successful realist foreign policy outside the EU is more broadly economic. It is widely expected that leaving the EU will have negative consequences on growth and inflation, which has already started to pick up to 3% annually following the fall of the pound after the referendum. In the first half of 2017 British growth was the lowest among G7 countries (1.6%). Whether the UK and EU achieve a deal on free trade before March 2019 (or during a transition period which would follow) or not would make a big difference to its economic outlook—up to 1.5% in GDP according to the OECD (2017). In any case, the financial and economic cost of Brexit will have an impact on foreign policy, or at least on defence, with less funding available than planned for the defence budget, which was already hit by large cuts between 2010 and 2015.[5]

Thirdly, one may wonder about the soundness of a strategy based on the strengthening of the "special relationship" with the US at a time when the American president, Donald Trump, consistently undermines multilateral organisations including, at least during the presidential campaign, NATO and claims that free trade agreements jeopardize American industry and jobs. Theresa May rushed to Washington to meet the new president in January 2017 and was at pains to underline the friendship between the two countries but her government had little impact on the new administration's foreign policy, whether it was on the Paris climate deal that Trump pledged to withdraw from or on Iran, when Trump refused to endorse the nuclear deal signed by President Obama, France, Britain, Germany (the EU-3), Russia and China. There is little evidence that a post-Brexit UK would have more influence on American policy, even under a different administration, as Europe has been receding from Washington's priorities since well before Trump was elected.

[5] 'PM's former security adviser warns of Brexit defence cuts', *The Observer*, October 14, 2014.

It is also interesting to notice that none of the countries hailed as future natural partners ever supported Brexit. During the referendum campaign, President Obama insisted that the UK outside the EU would not enjoy any privileged position in Washington and would be 'at the back of the queue' to sign a trade deal with the US.[6] Neither Canada, Australia or New Zealand stated anything different, with for instance the Australian trade minister saying that an agreement with the EU would have precedence over a free trade deal with the UK.[7] Similarly, Theresa May had limited success in promoting a free trade deal with India on an official visit in November 2016, especially when she opposed the Indian Prime Minister's demand to offer more visas to Indians citizens.[8] The same message was conveyed to Theresa May on an official visit to Japan in September 2017.[9]

More generally, Brexit is reinforcing a trend which had already become apparent in British foreign policy since 2010, which is one of a declining presence on the international scene, a result both of budget cuts and public opinion's increased reluctance towards foreign intervention following the Iraqi fiasco. London was largely absent from the diplomatic talks which followed the crisis with Russia over Ukraine. On the contrary, being part of the EU common foreign and security policy increased its international clout, whether it be as part of the original deal signed with Iran or in applying sanctions to countries such as Russia or Syria. This could be lost once the UK leaves the EU, even if the government hopes to maintain high levels of cooperation with the EU in these fields. It has a bargaining power in that it is the main European defence power with France and has built useful bilateral links such as the Lancaster House agreements signed with France in 2010. Yet it is hard to see how the UK will not lose some of its influence, not to mention

---

[6] 'Barack Obama: As your friend, let me say that the EU makes Britain even greater', *Daily Telegraph*, April 22, 2016.

[7] 'Australia says there will be no free trade deal with UK for years', *The Independent*, September 7, 2017.

[8] 'India: Theresa May's charm offensive leaves many unmoved', *BBC News*, November 13, 2016. Available at http://www.bbc.com/news/uk-politics-37950198. Accessed October 23, 2017.

[9] 'As missiles fly, Britain offers Japan whisky and Aston Martins', *The Economist*, September 2, 2017.

the fact that the time and energy spent on negotiating the terms of the exit and the future relations with the EU will also leave little space for active engagement elsewhere. Even a permanent seat in the UN Security Council will not provide unlimited influence over world affairs. One could argue that the reality is one of long-term relative decline being actually concealed rather than addressed by the repetitive discourse about "Global Britain". Rather than new opportunities, the near future seems more fraught with risks for British influence in the world (Chalmers 2017).

CONCLUSION

Realism has proved particularly relevant to understanding the evolution of British foreign policy sinced 1945. It has shaped perceptions of UK politicians and governments not just during the Cold War but also in its aftermath, when policy-makers have attempted to redefine (or not) the goals and means of British foreign policy. Even Tony Blair, in spite of his emphasis on liberalism, never broke completely with this tradition. But it was never based on a narrow definition of the national interest (territorial integrity and trade, for instance) and was combined with a focus on cooperation and multilateral institutions. As the UK joined the EC/EU and increased its commitment to a common foreign policy as well as humanitarian intervention, it seemed that it had accepted a less narrow definition of its national interest.

The vote to leave the EU in 2016 suggests instead a return, at least among many Conservatives and in Theresa May's government, to a more old-fashioned view of Britain's place in the world, based on its past glory, which is very far from its tradition of pragmatism and compromise and ill-adjusted to the realities of the world today, such as economic globalisation or the complex new threats coming from different parts of the world (from the classical state one to non-state actors). Indeed some of the arguments referring explicitly or implicitly to realism seem totally irrational in the world we are now in. Realism, therefore, remains helpful to understanding British foreign policy after Brexit if it is qualified with an analytical constructivist insistence on the power of emotions such as fear and nostalgia, as well as perceptions and a view of British exceptionalism still highly prevalent in the British political elites and the general public.

REFERENCES

Blair, Tony. 1999. "The Doctrine of the International Community", Speech to the Chicago Economic Club, April 22.

Blair, Tony. 2010. *A Journey*. London: Hutchinson.

Bratberg, Øivind. 2011. "Ideas, Tradition and Norm Entrepreneurs: Retracing Guiding Principles of Foreign Policy in Blair and Chirac's Speeches on Iraq." *Review of International Studies* 37 (1): 327–348.

Cameron, David. 2006. "A New Approach to Foreign Affairs—Liberal Conservatism", Speech to the British American Project, September 11. http://www.conservatives.com/News/Speeches/2006/09/Cameron_A_new_approach_to_foreign_affairs__liberal_conservatism.aspx.

Chalmers, David. 2017. "UK Foreign and Security Policy After Brexit", RUSI Briefing Paper, January. Available at https://rusi.org/sites/default/files/201701_bp_uk_foreign_and_security_policy_after_brexit_v4.pdf. Accessed October 24, 2017.

Daddow, Oliver, and Pauline, Schnapper. 2013. "Liberal Intervention in the Foreign Policy Thinking of Tony Blair and David Cameron." *Cambridge Review of International Affairs* 26 (2): 330–349.

Evans, Geoffrey, and Anand Menon. 2017. *Brexit and British Politics*. London: Polity Press.

Ford, Robert, and Matthew, Goodwin. 2014. *Revolt on the Right: Explaining Support for the Radical Right in Britain,* London: Routledge.

Ford, Robert, and Matthew, Goodwin. 2017. "A Nation Divided." *Journal of Democracy* 28 (1): 17–30.

Gaskarth, Jamie. 2013. *British Foreign Policy*. Cambridge: Polity Press.

Gaskarth, Jamie. 2014. "Strategizing Britain's Role in the World." *International Affairs* 90 (3): 559–581.

Gilmore, Jonathan. 2014. "The Uncertain Merger of Values and Interests in UK Foreign Policy." *International Affairs* 90 (3): 541–557.

Gribble, Rachael, Simon Wessely, Susan Klein, David A. Alexander, Christopher Dandeker, and Nicola T. Fear. 2012. "The UK's Armed Forces: Public Support for the Troops But Not Their Missions?" *British Social Attitudes* 29. Available at http://www.bsa.natcen.ac.uk/media/1150/bsa29_armed_forces.pdf. Accessed October 11, 2017.

Hadfield-Amkhan, Amelia. 2010. *British Foreign Policy, National Identity and Neo-Classical Realism*. Lanham, MD: Rowman and Littlefield.

Hague, William. 2010. "Britain's Values in a Networked World", Speech Given at Lincoln's Inn, September 15.

HM Government. 2010. *Securing Britain in an Age of Uncertainty: The Strategic Defence and Security Review*, Cm 7948. Available at https://www.gov.uk/government/uploads/system/uploads/attachment_data/file/62482/strategic-defence-security-review.pdf. Accessed October 13, 2017.

HM Government. 2017. *Foreign Policy, Defence and Development: A Future Partnership Paper*. Available at https://www.gov.uk/government/publications/foreign-policy-defence-and-development-a-future-partnership-paper. Accessed October 17, 2017.

Johnson, Boris. 2016. Conservative Party Conference Speech, October 2. Available at https://blogs.spectator.co.uk/2016/10/full-text-boris-johnsons-conference-speech/. Accessed October 16, 2017.

May, Theresa. 2016. Speech to the Conservative Party Conference, October 5. Available at http://www.independent.co.uk/news/uk/politics/theresa-may-speech-tory-conference-2016-in-full-transcript-a7346171.html. Accessed October 16, 2017.

May, Theresa. 2017. Speech to the Republican Party Conference, January 26. Philadelphia. Available at https://www.gov.uk/government/speeches/prime-ministers-speech-to-the-republican-party-conference-2017. Accessed October 24, 2017.

OECD. 2017. *OECD Economic Survey: UK*, October. Available at http://www.oecd.org/eco/surveys/United-Kingdom-2017-OECD-economic-survey-overview.pdf. Accessed October 18, 2017.

Sanders, David, and David Patrick Houghton. 2017. *Losing an Empire, Finding a Role: British Foreign Policy Since 1945*, 2nd ed. London: Palgrave.

Uberoi, Elise. 2016. *European Union Referendum* 2016. House of Commons Library Briefing Paper 7639, June 29.

Wallace, William. 1991. "Foreign Policy and National Identity in the United Kingdom." *International Affairs* 67 (1): 65–80.

Wellings, Ben. 2017. "The Anglosphere in the Brexit Referendum." *Revue Française de Civilisation Britannique* 22 (2). http://rfcb.revues.org/1354. Accessed October 15, 2017.

PART IV

Multilateral Actors and Issues

As NATO Looks East, Will It Stumble in the South? The Case of Protection of Civilians Policy

Sten Rynning

Realism has returned to the North Atlantic Treaty Organization (NATO) following more than a decade of a wide range of activities, such as expeditionary efforts to rebuild Afghanistan. The cause of newfound realism is Russia whose 2014 annexation of Crimea and continued offensive actions in Ukraine have brought NATO to rediscover the virtues of collective defense and deterrence. NATO's realism is durable, as the Alliance has announced that summits in 2018 and 2019 will be dedicated to sharpening the allied defense and deterrence posture. In effect, NATO has returned to its founding East-West axis—following the adage of Lord Ismay that NATO's purpose was to keep the United States engaged in Europe, keep Russia out, and then manage (keep down, as it was) Germany (Moore and Coletta 2017; Ringsmose and Rynning 2017).

S. Rynning (✉)
Center for War Studies, University of Southern Denmark,
Odense, Denmark
e-mail: sry@sam.sdu.dk

R. Belloni et al. (eds.), *Fear and Uncertainty in Europe*, Global Issues,
https://doi.org/10.1007/978-3-319-91965-2_11

This return to the East-West axis raises questions in regards to the type of realism that will take first seat in the Alliance. By the terms of this volume, regional fear and uncertainty invite a return to realism, but the meaning of realism could have changed on account of an evolving normative context. For NATO, the question is whether fear and uncertainty lead to a realism of days past when NATO mostly focused on a strong deterrence posture vis-à-vis Russia, or rather to an equally strong policy on southern threats and risks? The argument of this chapter is that the normative order in regards to the South has evolved considerably and, moreover, that NATO recognizes and seeks to incorporate it. The context of realism has changed, therefore. However, due in part to the ephemeral and intractable nature of southern risks and in part to national interest rivalries within NATO itself, this normative order is struggling to take root within the Alliance. Of the two realisms, NATO is clearly most comfortable with the familiar realism of East-West deterrence.

This chapter is thus the story of NATO's continuing struggle to act with foresight and coherence toward the South. The challenge was all the rage during the war on terror when NATO took command of the International Security Assistance Force (ISAF) in Afghanistan, ran a modest training mission in Iraq, extended new partnerships into the Persian Gulf (the Istanbul Cooperation Initiative) and further south into Africa (with the African Union), fought pirates off the coast of Somalia, and finally bombed Muammar Qaddafi's Libyan regime to pieces to protect the civilian population. The changing normative context is visible in regards to the crisis management umbrella under which these efforts took place and which aligned NATO with the international, UN-centric development and governance community that, from a NATO perspective, promised to bring greater legitimacy to out-of-area operations (Daalder and Stavridis 2017; Welsh 2011; see also Beadle 2010). In 2016, NATO capped off this record of engagement with its own Protection of Civilians (PoC) policy, which connected a range of past crisis management policies and, allegedly, paved a path for NATO's continued development (NATO 2016a).

If the outlook for NATO's anchoring in this normative context is grim, it is not entirely dismal. The chapter will first examine the lesson that NATO learned from mostly Afghanistan but also Libya and other crisis management operations and which brought NATO to adopt a unifying PoC policy in 2016. NATO proved pragmatic and political, as we would expect from a politico-military alliance, but also committed to humanitarian principles. The chapter then looks into the drivers of NATO pragmatism, which emerge from the crisis management track record as it formed in the 1990s and evolved in the 2000s. If NATO pragmatism can be read as restrictive when it comes to PoC principles, which at heart are universalist, the track record informs us of NATO's causes for restriction. The third section then asks whether NATO's hard-won lessons offer guidance for current NATO stabilization policy, mainly in regards to its southern flank. Defense and deterrence measures targeting Russia detract from NATO's southern focus, the section finds, but the main stumbling block is the allied effort to shift the southern engagement from one of crisis management operations to one of diplomatic-military partnership and defense capacity building. NATO is finding that doing something on the politico-diplomatic front can be as hard if not harder than doing something militarily. This lesson does not flow from realist theory per se, following Donnelly's chapter in this volume, but is consistent with realism's emphasis on social groups (i.e., NATO) and the responsibility of the individual group to define for itself an adequate balance of power and principle. NATO is still searching for its balance and thus for an adequate balance of power and principle. The implication is not that NATO must turn its back on Protection of Civilian principles but rather that NATO must reorder the strategic framework within which it engages them.

NATO AND THE PROTECTION OF CIVILIANS

The first thing to understand about NATO crisis management is how different it is from collective defense—the Alliance's Cold War remit. Collective defense is inherently legitimate and legal from the perspective of common law and the UN Charter (Article 51) and NATO prepared for it by drawing up defense plans that instructed armed forces on how to train, deploy, and connect to war-time command and control arrangements.

Crisis management is, in contrast, inherently ambiguous. Threats cannot be identified in advance; the legal and normative framework is subject to negotiation; the willingness of all allies to participate is uncertain; and an alliance such as NATO will only possess some of the tools required for conflict resolution, meaning that NATO, to execute its mission, must partner with other international organizations. Ultimately, crisis management pulls NATO into the orbit of a UN-based collective security system, bringing to light tensions between collective defense principles on the one hand and collective security principles on the other—between the regional alliance focused on external political-military threats and the global security system focused on risks from within its ranks of members.

Moreover, rules of engagement vary. In collective defense, armed forces prepare for war, which in legal speak is defined as "armed conflict," and which involves tried and tested principles of humanitarian law: that military forces can apply lethal force only in cases of military necessity, must distinguish between combatants and non-combatants, and use force proportional to the objective. In crisis management, rules of engagement blossom and flow from broader concerns with human security and development—as opposed to the defeat of an armed adversary. In this human terrain, human rights law predominates. It is the law of peacetime, where humanitarian law is for war ("armed conflict"). It is focused on humans' right to life, to due process, freedom of movement, freedom of speech, freedom of thought, conscience, and religion, and so on. If armed forces get involved in crisis management operations, they must protect and uphold these human rights.

NATO has developed doctrines step-by-step for such protection. The first step came in response to the Women, Peace, and Security resolution (1325) adopted in 2000 by the United Nations Security Council (UNSC). In December 2007, NATO adopted guidelines for implementing this resolution—meaning NATO's political authority (the North Atlantic Council) tasked its civilian staff and, not least extensive military authorities, including the collective chain of command, to develop guidelines for protecting women in armed conflict (NATO 2014a). As the UNSC amended the Women, Peace, and Security resolution to focus notably on sexual violence in armed conflict, NATO followed suit and in 2015 gained military guidelines on Sexual and Gender-Based Violence. In the meantime, the Alliance had responded to UNSC resolution 1612 of 2005, which concerned the Protection of Children in Armed Conflict. NATO adopted a policy on this topic at its Chicago summit in May 2012 and soon thereafter finalized a new set of military guidelines (NATO 2012: para. 9; see also NATO 2016b). At NATO's Warsaw summit in July 2016 the alliance took a broader step into the domain of "protection of civilians" (PoC)—which, as the name indicates, is not focused on a sub-group such as women or children but, quite simply, civilians. As before, NATO PoC policy was then followed by new military guidelines (NATO 2016a).

From a NATO perspective, it is no simple matter to "plan" for a real crisis management operation. As mentioned, things were relatively simple during the Cold War when the threat was clear and all allies could be expected to mobilize and fight. In contrast, a crisis response needs its own improvised operations plan (in NATO-speak, an OPLAN) and then also a set of military forces that must be generated on a case-by-case basis (in NATO-speak, a Force Generation Process). By 2005 NATO had learned enough lessons in this business to set up a proper Crisis Management Response System that involved six phases of indications and warning, strategic assessment, response options, military planning (the aforementioned OPLAN based on a Concept of Operations), execution, and transition and termination (Williams 2018).

Once NATO has settled on a plan and moves to "execution," doctrinal clarity becomes an issue. It is a matter of how clearly heads of state and government articulate the political ambitions; how easy it is to build "response options" on this basis; and then how easy it is to translate them into "military planning." Problems in this chain of doctrinal clarity dogged NATO's ISAF command (2003–2014) when broad ambitions and limited means to counter the Taliban insurgency led NATO/ISAF to actions that caused an alarming number of civilian casualties. Campaign adjustments followed (as we shall see), so much so that by mid-2015, in the wake of the ISAF mission, NATO's lesson-learned unit concluded that NATO/ISAF had successfully reduced civilian casualties over the period 2008–2014 and that the reduction was due to NATO/ISAF measures (JALLC 2015).

This experience of having had a long run as a crisis management actor, having built up both doctrinal commitment and a Response System, and yet getting involved in a crisis management operation (ISAF) that on account of its mounting civilian casualties threatened to spin out of political control, triggered NATO's commitment to the comprehensive PoC policy of July 2016. The PoC policy, NATO (2016a: para. 2) along with some of its partners concluded, results from "the need to bring together" all protection doctrine (examined above) "under one overarching policy" that can "address in a more coherent way, the protection of civilians in relevant NATO operations, missions and activities." The 2016 PoC policy is thus an umbrella policy tying past crisis management principles and experiences together, tracing a path forward for NATO. It does so in three remarkable ways (Rynning 2017).

First, NATO is strictly focused on civilian casualty mitigation and the threat of physical violence to civilians. As we have seen, this is just one piece in a large human security puzzle that involves, essentially, all the human rights of international conventions. NATO could have chosen to go broad and emphasize, for instance, a duty to secure civilians' access to clean water, health care, education—or any other human rights issue. Likewise but within the narrower part of the puzzle related to civilians in conflict, NATO could have emphasized a duty to provide for due process during detention, restitution for damaged property, or the clearance of unexploded ordnance in areas where NATO has operated. NATO did not. NATO instead stuck to the protection from physical violence as far as its core PoC mission is concerned. NATO does recognize that this can involve something broader, such as protecting civilians from "others' actions"—meaning the actions of the Taliban, for instance, or NATO support for "humanitarian action" that is critical to the establishment of a "safe and secure" area for civilians (NATO 2016a: para. 16–17). However, the ultimate signal from NATO is that it is a political-military actor that can help create secure spaces in conflict areas; that it will be particularly mindful of not causing harm to civilians and protecting them from violence as it does so; but that it does not assume responsibility for wider development and governance issues.

Second, NATO is inherently pragmatic when it comes to the source of authority of any given crisis management mission. Human rights advocates would in contrast tend not to opt for pragmatism but instead the legal and moral force of human rights doctrine. If human rights reign supreme, states have obligations under law, and if the law is ambiguous, states have a moral "responsibility" to act nonetheless.[1] NATO intervened in Libya in 2011 under such a "responsibility" to protect civilians, and its PoC policy broadly underscores this full range of "legal, moral, and political imperatives" (NATO 2016a: para. 4). However, the policy goes on to define NATO's highest authority—the North Atlantic Council—as the source of NATO mandates, which is to place the political imperative higher than legal and moral doctrine. Moreover, the policy does not prejudice force projection or collective defense obligations, it eschews the inherently tricky question of when to apply humanitarian and human rights law, respectively, and it underscores that NATO will

[1] The UN adopted such a "responsibility to protect" doctrine in 2005. See further UN (n.d.).

take all "feasible" measures to avoid, minimize and mitigate harms to civilians. Feasibility is, again, a reference to the political will of the North Atlantic Council.

Finally, NATO is inviting partnerships between itself and other crisis management actors. It does so by publishing its PoC policy—publication of policy is not a given for a military alliance. Moreover, it involved NATO partners in the drafting of the PoC policy. At one point, some partners, such as Austria and Sweden, got so involved in the policy's development that NATO allies and officials felt it appropriate to discuss amongst themselves how far non-NATO actors de facto could be allowed to shape NATO policy.[2] The issue was resolved, though, and the overarching PoC policy became the latest in NATO's panoply of partnership policies designed to advanced the network of actors that crisis management missions presuppose.

In sum, with the PoC policy of 2016 NATO gained a capstone policy building on nearly two decades' worth of crisis management engagement. It is, on the one hand, a policy that guards NATO's right to decide for itself what it should do, promising to keep NATO strictly focused on security tasks, and yet, on the other, it is an invitation to engagement and NATO's insertion in a wider policy network. In short, it is a balancing act. The question to which we now turn is how this balancing act came about, where the final section asks whether NATO is keeping or losing its balance.

Pains of Adjustment

NATO's reluctance to get drawn into wide-raging definitions of its crisis management role is in great parts motivated by the difficult transition from phase 3 to phase 4 in its crisis management response system: in phase 3 NATO defines its options in terms of political ambition; in phase 4 the military sets out options for action. Put differently, it is about managing the gap between political ambition and operational capacity.

At the end of the day, the military chain of command as well as the forces on the ground will want as clear guidelines as possible on the "key military tasks" and "key supporting tasks" that it must carry out on the ground. These tasks are defined by NATO's military authorities

---

[2] Author's interview with NATO official, December 2016.

in response to the "Initiating Directive" that comes out of phase 3—and which is thus politically driven—and then the Concept of Operations (CONOPS) that the supreme military commander (SACEUR) develops in response (beginning of phase 4). Once this framework is in place, the key tasks can be defined in an Operations Plan (OPLAN).

NATO's OPLAN for "big ISAF" that rolled out of Kabul to cover all of Afghanistan is illustrative (NATO 2005). It enumerates six "key military tasks" focused on "security sector reform" and thus the building of Afghan capacity, "stability and security operations" in coordination with Afghan forces, and related tasks. It then enumerates eleven "key supporting tasks" related to development, police training, border security, the return of refugees, disaster relief operations, evacuation operations, counter-terrorism, and mine clearance. Each supporting task is qualified with reference to NATO's level of engagement: on development, NATO/ISAF should only to "provide a coherent overview"; on counter-terrorism, NATO/ISAF could only "in-extremis" support such operations; on mine clearance, NATO/ISAF could engage the task only "when essential for mission accomplishment," and so on. In short, it is complicated.

The OPLAN then adds three appendixes on issues of which NATO/ISAF was not primarily in command: relations with Provincial Reconstruction Teams (PRTs), the development of Afghan national security and defense forces (ANSD), and counter-narcotics operations. Individual nations were in command of the PRTs, though NATO/ISAF was to provide perimeter security. Moreover, the G8 format of great powers had previously granted lead nations responsibility for ANSD development (the United States) and Afghan counter-narcotics support (the United Kingdom). These add-on issues were politically controversial inside NATO, and the OPLAN eschewed controversy by arguing that what mattered at the end of the day was "good governance at the local level" (NATO 2005: Annex C, Appendix 3).

The primary task of NATO/ISAF's main headquarters in Kabul, Afghanistan as well as subsidiary headquarters in the regions was then to translate the OPLAN into effects on the ground—and ultimately to enable transition and termination (phase 6). The challenge was complex from the outset, and the growing insurgency exacerbated difficulties. When during these early years of "big ISAF," 2006–2008, NATO's political-strategic headquarters in Brussels pushed for ISAF's greater engagement with protection of civilian issues, children in particular, the risk of mission creep as well as the difficulty of getting civilian advisors into the field made the same headquarters reluctant to open and amend the operations plan (OPLAN). The military chain of command was therefore faced not only with an already complex OPLAN but also political expectations that new tasks could quietly be slipped into it. For the soldiers doing patrols, it was simply not clear how they should manage a volatile security environment and then also, say, detect and report on suspicions of child abuse.[3]

The outcome was that the military chain of command focused on delivering concrete achievements on its "key tasks" for semi-annual periodic mission reviews. Moreover, as the campaign was under-resourced (or, as ambitions were excessive), the insurgency grew on ISAF and compelled it to acts of armed violence—to war. Lacking manpower, ISAF resorted again and again to air power, earning ISAF Commander General McNeill the unflattering nickname "Bomber McNeill." Somewhere in this gap between complex and under-resourced "key tasks" and a growing reputation for causing civilian casualties by excessive bombing, ISAF was slowly losing control of its crisis management mission.

The UN mission to Afghanistan, UNAMA, began tracking civilian casualties and issuing Protection of Civilians reports in mid-2007, adding to the urgency of the issue and the pressure for NATO/ISAF to adapt. In particular, the situation highlighted how a military campaign operates by certain procedures, including the level of risk accepted for own troops, the type of munitions used, and, by implication, the tolerance of the risk of civilian casualties. The regular use of 2000-pound bombs to strike at enemy forces, for instance, became one of the focal points of the criticism raised against ISAF procedures (Crawford 2017).

Inhibiting NATO/ISAF's rapid response to this deteriorating situation was the fragmented nature of the campaign. Most troop contributing nations were not so much focused on the overall campaign as their portion of it. They would typically have troops attached to a task force located in the vicinity of a PRT, thus in one of the provinces, and it would be the provincial situation, not the challenge of strategic reserves or the ability to move and coordinate troops at the national level that preoccupied them. Individual allies' national chain of command was thus

---

[3] Interview with NATO international staffer with ISAF experience, December 2016.

to an extent myopic, and for an obvious reason: the national media and public would primarily worry about the fate of national troops, and the government had to cater to these concerns (Graf et al. 2015).

However, by 2008–2009 civilian casualties had become a collective, strategic issue. Something had to be done to limit these casualties or NATO/ISAF would lose control of the campaign. At this stage it was clear that the recipe for managing a fragmented campaign was not working well: this was the so-called Comprehensive Approach that prescribed a coordinated division of labor between international organizations and other actors doing primarily security, development, and governance. NATO had tailored the Comprehensive Approach to suit "big ISAF" and to ensure that other organizations' advances in development and governance matched NATO's extended security presence throughout Afghanistan.[4] The plan came late in the game, though, and it was mired in a larger controversy that involved not least UN-NATO relations.

NATO commanded ISAF on a UN mandate that was renewed annually, and ISAF provided security for the UN's political mission (UNAMA) and thus governance, just as it provided security for a range of UN, national, and non-governmental development agencies. The theory of how this could work effectively was the Comprehensive Approach. In practice NATO/ISAF got caught up in two lines of fire from within the UN system. On the one hand, the development community has historically maintained an arms' length principle to militaries, basing its ability to provide aid and development in zones of conflict on its reputation for neutrality. The effective and thus visible coordination with ISAF was inherently unappealing to this community, and it opened a gap of institutional animosity into which UNAMA—the political mission—sank. By its political nature, UNAMA was fairly close to ISAF and thus a partner in the political-military coordination of the campaign, but it was also meant to coordinate and facilitate UN aid and development work. At the end of the day UNAMA made civilian casualties a focal point for its ISAF criticism, which aligned UNAMA with both the aid and development community and Afghanistan's president Karzai, who had grown frustrated with his lack of political control of national events. A number

---

[4] NATO allies had agreed to the principles of a Comprehensive Approach in 2006 when ISAF had become a national campaign, and it rolled out both an overarching Comprehensive Approach policy and an Afghan-related plan in 2008. See further Rynning (2015), Williams (2011), and Steinsson (2015).

of leading nations sought to stitch together a compromise in late 2007, which would effectively empower UNAMA, but President Karzai vetoed the deal, and from this point on the UNAMA-ISAF relationship never got effectively back on its feet. ISAF Commander General McKiernan issued an ISAF Tactical Directive in September 2008 that stressed "proportionality, restraint, and the utmost discrimination in the use of firepower," but UNAMA's head, Kai Eide, continued a public campaign to highlight the inadequate protection of civilians, stating he was not convinced the international community—by which most would understand ISAF—was listening to the concerns of President Karzai and the Afghan people (Bowman and Dale 2010: 32).

The other UN-NATO controversy took place in the UN headquarters in New York where NATO's attempt to operationalize the Comprehensive Approach by way of an institutionalized partnership between the UN and NATO failed. There are multiple causes for the breakdown but they all relate to NATO-Russia relations. NATO's comprehensive action plan emerged out of the Bucharest summit of April 2008 that also, to Russia's great consternation, foresaw Ukraine and Georgia's eventual inclusion as NATO allies. A few months later, in August 2008, Russia invaded Georgia's South Ossetia region—in an effective challenge to NATO policy that was not lost on NATO allies. A NATO-UN deal was thus off the table, and what remained was a Joint Declaration by the UN and NATO secretary-generals by which they agreed to work together "in a practical fashion." (Streit Council 2008).

There was thus limited hope in 2008 for a broad-based solution to the strategic challenge of limiting civilian casualties and, as part hereof, improving the course of events in Afghanistan. President Obama, who took office in January 2009, offered change but via the ability of his nation to mobilize a "surge" in the Afghan campaign. This shifted command responsibility even further in an American direction—the United States was always the first among equals in NATO/ISAF—and thus from NATO's OPLAN to the counter-insurgency campaign plans developed first by General McChrystal and then General Petraeus. Both issued new Tactical Directives to emphasize more clearly the need for judicious restraint in the use of force, and though civilian casualties declined significantly—from 622 (from aerial operations) in 2009 to 162 in 2014—they remained inherently controversial (UNAMA and UNHR 2015: 94). As the ISAF campaign in mid-2012 went into its final stage of transition (it terminated in December 2014), ISAF Commander General

Allen simply banned the bombing of civilian homes under any circumstance except self-defense (Perkins 2014).

Stock-taking began as ISAF drew down. In a review of ISAF periodic mission reports, NATO's lessons-learned unit concluded that ISAF had reduced ISAF-caused civilian casualties over the period 2008–2014 (JALLC 2015). Yet this organizational summary of campaign adaptation was a mere first step: the issue of protection civilians had attained strategic proportions, and it required an equally strategic lesson learned assessment from the politico-military headquarters of NATO. This lesson became the PoC policy (analyzed in the preceding section) that NATO allies concluded in mid-2016.

Given that NATO is a politico-military alliance, it can come as no surprise that NATO's approach to PoC issues—as defined by the new PoC policy—is concerned with military organization: how it can plan and conduct operations in respect of PoC principles, how it can train for such missions, and how it can help national and partner forces educate themselves and learn lessons.[5] Clearly, where military forces are educated in and trained to operate within the bounds of humanitarian law (the laws of war), the policy is asking for a similar persistent effort to ensconce PoC principles and (areas of) human rights law in the force. By February 2017, NATO's ministers of defense approved of an action plan to this effect, meaning the PoC policy went into full implementation mode.

The strategic adaptation of the Alliance remains to be assessed, though. The PoC policy is a stepping-stone but not more than that. According to NATO's Strategic Concept from 2010, crisis management continues to be a NATO core task on par with regional defense and deterrence (NATO 2010). Logically, therefore, as NATO reengages issues of defense and deterrence vis-à-vis Russia (covered elsewhere in this book), NATO must equally tend to the development of the policy framework for its southern flank. In principle, NATO has the choice of simply downgrading the southern flank in order to privilege defense and deterrence to the East, but the political reality of having a number of southern European allies exposed to other risks and threats than that from Russia precludes this NATO option. Thus, NATO must reconfigure its southern engagement not only to maintain the lessons it learned in Afghanistan but also to keep its wider strategic balance.

[5]NATO's PoC policy of June 2016 ends with a 10-point plan for military activities—effectively a political tasking of work the military authorities must carry out.

Lost in Translation? PoC and NATO's Return to Europe

Defense and deterrence are unmistakably NATO's new top priorities. The torrent of new East-West measures since 2014 testify to it: new reaction forces, new in-place trip-wire forces, new graduated response plans, an emerging new command structure, a revised and reinforced Crisis Response System to cope with hybrid threat scenarios, and carefully scripted references to nuclear deterrence.

It is likewise increasingly clear that NATO's continued southern engagement is largely indirect and, as a matter of fact, very modest. Most significant is the ongoing Afghanistan training mission (Resolute Support Mission) that gained an injection of energy following President Trump's espousal in July 2017 of a so-called conditions-based policy by which the United States promised to stay on to finish the job of stabilization in the country (Trump 2017). NATO followed suit: as the United States adds approximately 1500 troops to Resolute Support, allies will add an equal number, bringing the mission to around 16,000 troops.[6] Afghanistan thus remains a significant area of operation for NATO, even as the Alliance now is well into the "termination" phase of its engagement. Moreover, with the introduction of a conditions-based strategy, it is clear that this phase can drag on for quite some time.

Beyond Afghanistan, though, NATO's southern engagement is singularly modest. NATO's counter-piracy mission off the coast of Somalia (Operation Ocean Shield) terminated in December 2016; its partnership with the African Union is limited to small cases of staff training and liaisons; its maritime surveillance in the Mediterranean, Active Endeavor, transformed in October 2016 into a more flexible (reduced) Sea Guardian mission; it has offered maritime surveillance in the Aegean Sea to help reduce tensions related to refugee flows (and, once again, to manage relations between two of its allies, Turkey and Greece); and it maintains its usual partnership programs—the Mediterranean Dialogue and the Istanbul Cooperation Initiative.

Breaking new ground, though, NATO has offered so-called Defense Capacity Building (DCB) packages to Jordan and Iraq. NATO introduced these DCB packages at the Wales summit in 2014 as part of a

---

[6] The United States maintains app. 4000 troops in Afghanistan outside Resolute Support. The total number of Western troops is thus around 20,000. See further Emmott (2017).

so-called Defence and Related Security Capacity Building Initiative. This initiative was extended to Jordan at the 2014 summit, and then in 2015 to Iraq (NATO 2014b: para. 89). Defense Capacity Building is thus a growing agenda, and NATO signaled its intent to follow through on it by handing the dossier to its Deputy Secretary General, Rose Gottemoeller, which is quite high in the organizational hierarchy, and then also by setting up a "military hub" in NATO's integrated command structure to help ensure coordinated and focused efforts. This hub was eventually located within the Alliance's southern regional command in Naples, Italy, where the hub (app. 100 personnel) will help other NATO units assess threats, gather information, and plan NATO and partner training and exercises (Stoltenberg 2017a).

While there thus is some adaptation and forward engagement in policy along the Alliance's southern rim, the sum total of NATO's engagement is feeble or at the very least strictly measured, especially when compared to the high mark of engagement in 2011 when NATO commanded well beyond 100,000 troops in Afghanistan and was in the lead of the Responsibility to Protect air mission in Libya (Operation Unified Protector) that ultimately toppled the Qaddafi regime. Unquestionably, the resulting instability in Libya and the enduring cost of the Afghan effort have tempered the political appetite for large-scale crisis management operations and fed the search for smarter ways of engendering stability.

The fight against Islamic State illustrates the extent to which it is difficult for NATO to gain consensus for even a modest role in an area of conflict that lies on the doorstep of the Alliance's territory (i.e., Turkey is a next-door neighbor). When Islamic State burst forth in 2014 with its declaration of a Caliphate, a US-led Global Coalition formed (in fact, at the margins of NATO's Wales summit) to combat the terrorist movement. There was never any serious discussion of NATO taking command of the operation; rather, the question concerned the modalities of NATO support for the Global Coalition. The focal point of the ensuring debate became NATO's surveillance aircraft, AWACS, which could look into the Syrian and Iraqi airspace where the coalition operated. Considering that most of the coalition consists of NATO allies, the transmission of data to them would be straightforward. However, a number of allies—with France and Germany at the forefront—held back as they feared a re-run of the Afghan mission: what starts out small can grow into a major engagement. Thus, through 2015–2017 NATO was effectively sidelined. It was not until President Trump's first NATO visit in May 2017 that these allies as a goodwill gesture to the new American president drew back and allowed for the transfer of AWACS data to the coalition.[7] Operationally it did not make much difference, as the Global Coalition in any case relied on U.S. capabilities, but it was politically significant and not least revelatory of resistance to southern crisis management.

The same underlying conflict of views characterized the extension of a defense capacity building mission to Iraq. In the wake of the Wales summit that established this NATO policy platform, in 2015, Iraq requested its activation and thus NATO assistance. It was not a far-fetched request in so far as the Global Coalition was already partnering with Iraq in its request for self-defense assistance. However, while NATO approved the request in July 2015, it also got caught up in the aforementioned reticence expressed notably by France and Germany but also Turkey.[8] The initial Iraq assistance package NATO managed to agree to in mid-2015 thus offered Iraq out-of-country training (in the main explosive ordinance disposal and demining training in Jordan and Turkey). One year later, in July 2016, NATO allies managed to find sufficient common ground to allow an in-country capacity building mission that got under way in early 2017, but the allied agreement was hard fought (NATO 2016c: para. 95). The aforementioned reticent allies obviously shifted their positions, agreeing to move the mission inside Iraq, but in return they gained a commitment from key allies (i.e., notably the United States) that NATO will not train militias (on which the Iraq government has come to rely and which, critics argue, stoke sectarian violence) and also that NATO's training teams will be very modestly sized (8–12 personnel).[9]

The visible trend in NATO's engagement south of its border is therefore a shift from large crisis management operations (ISAF, Unified Protector) to small capacity building and training footprints (Jordan, Iraq, African Union). The latter may be agile and thus appear smart, but they are also small to the point of political tokenism. In the Iraqi case, the capacity building effort is operationally insignificant. Whether this will change in the latest case of defense capacity building, in Tunisia, remains to be seen. NATO secretary general Stoltenberg began soon

---

[7]Based on interview with NATO official, May 2017.

[8]Based on interviews at NATO headquarters, November 2016.

[9]Based on interviews at NATO headquarters, November 2016.

into his tenure (2014) to single out Tunisia—where the 2010 Arab Spring originated and which remains stable—as an obvious case for stability engagement and preventive conflict diplomacy. In mid-2016, at the same time as NATO agreed to move a small footprint inside Iraq, the Alliance offered Tunisia a capacity package tailored for its security needs: concretely, NATO will advice Tunisia on the development of an intelligence fusion center as well as training for Special Operations Forces (NATO 2016c: para. 104; NATO News 2016; *The New Arab* 2017).

As NATO ever so lightly steps into Tunisia, it is clear that NATO's new southern flank policy is diverging from the Comprehensive Approach to crisis management that ran deep in 2006–2014 and which directly informed NATO's Protection of Civilians policy. The Comprehensive Approach was NATO's answer to the challenge of coordinating lines of operations (security, governance, and development) in crisis management operations, and today the Comprehensive Approach is "totally dormant," as one NATO officer offered in an interview.[10] NATO is no longer undertaking "operations" to the south. Rather, it is engaged in a number of training and capacity building "missions" that grow out of a partnership and stability agenda. This is significant in a NATO context for several reasons.

First of all, in terms of strategic tasking, NATO's Strategic Concept foresees three equally important tasks: collective defense and deterrence; crisis management; and partnership and collaborative security. De facto, NATO emphasized the middle leg, crisis management, for as long as it led the ISAF operation. We know that collective defense and deterrence are back as top priorities for the East-West axis on account of Russia's actions, and to offer engagement along the North-South axis NATO has shifted its weight from crisis management to partnership and collaborative security. NATO has thus moved away from crisis management: it is privileging defense and deterrence, and it is trying to privilege partnership.

Secondly, this has real implications for NATO's military organization and the way in which priorities such as Protection of Civilians integrate in its work. Apart from the international staff at the strategic headquarters in Brussels, the bulk of NATO's organization is about command structure. The key point in regards to this analysis is that the command

---

[10] Interviewed by author, NATO headquarters, November 2016.

structure is all about military operations—about training and preparing military forces for operations that will come under NATO command. One part of the command structure is focused on current affairs (the Allied Command Operations headquarters in Belgium), another part on modernizing NATO forces (the Allied Command Transformation in the United States), and a supporting cast of military planners labor to ensure that NATO nations have the required number of forces to meet the allied level-of-ambition (a capacity to undertake two so-called Major Joint Operations and six smaller Joint Operations).

Crisis management operations fit into this organization as smaller Joint Operations (even if they grow to the point of big ISAF), and the organization is trained to adapt to changing and challenging operational circumstances: thus, when NATO political authorities demand an operational focus on counter-insurgency and the protection of civilians, the organization can adjust focus and operational mode. It might not be easy to do so, but operational command and adaptation are the focal points, and this is where the Protection of Civilians policy of 2016 takes aim: essentially, it asks the military organization to cope with the human rights dimension of military operations.

Capacity building with partnered nations is something different entirely and not the central focus of the command structure. NATO's regional south command in Naples was trained to respond to the political call in February 2011 for operational options against the threat posed by Muammar Qaddafi's regime to Libyan civilians; it was not trained to deliver capacity building to nations such as Iraq and Tunisia. The new capacity building "Hub" at Naples is the visible face of this underlying asymmetry built into the command structure—a recognition that capacity building has to be layered in via a new organizational offspring.

Moreover, capacity building will always be an offspring on NATO's military organization. After all, NATO's raison d'être is its ability to defend its member allies, and for this its command structure must be ready for war. The character of war may change over time—for instance as NATO singles out cyber as a distinct operational domain, which it did in mid-2016—but war and related operations will remain at the heart of the command structure. Capacity building is therefore an add-on, and for as long as defence and deterrence predominates along the East-West axis, the divide between war and operations, on the one hand, and capacity building on the other, will be stark. In fact, the risk is that the divide will grow as NATO grapples with collective defense weaknesses within its command structure that, the allies discover, has grown small and accustomed to crisis management operations.[11] Thus, rather than reinforcing the command structure for capacity building, the allies are reinforcing it for war.

Third and finally, NATO must look for tools to rebalance its commitments East and South, or else risk suffering an intra-Alliance decoupling. Decoupling traditionally refers to transatlantic relations but its intra-European dimension has grown in importance with NATO's return to realism in its own neighborhood. NATO has successfully managed to get every ally on board for the ramped up measures to counter Russia: Portugal and Spain, for instance, are every much a part of the new defence and deterrence measures as other allies. For NATO the challenge is to organize a return investment for southern allies. The Alliance has already picked low hanging fruits, such as underscoring how the reinforced NATO Response Force can operate both East and South. Realizing the inadequacy of just putting such "360 degree" labels on Alliance capabilities, the United States took the lead in the run-up to the 2014 Wales summit in launching a new Projecting Stability project that focused precisely on enhanced partnerships and capacity building. The underlying idea is that NATO security is enhanced when neighbors are stable, in the words of NATO secretary general Stoltenberg (2017b), and, as we have seen, NATO has partnership and defense capacity policies to show for it. And while Projecting Stability is another "360 degree" initiative, it is clearly designed to bring activity to the southern flank and thus (in part) manage the internal balance of interest in NATO.

Projecting Stability leaves much to be desired from an allied perspective. There is no fixed political agreement on what defense capacity building means, and while the case-by-case tailoring of capacity policy to specific partners is politically comfortable, the lack of wider political agreement prevents NATO from building a strong organization in support of policy. The Naples "Hub" will at best be able to deliver at the level of modest expectations, therefore. This hub, along with the broader ambition to protect civilians, build partner capacity, and promote

---

[11] NATO is thus introducing two new command components to facilitate troop movement and reinforcements along the East-West axis, connecting North America to Western Europe and then also Western Europe to the new allied territories in the East. See further Matthias Gebaur et.al. (2017). These new commands will likely be approved at a NATO summit in July 2018.

regional stability, will be strong only to the extent that NATO is able to clarify what it wants from the third leg of its Strategic Concept, namely cooperative security, and notably what this means at a practical level of day-to-day political-military activity.

CONCLUSION

One of NATO's main lessons learned from a decade's worth of Afghanistan warfare is the Protection of Civilian policy it started drafting in late 2014 and then finally endorsed in mid-2016. For as long as NATO does more than defend and deter its home territory, for as long as it engages in crisis management operations outside its protected domain, NATO must be better able to protect civilians. NATO will not accept full responsibility for protecting all human rights in violent conflicts, but it will do its part especially in regards to civilian casualties. Such was the lesson, and though it was framed in generic terms, it was clearly a lesson of special importance for the crisis management task inherent in its Strategic Concept.

NATO's return to European defence and deterrence was not antithetical to this lesson, at least in principle. On the one hand, modern defence and deterrence involves so-called "resilient" societies that should not be vulnerable to hybrid war and intimidation. On the other hand, protecting civilians goes hand-in-hand with narrower self-defence, counter-terrorist operations in the South. It is possible and indeed logical to fight terrorists such as Islamic State both with counter-terrorist offensives and then also stabilization policy that must protect the local civilian population. More than defence and deterrence in the abstract, it was the dogged and difficult nature of realizing effective crisis management in Afghanistan and also Libya that zapped NATO's enthusiasm for expansive, human security efforts.

If NATO PoC policy nowadays tends to wither on the vine, it is thus not because it is incompatible with defence and deterrence but because crisis management operations overwhelmed NATO and because the architecture of engagement along its southern flank is broken. Put differently, the PoC challenge is not about fear, uncertainty, and the return of realism in Europe but the persistence of fear and realism when it comes to nation-building in non-Western societies. The inability of Western allies to turn around the situation in Afghanistan even with an extraordinary infusion of American troops and leadership, in 2009–2010, has led them ever since into an extended transition and termination phase that evolves around the ongoing Afghan Resolute Support Mission. Beyond Afghanistan NATO's southern footprint is minimal, if not miniscule. The ambition for crisis management operations is gone, and NATO's Comprehensive Approach out of which its PoC policy emerged is at best dormant. NATO has sought to emphasize partnerships and capacity building missions as captured by the Projecting Stability agenda and as evidenced by small footprints in Iraq and Tunisia and also with the African Union. The ideas behind NATO's agenda are coherent enough, but the political momentum is weak and not growing.

NATO's return to Europe has de facto reordered the fundamental tasks of its 2010 Strategic Concept and thus reordered the framework within which NATO must think about the protection of civilians. The tasks are theoretically on par but effectively rank-ordered with defence and deterrence as the top priority, partnership and cooperative security as a struggling secondary task, and crisis management as a distant third order priority for which there is no political nostalgia. This is not necessarily negative from the perspective of advancing NATO's engagement with protection of civilian principles because, as mentioned, PoC principles are not incompatible with any of these strategic tasks. In fact, the defense against and deterrence of Russia along NATO's East-West axis might be a fearful task but is also a task with which NATO allies are familiar in terms of command-and-control and thus risk management. The fear of mission-creep, loss of strategic control, and internal dissent and division along the North-South axis runs deeper and is perhaps the ultimately realist challenge to the Alliance. It involves not least Turkey's role as an outcast ally that could become a spoiler of strategic unity, and it involves non-NATO partners that occasionally team up with NATO but have distinct views of the normative order from which PoC and human rights emerge. To move beyond fear and uncertainty, NATO must search for a realist policy somewhere between narrow counter-terrorism and broad transformative visions that caters to the special needs of southern allies, among them Turkey, but which remains principled enough to get southern partners to advance human rights principles. It will be a fine balancing act that NATO has only just begun.

Acknowledgements The author is grateful to the Gerda Henkel Stiftung for supporting research for this article and the overarching project *Can NATO Learn Afghan Lessons?*

References

Beadle, Alexander W. 2010. "Protection of Civilians in Theory—A Comparison of UN and Nato Approaches", *FFI-Report* 2010/02453. Kjeller: Forsvarets forskningsinstitutt. http://rapporter.ffi.no/rapporter/2010/02453.pdf.

Bowman, Steve, and Catherine Dale. 2010. *War in Afghanistan: Strategy, Military Operations, and Issues for Congress.* U.S. Library of Congress, Congressional Research Service. R40156, 32.

Crawford, Neta C. 2017. *Accountability for Killing: Moral Responsibility for Collateral Damage in America's Post-9/11 Wars.* Oxford: Oxford University Press.

Daalder, Ivo H., and James G. Stavridis. 2017. "NATO's Victory in Libya: The Right Way to Run an Intervention." *Foreign Affairs* 91 (2): 2–7.

Emmott, Robin. 2017. "NATO to Send More Troops to Afghanistan After U.S. Shift." *Reuters*, November 7. Available at https://www.reuters.com/article/us-nato-afghanistan/nato-to-send-more-troops-to-afghanistan-after-u-s-shift-idUSKBN1D71E0.

Gebauer, Matthias, Konstantin von Hammerstein, Peter Müller, and Christoph Schult. 2017. "NATO Grapples with Serious Organizational Shortcomings." *Der Spiegel*, October 20. Available at http://www.spiegel.de/international/world/nato-faces-serious-shortcomings-in-command-revamp-a-1173947.html.

Graf, Beatrice, George Dimitriu, J., and Jen Ringsmose, eds. 2015. *Strategic Narratives, Public Opinion and War: Winning Domestic Support for the Afghan War.* London: Routledge.

Joint Analysis and Lessons Learned Centre (JALLC). 2015. *Protection of Civilians: How ISAF Reduced Civilian Casualties.* Lisbon, Portugal: JALLC.

Moore, Rebecca, and Damon Coletta (eds.). 2017. *NATO's Return to Europe.* Washington D.C.: Georgetown University Press.

NATO. 2005. SACEUR OPLAN 10302 (Revise 1), December 2005, 106409, Unclassified.

NATO. 2010. "Active Engagement, Modern Defence: Strategic Concept for the Defence and Security of the Members of the North Atlantic Treaty Organization." *North Atlantic Treaty Organization*, November 19–20. Available at https://www.nato.int/cps/ua/natohq/official_texts_68580.htm.

NATO. 2012. "Chicago Summit Declaration Issues by the Heads of State and Government Participating in the Meeting of the North Atlantic Council in Chicago on 20 May 2012." *North Atlantic Treaty Organization*, August 1, 2012, paragraph 9. Available at https://www.nato.int/cps/en/natohq/official_texts_87593.htm?mode=pressrelease.

NATO. 2014a. "NATO/EAPC Policy for the Implementation of UNSCR 1325 on Women, Peace and Security and Related Resolutions," *North Atlantic*

Treaty Organization. June 24. Available at https://www.nato.int/cps/en/natohq/official_texts_109830.htm?selectedLocale=en.

NATO. 2014b. "Wales Summit Declaration," *North Atlantic Treaty Organization*, September 5, paragraph 89. Available at https://www.nato.int/cps/ic/natohq/official_texts_112964.htm.

NATO. 2016a. "NATO Policy for the Protection of Civilians, Endorsed by the Heads of State and Government Participating in the Meeting of the North Atlantic Council in Warsaw 8–9 July 2016." *North Atlantic Treaty Organization*, July 9. Available at http://www.nato.int/cps/en/natohq/official_texts_133945.htm?selectedLocale=en.

NATO. 2016b. "NATO and Children in Armed Conflict." *North Atlantic Treaty Organization*, July. Available at: https://www.nato.int/nato_static_fl2014/assets/pdf/pdf_2016_10/20161018_1610-children-armed-conflict-en.pdf.

NATO. 2016c. "Warsaw Summit Communiqué," *North Atlantic Treaty Organization.* July 8–9, paragraph 95. Available at https://www.nato.int/cps/en/natohq/official_texts_133169.htm.

NATO News. 2016. "NATO Steps Up Efforts to Project Stability and Strengthen Partners," *North Atlantic Treaty Organization*, July 14, 2016. Available at https://www.nato.int/cps/en/natohq/news_133804.htm?selectedLocale=en.

Perkins, Robert. 2014. *Air Power in Afghanistan: How NATO Changed the Rules, 2008–2014.* London: Action on Armed Violence.

Ringsmose, Jen and Sten Rynning. 2017. "Now for the Hard Part: NATO's Strategic Adaptation to Russia." *Survival: Global Politics and Strategy* 59 (3): 129–146.

Rynning, Sten. 2015. *NATO in Afghanistan: The Liberal Disconnect.* Stanford: Stanford University Press.

Rynning, Sten. 2017. "Rethinking NATO Policy on the Protection of Civilians." *Parameters* 47 (3): 1–11.

Steinsson, Sverrir. 2015. "NATO's Comprehensive Approach in Afghanistan: Origins, Development, and Outcome." *E-International Relations*, July 26. Available at http://www.e-ir.info/2015/07/26/natos-comprehensive-approach-in-afghanistan-origins-development-and-outcome/.

Stoltenberg, Jens. 2017a. "Press Conference." *North Atlantic Treaty Organization*, February 16. Available at https://www.nato.int/cps/ua/natohq/opinions_141109.htm?selectedLocale=en.

Stoltenberg, Jens. 2017b. "Projecting Stability Beyond Our Borders," *North Atlantic Treaty Organization*, March 2. Available at https://www.nato.int/cps/ic/natohq/opinions_141898.htm.

Streit Council. 2008. "Joint Declaration on UN/NATO Secretariat Cooperation," September 23. Available at http://streitcouncil.org/uploads/PDF/UN-NATO%20Joint%20Declaration.pdf.

The New Arab. 2017. "NATO to Launch 'Intelligence Hub' in Tunisia." *The New Arab*, April 11. Available at https://www.alaraby.co.uk/english/indepth/2017/4/11/nato-to-launch-intelligence-hub-in-tunisia.

Trump, Donald J. 2017. "Remarks by President Trump on the Strategy in Afghanistan and South Asia." *The White House*, August 21. Available at https://www.whitehouse.gov/the-press-office/2017/08/21/remarks-president-trump-strategy-afghanistan-and-south-asia/.

UNAMA and UNHCR. 2015. *Afghanistan: Annual Report 2014, Protection of Civilians in Armed Conflict*, 94. Kabul, Afghanistan: UNAMA/UNHCR.

United Nations. n.d. "Responsibility to Protect," *United Nations Office on Genocide Prevention and the Responsibility to Protect*. Available at http://www.un.org/en/genocideprevention/about-responsibility-to-protect.html.

Welsh, Jennifer. 2011. "Civilian Protection in Libya: Putting Coercion and Controversy Back into the RtoP." *Ethics and International Affairs* 25 (3): 255–262.

Williams, M. J. 2011. *The Good War: NATO and the Liberal Conscience in Afghanistan*. Basingstoke: Palgrave.

Williams, Nicholas. 2018. "Crisis Management versus Collective Defence," *Center for War Studies Policy Papers 1*. https://misc.sam.sdu.dk/files/P.pdf.

CHAPTER 12

Realism in the EU: Can a Trans-national Actor Be Strategic?

Vincent Della Sala and Roberto Belloni

The EU's two major strategic reviews in 2003 and 2016 represent book-ends that trace the evolution of its foreign policy from expectations to capabilities, to paraphrase Christopher Hill (1993). They capture the evolution of a foreign policy actor that initially seems focussed simply on projecting itself and its values onto a broader international canvas to one that wants to define more clearly priorities and develop the capacity to realise them. The two reviews also suggest that the context in which EU foreign policy is designed and applied has changed, from one that did not present serious threats to domestic and transnational security to one where fear and uncertainty have assumed a central position. They also present two different points in the evolution of European integration, with the first coming on the heels of the introduction of the single currency and on the cusp of the EU's most important enlargement to include former parts of the Soviet Union and the Warsaw Pact.

V. Della Sala (✉) · R. Belloni
Department of Sociology and Social Research,
University of Trento, Trento, Italy
e-mail: vincent.dellasala@soc.unitn.it

R. Belloni
e-mail: roberto.belloni@unitn.it

R. Belloni et al. (eds.), *Fear and Uncertainty in Europe*, Global Issues,
https://doi.org/10.1007/978-3-319-91965-2_12

From what was possibly the pinnacle of support for European integration, the second review thirteen years later saw the EU facing a number of serious challenges—economic crisis, migrants, tensions with Russia and Brexit—that led many national political leaders to talk of an "existential" crisis and an international order in which fear and uncertainty seemed to prevail.

The aim of this chapter is to examine some of the challenges that the EU faces in trying to act "strategically" in geopolitical spaces in close proximity and which have been traditionally sources of the fear and uncertainty that led to the reasons for the creation of the Union in the 1950s. We will focus on two areas that are particularly useful to illustrate the challenges the EU faces in being a strategic actor as well as the continuing or growing nationalization of foreign policy: its policy in the Balkans and the EU's relations with Russia. Our argument is that both areas present not only foreign policy challenges but also existential issues that point to the EU's lack of ontological security. They highlight the tension between the growing need to make strategic choices in both cases and remaining consistent with its narrative of a benign, normative power.

The chapter will be divided into two main sections. The first part will provide a broad picture of some of the debates about the EU's fledgling foreign policy and explores what realism may provide to inform debates about what kind of global actor it may be and become. The second part of the chapter will explore the EU's policy in the Balkans and with respect to Russia. Both cases will reveal the tension between the strategic choices the EU is forced to confront and how these may undermine some of the very same arguments that define the EU as a distinct global actor. The EU's "existential crisis" is that there may be an incongruity between what it thinks it is and how it must act in the international arena.

Realism and the EU

As Jack Donnelly points out in this volume, realism can be used in many different ways, from theory to heuristic device, and it can have many different meanings. What they share is the core notion that the fear and uncertainly that define international relations favours thin institutional and normative frameworks in guiding the behaviour of actors. In these terms, realism in whatever way it is used or understood would not be consistent with most conventional accounts of the European Union.

Scholars may disagree about the reasons for its creation and over what it is but the EU, especially with the end of the Cold War, has been seen as representing a different kind of international order than the one constructed by realism. It was to be an order based on a rich and textured multilateralism that placed primacy on the rule of law rather than material capability. It was not just hubris that led European leaders and commentators to argue that the new century would belong to the EU (Leonard 2005). It was fuelled by Europe's post-war experience, especially Franco-German relations, of using economic integration as the vehicle to enhance closer political ties and change the matrix of interests of member states. The structural constraints of the Cold War in Europe were glossed over to narrate the story of a project that had "surpassed realism" (Gilbert 2003). Not everyone shared in this belief of an international order free of power politics and geostrategic calculations. The dust had not yet settled after the crumbling of the Berlin Wall when John Mearsheimer warned of "going back to the future" in Europe. He foresaw that rather than ushering in a period of unbridled peace, the end of the Cold War would lead to multiple centres of power and power inequities on the continent and likely result in greater instability and likelihood of violence (Mearsheimer 1990). Mearsheimer may have anticipated developments that have led to greater fear and uncertainty in Europe but he was largely a lone voice in the 1990s, especially compared to the dominant almost hegemonic view amongst EU leaders and within EU studies that the end of bipolarism could only enhance the prospects for a thick institutional and normative order in Europe.

This belief that the EU was indeed the architect of an emerging order based on a thick institutionalism and normative foundation more than fear and uncertainty was captured in its first strategic review in 2003. Coming a decade after the formal introduction of the Common Foreign and Security Policy (CFSP), it was titled "A Secure Europe in a Better World" and opened by claiming that, "Europe has never been so prosperous, so secure nor so free" (Council of the European Union 2003: 1). Making arguments that seem consistent with liberal internationalism, the strategic review, known as the European Security Strategy (ESS), claimed that the opening of markets and the spread of democratic values and institutions were responsible for a more secure and peaceful Europe. Moreover, this successful management of relations within Europe was the basis for an assertive role in international relations and in extending the model to shape a new international order. Interestingly, the relatively brief report (15 pages compared to 55 in 2016) only refers to strategy once, on the title page, while there are only three references to "European interests". This suggests a vision of the EU that was charting a course for itself as the architect of an international order that was far from the power politics and geopolitical calculations that had shaped the continent in the modern era. Nonetheless, it marked a deliberate attempt to assume an international role for the EU as an important "strategic" actor (Mälksoo 2016).

The European Union Global Strategy (EUGS) was met with a great deal of fanfare and anticipation. As one of its architects, Natalie Tocci, claims, the EU needed more than just a vision that characterised the ESS. The EU was in the midst of an "existential crisis" and it needed a strategy to not only heal internal rifts but also to provide the basis to act in an increasingly unstable international order and to give meaning to that action (Tocci 2016: 462). Perhaps reflecting the bruising decade that had led to the EU's "existential crisis", the organising principle of the global strategy was to be "resilience", taking guidance from recent emphasis on the ability of states and societies to withstand and adapt to crises (Chandler 2012; Wagner and Anholt 2016). The emphasis on resilience was also seen as an attempt to distance EU foreign policy from the idealism of the ESS and to chart a more "pragmatic" course (Juncos 2017). The EUGS was seen as an attempt to begin to operationalize the EU's foreign policy by perhaps loosening the reins that resulted from an emphasis on the EU's thick institutional and normative approach. For instance, while the ESS had infrequent references to strategies and interests, nearly every page of the EUGS makes reference to one or both as the guiding principles for action.

The EU's two strategic reviews also represent the development of scholarship on the EU as a global actor and its foreign policy. Starting in the 1970s with the notion that the EU could be a "civilian power", many scholars largely perceived the fledgling foreign and security policy at the turn of the millennium as embodying "normative power" (Manners 2002). The EU as a global actor embodied the values that were instrumental in defining its reasons for being and which gave purpose to its relations with other states: a post-sovereign polity that operated on the basis of shared interests and values more than on clearly defined strategic interests backed by the security and defence architecture to realise them. The notion of normative power gained wide currency in the academic literature but by the time the EU began to reflect on a new strategic review, even scholarly research was taking a much more nuanced approach to foreign and security policy. Scholars began to ask if the EU could remain faithful to its liberal internationalist principles in a world that was increasingly reverting back to realist principles driven by geopolitical considerations (Krotz 2009; Smith 2011; Zimmermann 2007; Matlary 2006).

The EU's search for a strategic response to fear and uncertainty, evident in the second strategic review, is taking place in the midst of a broader questioning of the direction of the integration project. A useful lens to understand the evolution of CFSP and some of its shortcomings may be that of the notion of ontological security. The debate about the *sui generis* nature of the EU centres primarily on *what* it is—confederal, post-modern, compound, federalising, etc.—more than on who it is and why. However, as a social and collective actor, the EU may also seek out ontological security; that is, practices, routines and narratives that help define who it is and why it remains as a political community (Mitzen 2006a; Steele 2008). Drawing from its use by Giddens and international relations scholars, ontological security refers to a sense of confidence of one's identity (Berenskoetter 2014; Giddens 1991; Mitzen 2006b). Giddens claims that ontological security, "[r]efers to the confidence that most humans beings have in the continuity of their self-identity and in the constancy of the surrounding social and material environments of action" (Giddens 1990: 92). Ontological security claims that social actors need basic trust in the continuity of the factors that give them their sense of identity in order for them to have agency, to set objectives, define interests and act strategically. This continuity is rooted in habit and routine (Giddens 1990: 98) as well as in the stability of the environment that defines an identity. Routines are important in ordering the social world as they, "Serve the cognitive function of providing individuals with ways of knowing the world and how to act, giving them a felt certainty that enables purposive choice" (Mitzen 2006b: 347). In the face of perceived external threats and challenges, the EU seemed incapable of acting not because it did not know what to do, but because it was not clear what it was and why it should act.

The notion of normative power Europe, so central to so many academic debates and the EU's own narrative as a global actor, stands in contrast to many of the precepts of realism and geopolitics Being normative means replacing the state "as the centre of concern" (Manners), promoting values, using persuasion instead of brute force in foreign policy, etc. However, the concept of normative power may be understood differently, looking to the functions it might serve in trying to craft a foreign policy for a union of sovereign states (Bickerton 2011): that is, that the idea the EU is a benign global actor that behaves according to norms rather than interests serves as a lowest common denominator to mask that its member states have different interests and behave differently (Bickerton 2011: 34). The EU's foundational narrative is that it eschews power politics in favour of a rules-based international order, notwithstanding the possibility that its member states may not necessarily always behave accordingly. The argument here is that the EU's foreign policy is as much for internal consumption as it is for shaping the behaviour of other actors. It helps contribute to a biography of the EU that is consistent with relations between its member states, guided by a commitment to values and shared economic interests. The challenges arise, as they have in the last decade, when that biography needs to be reconciled with the need to make strategic decisions in parts of the world and with other actors who operate according to a realist logic and geopolitical considerations (Smith 2011). Academic scholarship, just like EU policy-makers, has begun to find ways in which to reconcile a commitment to liberal democratic values, as well as internal policy differences and a fledgling foreign policy architecture, with the need to deal with an international order that is increasingly characterised by fear and uncertainty (Wagner 2017; Simón 2013).

THE WESTERN BALKANS: THE CHANGING MEANING OF ENLARGEMENT

The EU's Strategic Review in 2003 declared the building of a "ring of well-governed countries" in the neighbourhood as a key strategic objective and elevated "good governance" as a guiding principle of its foreign policy. Geographically, it singled out the Balkans as the "best illustration" of the benefits of enlargement in supporting the democratic transformation of aspiring new EU members. Both policy makers and several scholars recognized enlargement as the key policy instrument in order to achieve political stability and support the process of democratic transformation in the region. The accession process entailed the application of a number of conditionalities, identified by the 1993 "Copenhagen criteria," which have been progressively tightened and made more stringent in the course of several enlargement rounds. This inherently top-down and material process, whereby the stronger actor (the EU) sets the conditions, while the weaker actors (western Balkan states) have to accept and apply them with relatively minor leverage to negotiate particular issues, was premised upon the EU's normative power of attraction. The EU believed that only in extreme cases, if at all, conditions should have been imposed through arm-twisting, sanctions and the like. Rather, because these conditions were expected to benefit aspiring new EU members by bringing them closer to universal values of democracy and human rights, they were inherently appealing and should have been subscribed to more or less voluntarily. Thus, by the time the first Strategic Review was published, the EU's own narrative highlighted its attractiveness as a beacon of universal values and principles.

Throughout the 2000s several policy analysts and think-tanks endorsed this EU's self-understanding. For example, in an influential report the International Commission on the Balkans (2005) described the options available to the EU as between "empire and enlargement." In dealing with the western Balkan region the strategic choices were essentially reduced to two: either the EU imposed a number of semi-protectorates and run them in a quasi colonial fashion, thus imposing the law of the stronger while violating basic principles of self-determination and human rights; or it provided the region with an enlargement perspective to support a process of domestically-driven political, economic and governance reforms. The Commission's own choice was stated explicitly: while the EU possessed the power to impose its own views (and institutions) on western Balkans states, such an imposition would have amounted to a short-term (and short-sighted) superficial change. By contrast, the International Commission on the Balkans believed that an enlargement perspective would have unleashed the EU's attractiveness, supported the domestic ownership of reforms, and thus led to a more profound and lasting restructuring of domestic institutions.

With the enlargement prospective, formally adopted in the early 2000s, the EU rejected power politics and the outside imposition of policies and institutions in favour of an approach more respectful of domestic sovereignty and local ownership (Belloni 2009). In the case of Bosnia-Herzegovina, for example, it was not the top-down implementation of the 1995 Dayton Peace Agreement that was expected to move the country forward. Rather, possible membership should have stimulated a pro-Europe, bottom-up, reformist zeal in both political elites and citizens desiring to join the European club (European Stability Initiative 2005).

In a memorable sentence by Lord Paddy Ashdown, then High Representative of the International Community in the country, with the integration perspective and the related unleashing of the EU normative power, "the pull of Brussels will replace the push of Dayton." The EU's engagement in the western Balkans may have involved techniques of governmentality and practices of domination and exclusion (Juncos 2011), but nonetheless the EU has been reluctant to openly impose solutions to domestic problems, as for example in the case of the unsuccessful attempt at constitutional reform in Bosnia (Aparicio 2014). Not all EU member states were equally enthusiastic about the prospect of integrating the region into the EU, but in the optimistic mood of the 2000s, they endorsed the policy strategy strongly promoted by the Commission.

In sum, the EU put forward an enlargement policy vis-à-vis the western Balkan region aimed at supporting domestic processes of political, economic and social transformation through the power of attraction, not through coercion or imposition. This approach was premised upon three main underlying ideas which run diametrically opposed to almost any version of political realism as conventionally understood in the theory and practice of international relations (see Donnelly's chapter in this volume). First, norms and principles were thought to be at least as influential as coercion in producing change. Second, because of its *sui generis* character, the EU should have undermined state-centric understandings of international relations. The EU, simply by virtue of what it was even regardless of what it did, could structure the environment around it in a way to supersede traditional conceptions of the state and of its external role (Manners 2002). Third, the EU's enlargement policy was grounded not on the promotion of its own self-interest, which, by definition, could conflict with the self-interest of other actors, but was premised upon the prominence of democracy and human rights, both understood as universal (as opposed to European) values. On this basis, the EU viewed its foreign policy not so much as a zero-sum competition with actual or potential competitors, or as an uneasy coexistence between superpowers, but primarily as the promotion of a world order governed by international law, transparency, and mutual recognition.

Since the outbreak of the Euro crisis in 2008, however, and above all since the entry of Croatia in the EU on 1 July 2013, the EU has largely lost interest for enlargement. Both the EU and its member states are preoccupied more by managing a profound political crisis that began as a financial problem but evolved into a deeper existential predicament, than to accept new states into the European club. Confronted with an unprecedented migration wave, the still unpredictable consequences of "Brexit", and a feeble and uneven economic recovery, the majority of EU member states are influenced by a so-called "enlargement fatigue" and consider further enlargement an afterthought. To the extent they support accepting new member states into the EU, they do so by subscribing to a rhetorical support but without actively engaging into enlargement politics (Balfour and Stratulat 2015).

This situation has several consequences for the Western Balkans. To begin with, the EU's persistent crisis, coupled with its inability to provide a credible enlargement prospective, has facilitated the rise of Turkey, China, the Gulf states and, above all, Russia as realistic competitors for influence. According to Dimitar Bechev, "Russia and Putin command a tremendous amount of support across countries with Eastern Orthodox majorities (Serbia, Bulgaria, Greece, Republika Srpska in Bosnia and the Greek part of Cyprus)" (Bechev 2017: 225–226). This support has been demonstrated on numerous occasions, for example when Bosnia-Herzegovina, Macedonia and Serbia refused to apply EU's sanctions imposed against Moscow because of its behaviour in Ukraine from 2014 onwards. While Russia is not recreating satellite states reminiscent of an old-style empire, it is nonetheless interfering with European plans. Most notably, Moscow has been supporting Bosnian Serbs' challenge to the authority of the central state in Bosnia; it has engaged in a profound security and defence cooperation with Serbia—the only country in the region not seeking full NATO membership; and, according to the government in Podgorica, it supported a failed coup in Montenegro in October 2016 aimed at disrupting the country's accession to NATO.

Thus, the EU's Global Strategy has repeatedly condemned the "illusion that international politics can be a zero-sum game" while at the same time affirming its belief that its "power of attraction can spur transformation and is not aimed against any country" (European Commission 2016: 4, 25) in reality the EU and its member states (above all Germany) have been keenly aware that Europe's weakness has been opening a space for Russia to act as a spoiler. Russia is viewed in several European capitals as an existential threat to Europe's values and norms, and as a credible alternative to the EU. As confirmed by David McAllister, Chair of the European Parliament Foreign Affairs Committee, "geopolitics has returned to the Balkans" (Rankin 2017). Similarly Federica Mogherini, EU High Representative for Foreign

Affairs and Security Policy, has warned how "the Balkans can easily become one of the chessboards where the big power game can be played" (EurActive 2017).

The ultimate consequences of Russian activism and the question of the most appropriate strategic response to it is a matter of debate. In the most pessimistic reading of the situation, the alliance between Russia and Serbia could ultimately lead to a new war in Kosovo, destabilize Bosnia-Herzegovina, and draw into military conflict even NATO member Croatia (Schindler 2017). By contrast, other analysts suggest that Russia's economic and diplomatic clout in the region is relatively limited (Relijć 2017), but it is exaggerated by all actors involved for self-serving reasons: while Russia presents itself as more powerful and influential than actually the case, domestic governing leaders are keen to accept these claims in order to increase their leverage vis-à-vis the EU. Local leaders in the western Balkans skilfully play one side against the other in order to extract resources and concessions by Brussels, in particular a more relaxed attitude with regard to accession conditions. In order to break this stalemate, some analysts argue the EU should call the bluff and maintain a robust engagement in the region; when pressured to make a choice, local leaders will choose Europe—and the United States (Bechev 2017). Be that as it may, while the response to Russia's increasing assertiveness may be subjected to debate, nonetheless both the EU and its member states have began to take seriously the previously refuted idea that international politics can involve a "zero-sum" game between superpowers.

In addition to paving the way for Russia's growing influence, the inability of the EU to provide a credible strategy vis-à-vis the region has undermined its credibility as a foreign policy actor and has favoured the return to state-centred approaches to the region. No longer is the European Commission the key enlargement actor. Enlargement has been increasingly "nationalised", with member states more and more involved in setting conditions for aspiring new members and in assessing progress towards fulfilling those conditions. Thus, in recent years the Commission has both adopted a more strong-armed attitude and has found itself discussing (and sometimes quarrelling) with member states with regard to the assessment of the situation on the ground and the related policy choices. Member states have gradually assumed a dominant position on enlargement vis-à-vis officials in Brussels, and have (re)asserted their role as gatekeepers (Hillion 2015). As a result, the re-nationalisation of

European foreign policy has reverted the relationship between Europe and the western Balkans to bilateral relationships and the related attempt to carve out spheres of influence.

The perception of an increasing Russian threat in the region has convinced Germany (supported by Austria, United Kingdom, France, Italy and EU regional members Slovenia and Croatia) of the need for a more proactive presence in the area. Germany has been at the forefront in favour of a policy of continuing engagement with the region, for example by attempting to sustain a reform process in Bosnia through the so-called German-British Initiative (Jukic 2014). Germany has taken a lead both in supporting further enlargement but also in applying strict enlargement accession conditionality (Adebahr and Töglhofer 2015). It has criticised the Commission for presenting an unrealistic, too rosy picture of the situation in aspiring EU members, has clarified formerly unspecified conditions (for example by linking Serbia's accession to Serbia-Kosovo relations) and has stimulated the enlargement process in the most difficult cases (for instance in Bosnia) and regionally by promoting cross-border collaboration on issues of common interest through the so-called "Berlin process" (Flessenkemper 2017).

Germany's activism has facilitated the EU's renewed engagement vis-à-vis the Western Balkans, which is increasingly perceived in Brussels as a "strategic" region. In his 2017 State of the Union address, Commission President Juncker explained that the enlargement process continues to move forward despite the political difficulties that the EU has been experiencing for years, in particular after the outbreak of the economic and financial crisis in 2008. Juncker reiterated that no new accessions will take place before the end of his mandate (that is, late 2019), but he added enlargement to both Serbia and Montenegro among the Union's objectives to reach by 2025. This re-affirmation of the enlargement prospect occurred in a political context very different from the optimistic period of the early 2000s, when the first Strategic Review was published. Indeed, rather than testifying to the EU's renewed commitment and reliance on its celebrated normative and transformative power, the re-affirmation of enlargement reflects a response to the regional dynamics of "fear and uncertainty" and the related need to safeguard the EU's threatened ontological security. In proposing a revamped enlargement process, the EU attempts to address its existential crisis by falling back on its established routines involving conditionality and the top-down assessment of domestic political, economic and social processes.

The 2016 Global Strategy is supposed to provide the EU with the new normative framework in foreign policy. However, the concept of resilience is of limited relevance to existing policies towards the Western Balkans (Balfour 2017: 17), as opposed to "principled pragmatism," which has been elevated to the guiding standard to navigate the new uncertainties and threats in the region. In practice, "principled pragmatism" has translated into the sidelining of transformative motivations. The EU's approach aimed at achieving "stability" through a leader-oriented method of engagement and, by so doing, it has favoured the development of an "unhealthy symbiotic relationship" (Bandović and Dimitrov 2017: 81) between Balkan strongmen and European political elites. The 2015–2016 refugee crisis along the so-called "Balkan route" has been decisive in shaping this relationship. For the most part, EU member states interpreted the mass arrival of asylum-seeking persons as a threat to their security, identity, and wellbeing, and decided to close their borders. As a result, the Commission could only take note of member states' unwillingness to accept asylum-seekers, and thus operated to block them along the frontiers of the Union by relying on the collaboration of domestic leaders. Despite concerns about democratic backsliding, local governments, in particular the Serbian and Macedonian ones, could benefit from European support because of their role in closing the Balkan route. The EU praised regional leaders and elevated them to "factors of stability," while simultaneously downplaying normative and human rights concerns. The EU-Turkey Agreement, reached on 20 March 2016, testified to the Union's willingness to interpret "principled pragmatism" as setting aside normative "principled" issues in order to find a "pragmatic" solution to the refugee problem (Amnesty International 2016). For their part, in addition to acting as border police, local leaders have skilfully exploited fears related to the rising influence of Russia and to simmering ethnic tensions in order to present themselves in Brussels as indispensible counterparts.

Overall, the EU approach has contributed to "the rise of a regional 'stabilitocracy,' weak democracies with autocratically minded leaders, who govern through informal, patronage networks and claim to provide pro-Western stability in the region" (BiEPAG 2017: 7). All major democracy indices (including Freedom House and Bertelsmann) show that the western Balkan states have been backsliding for about a decade. Patterns of semi-authoritarian political rule involving the exercise of power through party dominance and patron-client networks are ever more common. Domestic leaders are both increasingly authoritarian and self-proclaimed pro-European democrats, while the EU is willing to turn a blind eye to local politicians' practices as long as they deliver on issues which represent a priority for member states, such as border control, fighting terrorism or regional stability (Stratulat 2017). In sum, Western Balkan leaders have learned that good relations with the EU are facilitated by the delivery of key EU needs, perhaps even more so than the adoption of those reforms required by the accession process. Although this approach may achieve some short-term success, in the long-run it could undermine stability by fuelling popular discontent, damaging the appeal of the EU (which is seen by pro-democracy movements in the region an impediment to democratization), and thus opening the way for other geopolitical actors to gain influence.

The EU and Russia: Policies in Search of a Vision

Paradoxically, although the EU had a strategic partnership with Russia since 1997 and the two partners shared a number of important policy objectives in a confined geographic area, the EU's 2003 strategic review had very little to say about Russia except that it was an important partner in key areas such as the Balkans and the Middle East. There was little concern about Russia being a security threat as the review claimed, "We should continue to work for closer relations with Russia, a major factor in our security and prosperity. Respect for common values will reinforce progress towards a strategic partnership" (Council of the European Union 2003: 14). This was consistent with the EU's understanding of itself as a global actor and the kind of international order it wanted to create: rooted in norms, foreign policy would reflect shared values but also interests that emerged from economic interdependence. A little more than a decade later, the 2016 strategic review claimed that Russia represented a threat to security in Europe and the greatest strategic challenge faced by the EU's foreign policy (European Commission 2016: 33). This trajectory of seeing Russia as a partner to then becoming a threat also highlights how the EU's sense of self as a regional, if not global, actor has been challenged by its relations with Russia (Kazharski and Makarychev 2015).

The relationship with Russia and post-Soviet states presented opportunities and challenges for the EU. Geography and historical legacies have ensured that the two sides would be destined to share common challenges but also be rivals for spreading influence and pursuing interests (Haukkala 2010). The immediate post-Soviet period in the 1990s saw the EU confident that it could build a "partnership" with Russia to address common concerns as well as promote its understanding of how it saw order in a wider European space and its role in it. This found expression in the Partnership and Cooperation Agreement (PCA) in 1997, which set out the principal common objectives, established the institutional framework for bilateral contacts, and called for activities and dialogue in a number of areas. Major principles and objectives of the PCA (perhaps paradoxically) included promotion of international peace and security; support for democratic norms, as well as for political and economic freedoms. At the Moscow Summit in May 2005, they adopted the Common Spaces Road Maps as the short and medium term instruments for the implementation of these areas. The EU-Russia strategic partnership was further complemented by the Northern Dimension and Cooperation with the Baltic Sea Region, the Black Sea Cooperation, the Partnership for Modernization in 2010 and more recently dialogue on the Arctic. The growing intensity and frequency of these agreements suggested a relationship that was, until Russia's invasion and annexation of the Crimea, deepening and increasingly institutionalized, with regular progress reports and benchmarks (Averre 2010).

Yet, masking what once seemed like a linear trajectory is a relationship marked by tensions over not only how to manage the "common spaces" but basic values and norms. Russia's attempts to continue to exert influence on shared neighbors, such as the Ukraine, were always a source of tension (Haukkala 2017). The EU's resistance to extending visa-free travel to Russian officials travelling in the EU was seen as condescending by the Russian leadership. EU criticism of Russian legislation regarding homosexuality furthered the sense that the relationship was not necessarily between partners who see each other as equals. Even prior to the Crimean invasion, Commission President Barroso, in an interview ahead of the G8 summit in St Petersburg in 2006 claimed that Russia cannot be regarded as a "*full, European-style*" democracy (authors' emphasis) and it is unclear whether it will become one.[1] He later went on to say that, "human rights and rule of law are much more important than diplomacy

---

[1] Cited from the Independent, July 13, 2006. Accessed on May 22, 2012.

between two states", suggesting that the strategic partnership with Russia was perhaps not so important for the EU.[2]

The underlying tensions are rooted in a lack of shared understanding amongst the EU member states and between the EU and Russia of what was "strategic" and whether it was the basis for a "partnership". The PCA is based on the premise that the two sides share many problems, often with their source in Russia and their consequences in the EU. These range from environmental threats to regional instability and transnational organized crime. Not surprisingly, it seems that the 'common spaces' are venues of differences, quarrels, and even conflicts. A source of tension with these common spaces is how to manage relations with neighbors the two partners share, resulting in a wider Europe initiative that includes the European Neighborhood Policy (ENP) and the Eastern Partnership (EaP) (Lavenex 2004) even encroaching on areas which Russia has always seen as its backyard. Russia has long sought to construct a Eurasian Union that extends westwards to the Ukraine, which has, under Poroshenko, instead opted to become an associate member of the EU. The EU has been able to develop an effective framework of engagement with neighbors in the areas shared with Russia. By providing "everything but institutions" (Prodi 2002), the EU presents itself as a more attractive partner than Russia, armed with an ambitious external governance agenda to manage its new interdependence in a shared geopolitical environment.

These issues were at the centre of the EU's strategy with its eastern neighbours, called EaP, which was part of a broader policy framework called ENP, created in 2004 and included Armenia, Azerbaijan, Belarus, Georgia, Moldova and Ukraine (Noutcheva et al. 2013). The EaP was established in December 2008, in part as a response by member states such as Poland and Sweden to the attempt by French President Nicholas Sarkozy to create a Mediterranean Union to enhance relations with the EU's southern neighbours. It was also a response to the Russian intervention in Georgia earlier in the year. It emerged because different member states looked to the ENP for different reasons. Some, such as Britain,

---

[2] "Barroso clashes with Putin over human rights abuses in Russia," European Forum for Democracy and Solidarity, February 9, 2009. http://www.europeanforum.net/news/509/barroso_clashes_with_putin_over_human_rights_abuses_in_russia. Accessed September 23, 2013.

saw it as a means to strengthen internal security by dealing with issues such as immigration and terrorism; while others, such as Poland, saw it a way to promote common values and interests (Łapczyński 2009). The latter referred to the strategic interest in drawing closer into the EU's orbit the former Soviet states on its borders. The aim with the EaP was to go beyond the general ENP objective of trying to influence neighbours with carrots and to try to deepen relations with the partners with the promise of greater access to EU markets and institutions (Bosse 2009). The EaP fell short of offering the prospect of full membership in the EU in the near or medium-term but it did promise enhanced bilateral relations, the chance to enter into a free trade area and increased civil society exchanges. In addition, the EU and the partners would devise Action Plans to help the latter achieve objectives to more closely align their policies, rules and institutions to those of the EU (Korosteleva 2011). Full membership may not have been on the table but the prospect of a free trade area and the aligning of domestic policies and politics certainly suggested to the partners that it was legitimate to hope that it might eventually result from the EaP.

Post Crimean annexation, the EaP is in tatters and the EU's stance towards Russia casts doubts over the existence of an EU-Russia strategic partnership. The annexation has resulted in EU sanctions against Russian firms, officials and associates of Vladimir Putin, with more applied after Russia intervened militarily in Eastern Ukraine. It also led to the cancellation of a planned G-8 summit on Russian territory in Sochi, and effective Russian expulsion from the G-8 by a revived G-7. The EU's apparent inability to influence Russian policy, from energy to human rights issues, or even to persuade Russia to eschew the military conquest of a portion of territory of a sovereign neighboring state, has led to numerous calls for a more "strategic" foreign policy (Youngs 2014). What this means is not entirely clear and it has been interpreted in two, possibly conflicting, ways. The first suggests that the EU's lack of hard power instruments is a severe constraint when dealing with a contending regional power that may not be as convinced about the imminent transformation of the international order based on power and geopolitics to one where multilateralism and the rule of law reigned. Being "strategic" in this sense means a readiness to make sacrifices and to inflict harm on an adversary to change its behavior: hence the use of sanctions after the military intervention in the Ukraine. However, being "strategic" has also been interpreted as meaning that the EU should no longer have its foreign policy driven by its own normative map and openly accept that there are instances when its interests need to be given a greater weight in shaping its relations with other actors (Cebeci 2017). This has meant that while the 28 member states have hung together to maintain sanctions against Russia, these have been not been comprehensive. Rather than making them open-ended and applicable until Russia recognizes the Ukraine's sovereign borders, the sanctions are subject to renewal every six months, leading to regular speculation that one or more member states will withdraw their support. Moreover, any attempt to extend the sanctions to back up EU criticism of Russia's bombing in Syria has been rejected by one or more member states. Some member states, such as Italy and to a lesser extent France and Germany, have argued that the EU needs to find a way to dialogue and accommodate Russia, as this is its long-term strategic interest.

The EU's relationship with Russia serves a number of important roles in helping craft the EU's narrative of itself as an international actor. Its institutions present the EU as a benign, ethical and democratic actor while narrating Russia as authoritarian, a perpetuator of human rights abuses, and more recently, as a flagrant violator of the territorial sovereignty of states (Tsygankov 2012). The discursive practice of "common spaces" connotes that the two close neighbors are divided, with conflicts and contestations on a wide range of issues but also that they are destined to manage shared interests and challenges. The EU's ambiguous treatment of territoriality is presented as the cutting edge of an emerging international order while Russia can be presented as stuck in a nineteenth century understanding of territory and power (Casier 2016).

The EU's complex relationship with Russia is especially fraught when it comes to the question of energy (Kuzemko 2014). Russia is the EU's most important single source of oil and gas, with some member states, such as Bulgaria, importing over 90% of its natural gas from its eastern partner. Reducing energy dependency in general, but specifically with respect to Russia, has led to an acceleration of the development of an "energy union" that will not only create an internal market but also a common policy to deal with third parties. The EU's energy policy has been wrapped in language and ambitions of European integration: the creation of a single market, unleashing competitive forces, the need to reduce consumption of fossil fuels, taking a leadership role in forging a global and multilateral response to climate change. It has translated into policy choices and outcomes that, from a European perspective, are merely instruments derived from these broader objectives aimed at European integration but which have been perceived by Russia as strategic choices to upset an equilibrium. For instance, the EU has sought to reduce the monopolistic presence of firms in the production, transportation and distribution of energy sources, leading to investigations by its competition authorities and policies that force firms to "unbundle" their different energy components. While EU institutions present this as consistent with the long-standing aim to create a competitive internal market, it is perceived by Russia as an attempt to weaken Gazprom, the large Russia firm that delivers gas to over 25 European states.

Pressure from the EU and its energy policy architecture led Russia and some EU member states, such as Bulgaria, to abandon plans to develop pipelines delivering gas to member states in eastern and central Europe; while other states sought their own deals with Russia. Germany has developed the North Stream I pipeline (operative since 2011) and plans to double capacity are being negotiated with North Stream II. Other member states, such as Italy, have looked to develop other routes and agreements, some aimed at reducing reliance on Russia but others looking to bypass troublesome routes for Russia through the Ukraine. Competing contracts, pipelines and distribution networks have made it difficult for the EU to develop a coherent position when dealing with Russia on energy, as member states have tried to ensure that their energy needs are met without always remaining consistent with commitments made at the EU level.

Both the conflict in the Ukraine and energy questions present the EU and its member states with difficult choices while also revealing some of the internal tensions in formulating a coherent strategic vision (Makarychev 2015). The 2016 global strategic review underscores how Russia presents not just a geostrategic threat to European security but an existential one: that is, Russia's understanding of geopolitics as a zero-sum game is at odds with an international order that puts norms and the rule of law at its core. The EU has thus not been able to craft a coherent response to this possible existential threat. Its member states have hung together to continue with a limited range of sanctions but were not able to come up with any other instruments as it became clear that they were having only a limited effect on the Kremlin's behaviour. Moreover, thinking strategically with respect to Russia means exposing deep fissures between member states not just on what needs to be done but on whether something needs to be done and by whom.

CONCLUSION

As the EU was buffeted by its many crises in the last decade, tensions in its ability to craft a foreign policy became apparent. Its global strategic review acknowledged as much and tried to navigate between trying to set out a strategic vision—laying out priorities and spelling out how to achieve them—and remaining faithful to its narrative of a benign normative power. The tension is apparent in a range of cases, from the western Balkans to the EU's relationship with Russia but also in relations with the United States and the Middle East. What emerges in the 2016 strategic review is that nearly twenty-five years of formally crafting a common foreign policy and sixty years of building an ever closer union has made acting with a single coherent voice in international relations a common good that gives meaning to the EU and could serve the strategic needs of its member states. In this sense, realism and geopolitics are not useful instruments to understand the emergence of a global power that is not a state.

While a common foreign policy might be in the long-term interest of the EU and its member states, especially in dealing with a military power such as Russia or a complex situation such as the western Balkans, there has yet to emerge a common understanding of what it should be and how it should be exercised. Our two cases reveal that a common foreign policy in the EU still is driven by member states, who do not hesitate to seek out their own interests bilaterally if need be. Moreover, they are increasingly driven by the pressures of fear and uncertainty, which render the EU's objective of creating a thick institutional and normative framework less tangible. In this way, realism does provide a useful interpretative key in that state actors continue to drive the process and pursue their own interests even at the expense of a collective and common policy. A dynamic that is not unlike a tragedy of the commons can develop, where each member state pursues their own strategic interests but still wants the cover of a common European policy.

REFERENCES

Adebahr, Cornelius, and Theresia Töglhofer. 2015. "Germany." In *EU Member States and Enlargement Towards the Balkans*, edited by Rosa Balfour and Corina Stratulat. Brussels: European Policy Centre, Issue Paper No. 79, July.

Amnesty International. 2016. *No Safe Refuge: Asylum Seekers and Refugees Denied Affective Protection in Turkey*. June 3, EUR 44/3825/2016.

Averre, Derek. 2010. "The EU, Russia and the Shared Neighbourhood: Security, Governance and Energy." *European Security* 19 (4): 531–534.

Balfour, Rosa. 2017. "Enlargement: What Role for Resilience?" In *Resilience in the Western Balkans*, edited by Sabina Lange, Zoran Nechev, and Florian Trauner. Paris: EU Institute for Security Studies, Report No. 36, August.

Balfour, Rosa, and Corina Stratulat (eds.) 2015. *EU Member States and Enlargement Towards the Balkans*. Brussels: European Policy Centre.

Bandović, Igor, and Nikola Dimitrov. 2017. "Balkan Strongmen and Fragile Institutions." In *Resilience in the Western Balkans*, edited by Sabina Lange, Zoran Nechev, and Florian Trauner. Paris: EU Institute for Security Studies, Report No. 36, August.

Bechev, Dimitar. 2017. *Rival Power: Russia in Southeast Europe*. New Haven and London: Yale University Press.

Belloni, Roberto. 2009. "European Integration and the Western Balkans: Lessons, Prospects and Obstacles." *Journal of Balkan and Near Eastern Studies* 11 (3): 313–331.

Berenskoetter, Felix. 2014. "Parameters of a National Biography." *European Journal of International Relations* 20 (1): 262–288.

Bickerton, Christopher J. 2011. *European Union Foreign Policy: From Effectiveness to Functionality*. London: Palgrave Macmillan.

BiEPAG (Balkans in Europe Policy Advisory Group). 2017. *The Crisis of Democracy in the Western Balkans: Authoritarianism and EU Stabilitocracy*. Graz: BiEPAG.

Bosse, Giselle. 2009. "Challenges for EU Governance Through Neighbourhood Policy and Eastern Partnership: The Values/Security Nexus in EU–Belarus Relations." *Contemporary Politics* 15 (2): 215–227.

Casier, Tom. 2016. "Identities and Images of Competition in the Overlapping Neighbourhoods: How EU and Russian Foreign Policies Interact." In *Security in Shared Neighbourhoods*, edited by Rémi Piet and Licínia Simão, 13–34. Basingstoke: Palgrave Macmillan.

Cebeci, Münevver. 2017. "Deconstructing the 'Ideal Power Europe' Meta-Narrative in the European Neighbourhood Policy." In *The Revised European Neighbourhood Policy*, edited by Dimitris Bouris and Tobias Schumacher, 57–76. Basingstoke: Palgrave Macmillan.

Chandler, David. 2012. "Resilience and Human Security: The Post-Interventionist Paradigm." *Security Dialogue* 43 (3): 213–229.

Council of the European Union. 2003. *A Secure Europe in a Better World: European Security Strategy*. Brussels: Council of the European Union.

European Commission. 2016. *Shared Vision, Common Action: A Stronger Europe—A Global Strategy for the European Union's Foreign and Security Policy*. Brussels: European Commission.

European Stability Initiative. 2005. *The Helsinki Moment—European Member State Building in the Balkans.* Berlin: European Stability Initiative, 1 February.

Flessenkemper, Tobias. 2017. "The Berlin Process: Resilience in the EU Waiting Room." In *Resilience in the Balkans*, edited by Sabina Lange, Zoran Nechev, and Florian Trauner, 23–29. Paris: EU Institute for Security Studies.

Giddens, Anthony. 1990. *The Consequences of Modernity.* Cambridge: Polity Press.

Giddens, Anthony. 1991. *Modernity and Self-Identity.* Cambridge: Polity Press.

Gilbert, Mark. 2003. *Surpassing Realism.* Lanham, MD: Rowman and Littlefield.

Haukkala, Hiski. 2010. *The EU-Russia Strategic Partnership: The Limits of Post-Sovereignty in International Relations.* London: Routledge.

Haukkala, Hiski. 2017. "The EU's Regional Normative Hegemony Encounters Hard Realities: The Revised European Neighbourhood Policy and the Ring of Fire." In *The Revised European Neighbourhood Policy*, edited by Dimitris Bouris and Tobias Schumacher, 77–94. Basingstoke: Palgrave Macmillan.

Hill, Christopher. 1993. "The Capability-Expectations Gap, or Conceptualizing Europe's International Role." *Journal of Common Market Studies* 31 (3): 305–328.

Hillion, Christophe. 2015. "Masters or Servants? Member States in the EU Enlargement Process." In *EU Member States and Enlargement Towards the Balkans*, edited by Rosa Balfour and Corina Stratulat. Brussels: European Policy Centre, Issue Paper No. 79, July.

International Commission on the Balkans. 2005. *The Balkans in Europe's Future.* Sofia: Centre for Liberal Studies.

Jukic, Elvira. 2014. "UK, Germany Launch Joint Initiative on Bosnia." *Balkan Insight*, 5 November.

Juncos, Ana E. 2011. "Power Discourses and Power Practices: The EU's Role as a Normative Power in Bosnia." In *Normative Power Europe*, edited by Richard G. Whitman. Houndmills: Palgrave.

Juncos, Ana E. 2017. "Resilience as the New EU Foreign Policy Paradigm: A Pragmatist Turn?" *European Security* 26 (1): 1–18.

Kazharski, Aliaksei, and Andrey Makarychev. 2015. "Suturing the Neighborhood? Russia and the EU in Conflictual Intersubjectivity." *Problems of Post-Communism* 62 (6): 328–339.

Korosteleva, Elena A. 2011. "Change or Continuity: Is the Eastern Partnership an Adequate Tool for the European Neighbourhood?" *International Relations* 25 (2): 243–262.

Krotz, Ulrich. 2009. "Momentum and Impediments: Why Europe Won't Emerge as a Full Political Actor on the World Stage Soon." *Journal of Common Market Studies* 47 (3): 555–578.

Kuzemko, Caroline. 2014. "Ideas, Power and Change: Explaining EU–Russia Energy Relations." *Journal of European Public Policy* 21 (1): 58–75.

Łapczyński, Marcin. 2009. "The European Union's Eastern Partnership: Chances and Perspectives." *Caucasian Review of International Affairs* 3 (2): 143–155.

Lavenex, Sandra. 2004. "EU External Governance in 'Wider Europe'." *Journal of European Public Policy* 11 (4): 680–700.

Leonard, Mark. 2005. *Why Europe Will Run the Twenty-first Century*. London: Atlantic.

Makarychev, Andrey. 2015. "A New European Disunity: EU–Russia Ruptures and the Crisis in the Common Neighborhood." *Problems of Post-Communism* 62 (6): 313–315.

Mälksoo, Maria. 2016. "From the ESS to the EU Global Strategy: External Policy, Internal Purpose." *Contemporary Security Policy* 37 (3): 374–388. https://doi.org/10.1080/13523260.2016.1238245.

Manners, Ian. 2002. "Normative Power Europe: A Contradiction in Terms?" *Journal of Common Market Studies* 40 (2): 235–258.

Matlary, Janne Haaland. 2006. "When Soft Power Turns Hard: Is an EU Strategic Culture Possible?" *Security Dialogue* 37 (1): 105–121.

Mearsheimer, John J. 1990. "Back to the Future: Instability in Europe After the Cold War." *International Security* 15 (1): 5–56.

Mitzen, Jennifer. 2006a. "Anchoring Europe's Civilizing Identity: Habits, Capabilities and Ontological Security." *Journal of European Public Policy* 13 (2): 270–285.

Mitzen, Jennifer. 2006b. "Ontological Security in World Politics: State Identity and the Security Dilemma." *European Journal of International Relations* 12 (3): 341–370.

Noutcheva, Gergana, Karolina Pomorska, and Giselle Bosse (eds.). 2013. *The EU and Its Neighbours. Values Versus Security in European Foreign Policy*. Manchester: Manchester University Press.

Prodi, Romano. 2002. "Speech to the Opening Session of the Convention on the Future of Europe."

Rankin, Jennifer. 2017. "Russian Destabilisation of Balkans Rings Alarm Bells as EU Leaders Meet." *The Guardian*, 9 March.

Relijć, Dušan. 2017. "The Impact of Russia." In *Resilience in the Western Balkans*, edited by Sabina Lange, Zoran Nechev, and Florian Trauner. Paris: EU Institute for Security Studies. Report No. 36, August.

Schindler, John R. 2017. "President Trump's First Foreign Policy Crisis." *The Observer*, 25 January.

Simón, Luis. 2013. No Might, No Right: Europeans Must Re-discover Military Power. In *European Global Strategy Project*. Madrid: Real Instituto Elcano.

Smith, Michael E. 2011. "A Liberal Grand Strategy in a Realist World? Power, Purpose and the EU's Changing Global Role." *Journal of European Public Policy* 18 (2): 144–163.

Sofia, Sebastian-Aparicio. 2014. *Post-War Statebuilding and Constitutional Reform*. Houndmills: Palgrave.

Steele, Brent J. 2008. *Ontological Security in International Relations: Self-Identity and the IR State*. London: Routledge.

Stratulat, Corina. 2017. "Democratisation via European Integration: Fragile Resilience and Resilient Fragility." In *Resilience in the Balkans*, edited by Sabina Lange, Zoran Nechev, and Florian Trauner. Paris: EU Institute for Security Studies. Report No. 36, August.

Tocci, Nathalie. 2016. "The Making of the EU Global Strategy." *Contemporary Security Policy* 37 (3): 461–472. https://doi.org/10.1080/13523260.2016.1232559.

Tsygankov, Andrei P. 2012. *Russia and the West from Alexander to Putin: Honor in International Relations*. Cambridge: Cambridge University Press.

Wagner, Wolfgang. 2017. "Liberal Power Europe." *Journal of Common Market Studies* 55 (6): 1398–1414.

Wagner, Wolfgang, and Rosanne Anholt. 2016. "Resilience as the EU Global Strategy's New Leitmotif: Pragmatic, Problematic or Promising?" *Contemporary Security Policy* 37 (3): 414–430.

Youngs, Richard. 2014. *The Uncertain Legacy of Crisis: European Foreign Policy Faces the Future*. Brussels: Carnegie Endowment for International Peace.

Zimmermann, Hubert. 2007. "Realist Power Europe? The EU in the Negotiations about China's and Russia's WTO Accession." *JCMS: Journal of Common Market Studies* 45 (4): 813–832.

CHAPTER 13

Realism, Neocolonialism and European Military Intervention in Africa

Catherine Gegout

This chapter argues that the realist approach, with an emphasis on the concepts of fear and uncertainty, supplemented with neo-colonialist approaches, provides the best way to understand European military intervention in Africa since the end of the Cold War. Military intervention includes arms sales, the deployment of ground troops, aerial bombing, and the setting of no-fly zones. European military intervention in the region is essentially French intervention. It mostly takes place in former colonies, for security and prestige motives. French foreign policy in Africa is moving away from some aspects of neo-colonialism. British military intervention has been very rare, but it is now increasing with the fight against terrorism and the desire to promote British prestige with the United States. Motives for EU intervention have changed. In the

This chapter (including the table in this chapter) draws extensively from my book on *Why Europe Intervenes in Africa: Security, Prestige and the Legacy of Colonialism* published in 2017 with Hurst, and in 2018 with Oxford University Press.

C. Gegout (✉)
University of Nottingham, Nottingham, UK
e-mail: Catherine.Gegout@nottingham.ac.uk

© The Author(s) 2019
R. Belloni et al. (eds.), *Fear and Uncertainty in Europe*, Global Issues,
https://doi.org/10.1007/978-3-319-91965-2_13

2003–2008 period, it was to acquire prestige, but since 2008 it has been to bring stability to African regions in conflict, protect EU economic interests and show a humanitarian face to the world. European actors make strategic choices to enhance their power (Guzzini 2013). They pursue their own interests, but this is not necessarily at the detriment of the "European spirit", which is to promote democracy and human rights. The first section of the chapter analyses the realist and neo-colonial approaches to motives for intervention. The second looks at the rhetoric related to relations with Africa of France, the United Kingdom and the European Union and argues that these actors emphasise the importance of humanitarianism because of their fear of uncertainty and instability. The third gives an overview of motives for intervention of these three actors and demonstrates that security and prestige interests matter for all actors, whereas neo-colonialism is waning.

REALIST AND NEO-COLONIAL APPROACHES TO MOTIVES FOR INTERVENTION

The realist approach and neo-colonialism are the most convincing approaches to explain European military intervention in Africa. First, a broader understanding of realism is necessary in order to explain intervention. This argument is similar to that of Jack Donnelly (2000, and his chapter in this volume) who has shown that there are different currents of realist thought. For realists, security prevails over all other motives for intervention. This is different from liberalism, as it could foresee that other motives such as humanitarianism could be as important as security. I distinguish between four types of realist thinking: core realism, economic realism, normative realism and ethical realism. Core realism focuses on security. It includes the definition of realism given by Roberto Belloni and Vincent Della Sala in the introduction of the book: self-interested states (and by extension, the European Union) are driven by fear and uncertainty in a system based on states seeking power, at a minimum, to guarantee their survival. Economic realism looks at economic motives for intervention, while normative realism invokes norms such as prestige. Prestige involves one actor impressing others with its own power or with the power it believes, or wants others to believe, that it possesses (Morgenthau 1948/1985: 87). Ethical realism considers humanitarianism a motive for intervention. It is in this respect very close theoretically to constructivism, which acknowledges both the importance of power and the impact of ideas and norms, but it is different in that humanitarianism is only allowed to be a motive when the intervening actor does not harm the security, economic interest and prestige of European states in the world.

Core realists believe that great powers think strategically, and maintain their own security by preventing conflicts, blocking migration into their own states, disrupting terrorist activities and the creation of weapons of mass destruction, and protecting their strategic military bases and their own citizens and embassies. Realists also argue that Europe, as a middle range power, fearful of other powers, is likely to jump on the United States' bandwagon, and follow US policy of intervention or non-intervention.

There are two types of core realist assumptions: defensive and offensive. Defensive realists do not see grounds for US military intervention in any conflict in the developing world, as they believe no strategic or economic advantages would be gained (Layne 1993; Bandow 1994; Krauthammer 2004). The same could be said of European military intervention in Africa. Defensive realists expect European actors not to intervene in conflicts in Africa, and more generally, to withdraw from the African continent: with the end of the Cold War, the Western powers no longer need to be involved in Africa, as Africa is not a threat to Europe, and they should act as "neo-isolationists". Stephen Van Evera (1990: 34) says that 'the security case for involvement [in the developing world] is ... weak, and other reasons for involvement are marginal.' Offensive realists argue that intervention is rational when it helps an actor control and shape the international environment, as long as this is done at low cost in terms of military risk (Smith 1994; Zakaria 1998). Offensive realists expect European actors to intervene in an African conflict in order to ensure their own security, but only at low human and financial cost. To sum up, for core realists, actors are only interested in security gains when they consider intervening or not in another state.

Both defensive and offensive realists consider fear or uncertainty as motives for policies (Lebow 2016: 2; Pashakhanou 2017). The idea of fear has been present in "realist" writings since Thucydides. He showed how Sparta feared the growth of Athenian power. For him, fear is the main motive for policy, followed by honour and interest. Machiavelli mentioned the importance of fear for a leader (for whom it is better to be feared than loved), and Hobbes argued that man is in constant fear for his life, and fear can serve as an important source for justifying collective political and moral foundations (Bleiker and Hutchison 2008: 119). Morgenthau explained how the United States feared the rise of a superpower in Europe (1950: 835). In this volume, Paul Van Hooft and Annette Freyberg-Inan remind us that smaller states fear being abandoned by their bigger allies and that big states are afraid of erratic behaviour by smaller allies. The latter type of fear can be applied to the relation between European and African states, even if the latter are not considered allies but rather vassals. Benedikt Erforth mentions in this volume that France intervened in Mali to avoid the consequences of a failed state on Europe's southern shore, and tells us that this would have been expected by Machiavelli, as order needs to be kept.

Economic realists argue that states are not only security maximisers but also economic maximisers. As long as states are protected in terms of security, they want to enhance their economic power, in order to improve their position in the world, the well-being of their people and their wealth (Carr 1939/2001: 120; Gilpin 1981: 50; Hyde-Price 2009: 26). For economic realists, therefore, when an actor is considering intervening in another state, security interests are essential, but economic gains are important too.

One norm which is often overlooked in modern realism, but which can have considerable impact on a decision to intervene in a state facing a conflict is that of prestige (Markey 1999: 126). Prestige derives from the perceptions other states have of a state's capacities and its ability and willingness to exercise its power (Gilpin 1981: 31). These perceptions can be constructed over a long period of time. For Edward Keene, the EU's prestige is built on over two centuries of European culture and history (Keene 2012: 12–14). But they can also be short-term (for instance, the prestige earned by Chancellor Angela Merkel for Germany). Prestige helps make principles, threats and promises credible, and it is especially valuable for bargaining situations (Mercer 1996: 18; Desch 1996: 359; Khalil 2000). I identify three types of prestige: individual, state and international prestige. At the individual level, leaders have a personal aim, which is to feel pleased with their own performance and a political aim, which is to remain in power as long as possible. At the level of the state, politicians will praise the strength of their own nation, to enhance its prestige, reinforce its legitimacy, and rally the support of its citizens. At the level of the international community, prestige is felt as the *rayonnement* effect, that is, as the projection of a positive image by the intervening actor to other international actors. Officials are "acutely sensitive" to questions of prestige when dealing with the great powers (Taliaferro 2004: 196). Prestige can be gained by intervening in order to protect or gain territory and economic interests, or to protect people who live either in the intervening or the targeted state. For Steve Wood (2015: 311, 313), prestige is only gained by implementing policies which have a positive impact on the ground. He argues that the European Union does not have much prestige in terms of global influence. This article does not look at the impact of EU policies on EU prestige, but rather on the relevance of prestige to explain policies.

Proponents of core, economic, and normative realism do not assume a priori that morality influences decision-makers. However, some realists do allow for the possibility of leaders having humanitarian motives when agreeing to intervene in a conflict, and will accept that states have both material and moral interests (Posen and Ross 1996–1997; Rose 1998; Donnelly 2000; Fiott 2013). I call these realists "ethical realists". Scott Sagan (2004: 75) sums up the ethical realist position: ethical norms *sometimes* have an important impact on states, and this impact depends on the context of power relations in the anarchic and competitive international system.

The reason why some realists allow for the possibility of intervention on moral grounds is that it is instrumental for other security and prestige interests. Promoting humanitarianism, they argue, leads to a safer world for all concerned; it perpetuates the supremacy of the intervening state, and it enhances its prestige (Carr 1939/2001: 74; Sagan 2004: 76). Even if states initially proclaim that they are acting in defence of human rights, they are also inevitably defending their own national interests (Franck and Rodley 1973: 275–305; Rieff 1995; Cooper 2005). Michael Walzer (2003: 26) argues that a "pure moral will does not exist in political life." However, according to Jack Donnelly, in a realist model "there is space for rare but genuine, even legitimate, humanitarian interventions" (1993: 618). Wanting peace in the world as an ultimate end is ethical in itself, and both E. H. Carr and Hans Morgenthau, the founders of classical realism, were proponents of peace.

Second, neo-colonialism has been described as the most recent and worst form of imperialism: "for those who practice it, it means power without responsibility, and for those who suffer from it, it means exploitation without redress" (Young 2001: 44). In 1965, Kwame Nkrumah, Ghana's first post-independence President, published *Neo-Colonialism: The Last Stage of Imperialism*, which analyses the neo-colonialism of the United States. Political control, he says, is exercised through institutional models and through espionage (he gives the example of Congo and the murder in 1961 of Patrice Lumumba, the first Prime Minister of the Congo, by the Belgian government, and according to Nkrumah, the CIA). Economic control is conducted through price control, interest rates and debts, and aid from international organisations, which comes with conditions attached, such as the requirement for a say in economic policies. Cultural control is exercised through language, by describing a people struggling for independence as rebels and terrorists; religious control is developed by evangelism; and military control comes through the Peace Corps. Neo-colonialism is about the subordination of African states in ways that allow foreign domination to continue without giving rise to challenges of re-colonisation (Anise 1989; Bass 2008: 379). It contributes to continued underdevelopment, stagnation, and low integration of economic sectors across the continent (Rodney 1972; Amin 1976).

In the perspective of neo-colonialism, hypotheses regarding intervention are the following: (1) if an actor has no colonial past in an African state and a former colonial power is already engaged in this state, it is unlikely to intervene in this state; and (2) if a state has a colonial past in an African state and acts as a neo-colonial power, it is likely to intervene militarily in this state if it is in the security and economic interest of the neo-colonial state, and if it provides the neo-colonial state with prestige.

Neo-colonialism is often studied together with Eurocentrism. It means that leaders see the West as superior to the South. It can paradoxically lead to two different policies. It might lead to inaction or indifference to the plight of the people in regions in conflict, and therefore encourage a decision for non-intervention. Alternatively, Eurocentrism might produce an intervention according to European rules, one that is paternalistic or patronising, and involves limited cooperation with African leaders as equals (Hobson 2012: 291). I will now turn to showing the relevance of realism and neo-colonialism in the rhetoric of European actors and in their motives for military intervention in African states since the end of the Cold War.

HUMANITARIAN RHETORIC IN FRANCE, THE UNITED KINGDOM AND THE EUROPEAN UNION ON RELATIONS WITH AFRICA

Roberto Belloni and Vincent Della Sala remind us that different "cultural-institutional contexts" have produced interesting and original perspectives and approaches to international relations, some of which squarely outside of the realist tradition. However, although France, the United Kingdom and the European Union have different political cultures, their rhetoric clearly fits into a realist framework (Jorgensen 2000). They emphasise their desire to act for humanitarian motives, but they also clearly show that security and economic interests also drive their policies. These actors do not emphasise the importance of humanitarianism because of their fear of uncertainty and instability, instead they do so in order to gain internal and international prestige. Humanitarianism is high on the list of motives given by EU actors in rhetoric, but as we will see in the following section, it is never the main motive for intervention or its absence.

The European Union argues it is motivated by responsibility. It states that: "We will engage responsibly across Europe and the surrounding regions to the east and south. We will act globally to address the root causes of conflict and poverty, and to promote human rights" (EUISS 2016: 8). The European Union wants to engage in the resilience of third parties, contribute to prevention of conflicts and peacebuilding, and foster human security. France aims to stabilise Europe's neighbourhood and the Middle East, and to contribute to peace in the world. The United Kingdom wants to strengthen the rules-based international order, tackle conflict and build stability abroad (UK Government 2015: 47). The three European actors have a position, which is completely different from the Russian one presented by Natalia Morozova in this book. She explained that Russia strongly condemns the use of human rights issues as a pretext to intervene in the internal affairs of states.

However, humanitarianism is not the only motive mentioned in official European documents. France and the United Kingdom want to protect their territories and citizens. Terrorism and migration, both directly related to European security interests, have become the highest priority for European actors. The fight against terrorism concentrates on the Sahel, Somalia and Nigeria. France is also concerned with criminal flows in Western Africa. The United Kingdom wants to invest in strengthening its network of counter-terrorism experts in both North Africa and Sub-Saharan Africa. By focusing on terrorism, the United Kingdom is establishing relations with states closely linked to France. It wants to cooperate with Algeria on good governance and energy security, with Tunisia on security and economic reform, and in Morocco on good governance, business and cultural links. The European Union wants to concentrate on issues such as border security, trafficking, counter-terrorism, non-proliferation, water and food security, energy and climate, infrastructure and disaster management (EUISS 2016: 35). All three actors are concerned with migration. The United Kingdom says it wants to strengthen its ability to control migration, and also 'help improve livelihoods and give displaced people the best possible prospects as close to home as possible' and to 'offer protection to those who need it' (UK Government 2015: 17). France is concerned with illegal migration and the European Union wants to address and prevent the root causes of displacement, manage migration, and fight trans-border crime (French Ministry of Defence 2013: 51; EUISS 2016: 27).

All three actors want to act in a multilateral framework. This also corresponds to the realist idea that cooperation is welcome as long as it contributes to the security of states. The three European actors want to support the institutional development of the United Nations, the African Union and of regional security organisations in Africa. The European Union wants practical cooperation, including on security issues through the Union for the Mediterranean, African regional organisations including ECOWAS and the G5 Sahel.

In terms of military intervention, European actors openly declare their intentions to act according to their own security interests. France and the United Kingdom favour two different types of military intervention: France intends to have military capabilities in the regions on the fringes of Europe, the Mediterranean basin, part of Africa (from the Sahel to Equatorial Africa), the Arabo-Persian Gulf and the Indian Ocean (French Ministry of Defence 2013: 79). It wants to act via NATO and the European Union. It is also prepared to work in an ad hoc multilateral framework, as it proposed in 2017 the creation of a European Intervention Initiative (French Ministry for Defence 2017: 64). French exceptionalism is still present in its doctrine: "the Sahel and part of sub-Saharan Africa are regions of priority interest for France 'due to a common history, the presence of French nationals, the issues at stake and the threats confronting them" (French Ministry of Defence 2013: 54).

The United Kingdom, rather, focuses on training. It wants to establish British Defence Staffs in Africa in 2016, and increase training in Kenya, Somalia and South Africa. The EU Global Strategy (EUISS 2016: 47) favours increased EU capacity to deploy military and civilian operations, but states that the EU needs to "tackle the procedural, financial and political obstacles" which prevents it from doing so.

In terms of economic relations, France stated its economic interests in having strong relations with Nigeria and South Africa. The United Kingdom has made clear that development aid would depend on the level of poverty of another state and on the UK national interest. Unlike France and the United Kingdom, the European Union is mainly focused on the fight against poverty, but this also fits in a security framework:

> The Economic Partnership Agreements will build stronger links between our trade, development and security policies in Africa, and blend development efforts with work on migration, health, education, energy and climate, science and technology, notably to improve food security. (EUISS 2016: 34)

Motives for European Military Intervention: Security and Prestige

This section shows that security and prestige interests matter for all actors, whereas neo-colonialism is waning. In terms of indirect military intervention, arms sales are directly related to European security interests. France stated in its 2013 strategy that it:

> [b]elieves that collective security and disarmament are linked. It therefore considers that a sustained effort is necessary in support of disarmament, enhanced monitoring of technological transfers and conventional equipment, the fight against proliferation of weapons of mass destruction and their means of delivery, likewise the combat [sic] against arms and ammunition trafficking. (French Ministry of Defence 2013: 25)

However, this statement is what realists would consider rhetoric, which masks the French national interest. Even if only a small percentage, 3.5%, of French arms exports went to African states in the 2000s, France was the biggest exporter of arms to Africa, North Africa and Sub-Saharan Africa in the European Union from 2004 to 2012. It was followed by

Italy, Germany and the United Kingdom. Between 2004 and 2008, three-quarters of French arms exports to Sub-Saharan Africa went to South Africa, and five per cent to each of Chad, Angola, Cameroon and Nigeria. France is known to have sold arms to Sudan, together with Russia, China, Iran and Saudi Arabia. Some high-level French officials also sold arms to Angola in the early 1990s without the authorisation of the French state in what became as the Falcone Affair.

More generally, in terms of the value of arms sold per head by all EU states in the same period 2004–2012, Libyans received by far the largest amount of arms. This indicates the overwhelming military might of the Gaddafi regime at the time of the Arab Spring. Algeria, Morocco, Egypt and Tunisia are also important importers of arms, which can be used for both foreign action and internal repression. Djibouti, the strategic base for France and the United States, is also a major recipient of arms. Gabon, Equatorial Guinea, Chad, Mauritania and Cameroon are also recipients, and considered 'not free' states, that is, states where basic political rights are absent, and basic civil rights are widely and systematically denied. Motives for indirect military intervention are far from humanitarian, with most arms sales are directed to former colonies.

In terms of direct military intervention, as expected by realists, France and the United Kingdom both have military bases in Africa. In 2017, France still had three permanent military bases in Africa, namely in Djibouti (1450 troops), Gabon (350), and Reunion (1600). Although the Senegal base officially closed in 2010, 350 French troops remained. Likewise, the Ivory Coast base officially closed in 2009, but 950 troops are currently stationed there. France also has troops deployed in the Gulf of Aden and the Gulf of Guinea. In 2014, France announced a new approach for the Sahel, known as Operation Barkhane. The 4000 French soldiers already stationed in the Sahel were re-organized into "specialized posts" based in Chad, Burkina Faso, Niger, Mali and Mauritania. The United Kingdom has an important military base in the Indian Ocean, Diego Garcia. It uses Kenya as a base for action against Somalia and groups supporting terrorist activities. In addition, British military ships are docked in Mombasa. Again, bases are present in former colonies.

Motives for direct intervention are different at the state level and EU level, as states and the European Union have different interests, legal frameworks and rules. When European actors decide to intervene at the state level, the imperatives of security and prestige, and the inheritance of the colonial past can explain policy decisions by large member states.

At the EU level, these three concepts need to be supplemented with the requirements of the principle of legality. Humanitarianism does not appear to be a primary motive for intervention at either level. The following table sums up the motives for French, British and EU direct military interventions in Africa since the end of the Cold War. The section then shows the importance through support to African security organisations; and realism and of neo-colonialism to explain intervention.

Core Realism

Core realism emphasises the importance of security for European states. The most important security interest is the stability of a state and region. Other motives related to European security interests on the African continent, and traditionally found in the literature on realism, are also valid: European actors want to protect their military bases, address the threat of terrorism and protect their own citizens. However, contrary to realist expectations, fear of migration was not a factor for intervention. Another crucial motive is the necessity for European actors to obtain US support. Finally, still as expected by realists, European actors do not intervene every time the United Nations asks for support, and they do not systematically follow UN policy.

Stability is favoured over regime change and humanitarian emergency: there is a fear of the unknown and uncertain, the opposition whose agenda is unclear in comparison with the certainty of a same regime remaining in power. Most French interventions were conducted in order to make sure African states remained stable, whether under the same leadership or not. For instance, France intervened in Chad and refused to intervene in Darfur because it wanted Chad and Sudan to remain stable. France chose not to intervene militarily in Algeria, Senegal and Madagascar, as it believed non-intervention was best for stability. The United Kingdom was also concerned with the stability of its former colonies in conflict, and preferred avoiding direct intervention: it did not intervene in Kenya, Uganda and Zimbabwe. In particular, the United Kingdom did not intervene in Uganda to fight the LRA, as it had special relations with the Ugandan regime, which did not request an intervention. The United Kingdom relied on Uganda for its relations with Sudan and Somalia, despite Uganda's problematic human rights record. However, the United Kingdom authorised an EU force in Chad because it did not want Sudan to take control of Chad and the surrounding region.

Motives for French, British, and EU Direct Military Interventions and Absence of Intervention in Africa (1986–2016)

French motives

Security	Economic	Prestige in the international community	Prestige in African states	Humanitarianism	Neo-colonialism	Neo-colonialism in transition: (no support for the government)
Togo 1986, 1991	Gabon 1990	Somalia 1992–1993	Togo 1986	Somalia 1992–1993	Togo 1986 and 1991	Ivory Coast 1999, 2002, 2003, 2004–2011
Comoros 1989, 1995, 2008	Algeria 1991–2002	Rwanda 1994, Operation Turquoise	Comoros 1989, 1995	Ivory Coast 2004–2011	Gabon 1990	Mali 2012
Gabon 1990	Senegal, Casamance 1992	DRC, 2003, 2006	Gabon 1990	Libya 2011	Comoros 1989, 1995, 2008	CAR December 2012–April 2013
Djibouti 1991–1992	Madagascar 1991, 2002, 2009	Ivory Coast 2003–2011	Djibouti 1991–1992	CAR December 2013	Djibouti 1991–1992	
Western Sahara 1991–today	Congo-Brazzaville 1997	Libya 2011	Rwanda 1990–1994	Nigeria 2014	Western Sahara 1991–today	
Algeria 1991–2002	Cameroon 1996–2008	Mali 2013	Cameroon 1996–2008		Algeria 1991–2002	
Madagascar 1991, 2002, 2009	Ivory Coast 2003	CAR December 2013	Congo-Brazzaville 1997		Madagascar 1991, 2002, 2009	
Senegal, Casamance 1992	Mauritania, Niger, Algeria, Nigeria 2008–today		Chad 2006, 2008		Senegal, Casamance 1992	
Somalia 1992–1993			Burkina Faso, 2014		Rwanda 1990–1993, 1994, Operation Turquoise	
Rwanda 1990–1994					Cameroon 1996–2008	

(continued)

(continued)

Security	Economic	Prestige in the international community	Prestige in African states	Humanitarianism	Neo-colonialism	Neo-colonialism in transition: (no support for the government)
Cameroon 1996–2008					CAR 1996–1997, 2003, 2006–2007, December 2013	
DRC 1996–2003, 1998, 2003, 2006					Congo-Brazzaville 1997	
CAR 1996–1997, 2003, 2006–2007, December 2012 and April 2013, December 2013					Sierra Leone 2000	
Congo-Brazzaville 1997						
Ivory Coast 2002, 2003, 2004, 2010–2011					Ivory Coast 2003	
Darfur 2003–2005					Chad 2006, 2008	
Chad 2006, 2008						
Guinea 2008–2009					Guinea 2008–2009	
Mauritania, Niger, Algeria, Nigeria 2008–today					Mali 2013	
Libya 2011, 2015–2016					Burkina Faso 2014, 2016	
Mali 2012, 2013						
Nigeria 2014						
Burkina Faso 2014, 2016						

British motives

Security	Economic	Prestige	Humanitarianism	Neo-colonialism	Neo-colonialism in transition
Uganda 1987–ongoing	N/A	**Somalia 1992–1993**	**Somalia 1992–1993**	Rwanda 1994	*Chad/CAR 2008–2009*
Somalia 1992–1993		Rwanda 1994	**Sierra Leone 2000**	**Sierra Leone 2000**	*Mali 2013*
Kenya 1992, 1997, 2007–2008		**Sierra Leone 2000**	**Libya 2011**	Ivory Coast 2002–2003, **2004**, 2010–2011	*CAR 2014–2015*
Rwanda 1994		**DRC 2003**, *2006*	**Nigeria 2014**	Zimbabwe 2008	
DRC 1996–2003, **2003**, *2006*		**Libya 2011**		Ivory Coast 2011	
Lesotho 1998		*Chad/CAR 2008–2009*		**Nigeria 2014**	
Sierra Leone 2000		*Mali 2013*			
Darfur 2003–2005		*CAR 2014–2015*			
Ivory Coast 2004					
Chad/CAR 2008–2009					
Zimbabwe 2008					
Libya 2011, 2015–2016					
South Sudan 2013					
Mali 2013					
CAR 2014–2015					
Nigeria 2014					

EU motives

Security	Economic	Prestige	Humanitarianism	Neo-colonialism	Neo-colonialism in transition (support for EU intervention)
Angola 1975–2002	**Gulf of Aden 2008–today**	**DRC 2003, 2006**	**DRC 2003, 2006**	Uganda 1987–ongoing	**DRC 2003**
Sudan (intra-state conflict in South, 1983–2005)		*Darfur 2005–2007*	*Darfur 2005–2007*	Rwanda 1994	**Chad/CAR 2008–2009**
Burundi 1993–2005		**Chad/CAR 2008–2009**	**Chad/CAR 2008–2009**	Sierra Leone 2000	**CAR 2014–2015**
Rwanda 1994, Operation Turquoise		**Gulf of Aden 2008–today**	**CAR 2014–2015**	Ivory Coast 2003–2011	
DRC 1996–2003, **2003, 2006, 2008**		**CAR 2014–2015**		Zimbabwe 2008	
Darfur 2003–2005, *2005–2007*				*Mali 2013*	
Chad/CAR 2008–2009					
Gulf of Aden 2008–today					
Tunisia and Egypt 2011					
Libya 2011					
Mali 2013–2016					
South Sudan 2013–today					
CAR 2014–2015					
Burundi 2015					

Bold: Intervention. Regular text: No intervention. *Italics: Indirect intervention* (for France and the European Union through support to African security organisations; and for the United Kingdom through support to the European Union and France)

Stability was also one of the motives for EU interventions in the DRC in 2006, Chad/CAR in 2008–2009, and the CAR in 2014.

Protection of military bases and the fight against terrorism in the Sahel are imperatives, for France in particular. France has deployed troops to Mali and to the wider Sahel with the support of the United States. It acted, as expected by core realists, in order to protect its own security. The United Kingdom indirectly supported France in Mali in 2013 and it intervened directly in Libya in 2015 and 2016. The British training operation in Tunisia in 2016 meant that the United Kingdom was now ready to intervene unilaterally in the French zone of influence. European states have intervened in order to protect their own citizens, but only if there are no more important security threats. For instance, France decided to intervene in Mali in 2013 despite the fact that French citizens had been kidnapped by Islamist groups: fighting terrorism, and therefore protecting French citizens in France in the long term, trumped the protection of a few French citizens on the ground.

Core realism highlights the relevance of the US hegemon for European powers: European actors are unlikely to carry out interventions without US agreement and/or support. This is the case for the United Kingdom (as in Sierra Leone in 2000 and Libya in 2011), and it is also usually the case for France, although France does act without US support in states where the United States has few security and economic interests. France prefers not to work through NATO, as this means losing control of the intervention to the advantage of the United States, but this happens: French leaders cannot militarily afford to opt out from a US-led alliance. In the case of Libya, there would not have been any intervention without US participation and the corresponding involvement of NATO. US support is indispensable when European states intervene with a large-scale operation, as European capabilities alone are insufficient to conduct a successful mission. EU missions are also conditioned by the US position: if the United States wants to intervene in Africa, NATO will be one of the privileged institutions to deal with a conflict. This was the case in Darfur in 2005, when both NATO and the European Union helped the African Union to deploy troops there.

As core realists would expect, European actors do not intervene in Africa because the United Nations asks them to intervene. For instance, despite several requests by the UN Secretary General, they intervened neither in Darfur nor in the DRC. Unlike the European Union,

European states do not systematically intervene in Africa with the support of the United Nations. The British mission in Sierra Leone in 2000 supported the UN missions there, but was not incorporated into it. The United Kingdom seemed prepared to intervene in Libya in 2011 without UN support. France was determined to obtain UN support for its intervention in the Ivory Coast in 2003 and it received support from the UN Security Council for its intervention in Chad in 2008, in the Ivory Coast in 2011, in Mali, and in the CAR in 2013. However, it conducted many interventions in Africa without a UN mandate: in the 1990s, in Togo, Gabon, the CAR, Comoros, Rwanda before the genocide, and Congo-Brazzaville; and since 2000, in the CAR, Niger and Mauritania. It also seemed to consider going into Libya in 2011 without the support of the United Nations.

Economic Realism

Economic aims were primary motives for intervention in the following cases: when France intervened in African states in the early 1990s, and when the European Union intervened in the Gulf of Aden with Operation EUNAVFOR Atalanta from 2008 until now. More importantly, economic realism is useful to highlight the fact that European actors always make sure that their decisions on intervention do not harm their economic interests. I prefer this formulation ('do not harm') to traditional explanations, which overemphasise the influence of geostrategic and economic motives (Bordat 2009: 61; Cameron 2013). The best example for this is when France, less than four weeks into its intervention in Libya in 2011, sent a delegation of businesses to the transitional government to make sure it would be rewarded in economic terms.

Normative Realism

When security and economic interests are not under threat, prestige can be a motive for French, British and EU military intervention. French leaders have intervened in Africa to be viewed favourably by their own citizens. They emphasised their commitment to humanitarianism in the following operations: Operation Turquoise in 1994 in Rwanda, Libya in 2011, and the CAR in 2013 and their commitment to fighting terrorism in Mali in 2013. They are eager to impress their American counterparts; French interventions in Somalia in 1992, Libya in 2011 and Mali in 2013 were viewed positively in the United States. France is careful to ensure that its policies towards Africa are perceived favourably by the Arab world. This was especially the case with Libya in 2011: it had damaged its image with its policy in Tunisia at the start of the Arab Spring and it acted in Libya in order to redeem this. France also wants to be viewed positively by African leaders. Good relations with African leaders entail support to France for its policies at the United Nations and in other African states. Its last interventions motivated by prestige in African states were in Chad in 2006 and 2008, and in Burkina Faso in 2014, when France evacuated the ousted President.

For British leaders, prestige is based on acting in the name of humanitarianism, and/or acting in order to satisfy the United States, the international community, their own electorate, the European Union and France. The United Kingdom wanted to show its electorate and the United States that it was capable of acting in the name of humanitarianism in Somalia, Sierra Leone and Libya. It wanted to show European states that it was committed to the idea of European integration in all its direct and indirect contributions to EU operations in Africa. And when the United Kingdom indirectly supported the French unilateral intervention to fight terrorism in Mali in 2013, it was also concerned with its reputation in France.

For the United Kingdom, prestige was about repairing a previous loss of prestige. In Sierra Leone, the United Kingdom had damaged its image with the Sandline affair in 1997 and this could have been one of the motives for the British intervention there in 2000. On one occasion, prestige with an African leader might have led to non-intervention. In Rwanda, preserving good relations with the RPF could have been one of the reasons for British non-intervention, and refusal to support a UN intervention.

Normative realism is also useful to explain EU interventions in the DRC in 2003 and 2006, in Darfur from 2005 to 2007, in Chad/CAR from 2008 to 2009, in the Gulf of Aden from 2008 to today, and in the CAR from 2014 to 2015. European member states, especially France, were keen to promote the prestige of the European Union on the international scene, especially where the United States was involved, in order to show that the European Union was as 'capable' as NATO. They also wanted to show that Europeans were doing something about humanitarian crises and potential crises, such as the one feared when elections were held in the DRC in 2006.

Ethical Realism

Humanitarianism seems to be either non-existent or simply one motive among others, and often a means to a different realist aim, that is, prestige. European actors could be said to show a lack of moral sense, as they fail to intervene in many conflicts in Africa; there is an overwhelming prevalence of non-humanitarian non-intervention (Chesterman 2003: 54; Welsh 2011: 1194). The decisions made by France, the United Kingdom and the European Union in Rwanda in 1994 undermine any claim that Europe practises humanitarian intervention. France and the other European actors elected to pursue morally unacceptable policies: France took an active part with the Rwandan government in the preparation for genocide and adopted a controversial policy at the end of it. Both France and the United Kingdom encouraged the United Nations not to respond to the genocide and failed to act while it was going on.

When European actors intervene militarily in an African state, humanitarianism can be a motivating factor for them, but it is never the only motive for intervention. In the 1990s, only one intervention with a humanitarian motive—amongst others—happened: Somalia in 1992–1993. Given the conditions under which Operation Turquoise took place in 1994, a feeling of guilt or, specifically for France, a desire to protect Hutus from the PRF is more likely to be a motive than humanitarianism. After 2000, operations that had humanitarian motives among others presented the characteristic of being multilateral, with the exception of the British intervention in Sierra Leone in 2000. France intervened in the Ivory Coast, CAR and Libya for humanitarian reasons, but again this was not the primary motive. All EU operations, with the exception of operation Atalanta, had a humanitarian motive, but in all these operations, European actors made sure that there were very limited risks for their security, trade interests and prestige. They never conducted a "humanitarian intervention' in the sense that humanitarianism was the main motive for military intervention. They were 'opportunistic in their humanitarianism' (Bass 2008: 317).

Neo-Colonialism

Historical relations still condition European interventions today. The study of non-intervention revealed that the United Kingdom and France had radically different policies in Rwanda in 1994 and in the DRC in 1996. In 2013, a French diplomat said: 'there is a shared responsibility: we had to deal with Mali, the Americans with Sudan, and the British with Somalia. And for the British and the Americans, the Central African Republic was the responsibility of the French' (*Jeune Afrique* 2013). The attitude of European leaders is changing slightly: the United Kingdom agreed that the European Union should intervene in Chad and the CAR in 2008–2009, even if it did not send any troops there. Britain deployed a unilateral military training operation in 2016 in Tunisia, the former French zone of influence. In 2004, France decided to abandon its leadership role in the Ivory Coast and to negotiate peace with regional security organisations, and in 2014, for the first time, France intervened indirectly with logistical support in the British zone of influence, that is, in Nigeria. However, France still retains full discretion whether to support or not an African state with which it has a defence agreement.

The concept of Eurocentrism has been useful for understanding motives for non-intervention and intervention in Rwanda in 1994 and is one to be kept in mind when analysing future military interventions and other types of intervention—especially when the extreme-right is gaining impetus in European politics. When European leaders today fail to take action against leaders in African states who are murdering their own citizens, they show the same passivity as their predecessors during the rule of Idi Amin in 1979, when at least 100,000 Ugandans were killed. In 1978, the President of Tanzania, Julius Nyerere, commented:

> If Amin was White, we would have passed many resolutions against him. But he is Black, and Blackness is a licence to kill Africans. And therefore there is complete silence; no one speaks about what he does. (Cited in Wheeler 2000: 115–116)

Eurocentrism must especially be taken into consideration when humanitarian motives are adduced. Anne Orford (2003: 166) has suggested that European actors see themselves as conforming to universal stereotypes of "good" Western states, in opposition to rogue states headed by ruthless dictators: these "heroes" of new interventionism, with their "white" masculine characteristics, believe they represent progress, democracy, peace and security.

Conclusion

The European Union and its member states do not respond to crises in Africa in a similar way. They are all concerned with fear of terrorism (and of migration since 2015), and with uncertainty and instability in African states. While the European Union focuses on multilateralism and on a desire for economic security and limited humanitarianism, an EU state can act independently from other EU states, and always for mainly security motives. EU states are now sometimes willing to intervene in an EU state's former colony, but their leaders will still expect the former colonial state to take the lead in the intervention. For both the European Union and its member states, humanitarianism was never the main motive for intervention. The 1994 genocide in Rwanda showed a complete lack of humanitarianism, but today a few cases have revealed some humanitarianism, the most recent one being CAR in 2014–2015.

Future interventions are likely to take place when similar motives as above are present, and at the state level rather than at the EU level. When deciding on the highly sensitive issue of intervention, power politics in Europe are likely to prevail. Stefan Lehne (2017) explains that "the sum of national viewpoints and the willingness to take responsibility falls far short of the total potential of the union as an international actor." In 2017, French President Emmanuel Macron did not coordinate his response to the Libya crisis with other EU states (Foreign Affairs 2017). The fact that France is calling on states such as Germany and the United Kingdom to develop common security structures confirms the fact that the European Union is only one of the instruments possible for intervention.

References

Amin, Samir. 1976. *Unequal Development. An Essay on the Social Formations of Peripheral Capitalism*. Hassocks: The Harvester Press.

Anise, Ladun. 1989. "Foreign Military Intervention in Africa: The New Co-operative-Competitive Imperialism." In *Africa in World Politics*, edited by Ralph I. Onwuka and Timothy M. Shaw. Wiltshire: Macmillan.

Bandow, Doug. 1994. *The Politics of Envy: Statism as Theology*. New Brusnwick, NJ: Transaction Publishers.

Bass, Gary J. 2008. *Freedom's Battle: Origins of Humanitarian Intervention*. New York: Alfred A. Knopf.

Bleiker, Roland, and Emma Hutchison. 2008. "Fear No More: Emotions and World Politics." *Review of International Studies* 34 (1): 115–135.

Bordat, Josef. 2009. "Globalisation and War: The Historical and Current Controversy on Humanitarian Interventions." *International Journal of Social Inquiry* 2 (1): 59–72.

Cameron, Hazel. 2013. *Britain's Hidden Role in the Rwandan Genocide: The Cat's Paw*. Abingdon: Routledge.

Carr, Edward H. 1939/2001. *The Twenty Years' Crisis, 1919–1939*. New York: Perennial.

Chesterman, Simon. 2003. "Hard Cases Make Bad Law: Law, Ethics, and Politics in Humanitarian Intervention." In *Just Intervention*, edited by Anthony F. Lang Jr., 46–54. Washington, DC: Georgetown University Press.

Cooper, Robert. 2005. "Imperial Liberalism." *The National Interest* 79: 25–34.

Desch, Michael C. 1996. "Why Realists Disagree About the Third World (and Why They Shouldn't)." *Security Studies* 5 (3): 358–384.

Donnelly, Jack. 1993. "Human Rights, Humanitarian Crisis, and Humanitarian Intervention." *International Journal* 48 (4): 607–640.

Donnelly, Jack. 2000. *Realism and International Relations. Themes in International Relations*. Cambridge: Cambridge University Press.

EUISS. 2016. "A Global Strategy for the European Union." https://eeas.europa.eu/top_stories/pdf/eugs_review_web.pdf.

Fiott, Daniel. 2013. "Realist Thought and Humanitarian Intervention." *The International History Review* 35 (4): 766–782.

Foreign Affairs. 2017. "How France Is Making Libya Worse." September 21. https://www.foreignaffairs.com/articles/france/2017-09-21/how-france-making-libya-worse.

Franck, Thomas M., and Nigel S. Rodley. 1973. "After Bangladesh: The Law of Humanitarian Intervention by Military Force." *American Journal of International Law* 67: 275–305.

French Ministry of Defence. 2013. "French White Paper on Defence and Security." https://otan.delegfrance.org/White-Paper-on-Defence-and-National-Security.

French Ministry for Defence. 2017. "Revue Stratégique de Défense et de Sécurité Nationale." http://www.defense.gouv.fr/dgris/presentation/evenements/revue-strategique-de-defense-et-de-securite-nationale-2017.

Gilpin, Robert. 1981. *War and Change in World Politics*. Cambridge: Cambridge University Press.

Guzzini, Stefano, ed. 2013. *The Return of Geopolitics in Europe? Social Mechanisms and Foreign Policy Identity Crises*. Cambridge: Cambridge University Press.

Hobson, John M. 2012. *The Eurocentric Conception of World Politics: Western International Theory, 1760–2010*. Cambridge: Cambridge University Press.

Hyde-Price, Adrian. 2009. "Realist Ethics and the 'War on Terror'." *Globalizations* 6 (1): 23–40.

Jeune Afrique. 2013. "En Afrique, Paris aimerait n'être plus que "l'ultime recours." December 1. http://www.jeuneafrique.com/Article/DEPAFP2013 1201113708/france-diplomatie-paris-laurent-fabius-france-afrique-en-afrique-paris-aimerait-n-etre-plus-que-l-ultime-recours.html.

Jørgensen, Knud Erik. 2000. "Continental IR Theory: The Best Kept Secret." *European Journal of International Relations* 6 (1): 9–42.

Keene, Edward. 2012. "Social Status, Social Closure and the Idea of Europe as a 'Normative Power'." *European Journal of International Relations* 19 (4): 939–956.

Khalil, Elias L. 2000. "Symbolic Products: Prestige, Pride and Identity Goods." *Theory and Decision* 49 (1): 53–77.

Krauthammer, Charles. 2004. "In Defense of Democratic Realism." *The National Interest* 77 (Fall): 1–12.

Layne, Christopher. 1993. "The Unipolar Illusion: Why New Great Powers Will Rise." *International Security* 17 (4): 5–51.

Lebow, Richard Ned. 2016. *Essential Texts on Classics, History, Ethics, and International Relations.* New York: Springer.

Lehne, Stefan. 2017. Is There Hope for EU Foreign Policy? December 5. http://carnegieeurope.eu/2017/12/05/is-there-hope-for-eu-foreign-policy-pub-74909.

Markey, David. 1999. "Prestige and the Origins of War: Returning to Realism's Roots." *Security Studies* 8 (4): 126–172.

Mercer, Jonathan. 1996. *Reputation and International Politics.* Ithaca: Cornell University Press.

Morgenthau, Hans J. 1948/1985. *Politics Among Nations: The Struggle for Power and Peace*, 6th ed. New York: McGraw-Hill.

Morgenthau, Hans J. 1950. "The Mainsprings of American Foreign Policy: The National Interest vs. Moral Abstractions." *The American Political Science Review* 44 (4): 833–854.

Orford, Anne. 2003. *Reading Humanitarian Intervention.* Cambridge: Cambridge University Press.

Pashakhanlou, Arash Heydarian. 2017. *Realism and Fear in International Relations: Morgenthau, Waltz and Mearsheimer Reconsidered.* Cham: Springer.

Posen, Barry R., and Andrew Ross. 1996–1997. "Competing Visions for US Grand Strategy." *International Security* 21 (3): 5–53.

Rieff, David. 1995. "The Lessons of Bosnia: Morality and Power." *World Policy Journal* 12 (1): 76–88.

Rodney, Walter. 1972. *How Europe Underdeveloped Africa.* Washington, DC: Howard University Press.

Rose, Gideon. 1998. "Neoclassical Realism and Theories of Foreign Policy." *World Politics* 51 (1): 144–172.

Sagan, Scott D. 2004. "Realist Perspectives on Ethical Norms and Weapons of Mass Destruction." In *Ethics and Weapons of Mass Destruction: Religious and*

Secular Perspectives, edited by Sohail H. Hashmi and Steven P. Lee, 73–95. Cambridge: Cambridge University Press.

Smith, Tony. 1994. "In Defense of Intervention." *Foreign Affairs* 73 (6): 34–46.

Taliaferro, Jeffrey. 2004. "Power Politics and the Balance of Risk: Hypotheses on Great Power Intervention in the Periphery." *Political Psychology* 25 (2): 177–211.

UK Government. 2015. "National Security Strategy and Strategic Defence and Security Review 2015." https://www.gov.uk/government/uploads/system/uploads/attachment_data/file/555607/2015_Strategic_Defence_and_Security_Review.pdf.

Van Evera, Stephen. 1990. "Why Europe Matters, Why the Third World Doesn't: American Grand Strategy After the Cold War." *Journal* of *Strategic Studies* 13 (2): 1–51.

Walzer, Michael. 2003. "The Argument about Humanitarian Intervention." In *The New Killing Fields: Massacre and the Politics of Intervention*, edited by Nicolaus Mills and Kira Brunner, 19–36. New York: Basic Books.

Welsh, Jennifer. 2011. "A Normative Case for Pluralism: Reassessing Vincent's Views on Humanitarian Intervention." *International Affairs* 87 (5): 1193–1204.

Wheeler, Nicholas J. 2000. *Saving Strangers: Humanitarianism in International Society*. Oxford: Oxford University Press.

Wood, Steve. 2015. "Does the European Union Have Prestige?" *European Politics and Society* 16 (2): 301–320.

Young, Robert J. C. 2001. *Postcolonialism: An Historical Introduction*. Oxford: Blackwell.

Zakaria, Fareed. 1998. *From Wealth to Power: The Unusual Origins of America's World Role*. Princeton, NJ: Princeton University Press.

INDEX

© The Editor(s) (if applicable) and The Author(s) 2019
R. Belloni et al. (eds.), *Fear and Uncertainty in Europe*, Global Issues,
https://doi.org/10.1007/978-3-319-91965-2

Printed by Printforce, the Netherlands